Rosemary Manning has worked in business and in teaching, and has been a writer for most of her adult life.

Her novels include *Look, Stranger* (1960), *The Chinese Garden* (1962, republished 1984). *A Time and a Time*, her autobiographical account of a lesbian love affair that ended in her attempted suicide, was published under the pseudonym Sarah Davys in 1971, and reissued in 1986 under her own name.

Among her books for children are *Green Smoke* (1957), *Dragon in Danger* (1959), *The Dragon's Quest* (1961), *Dragon in the Harbour* (1980) and *Arripay* (1963).

Rosemary Manning

A Corridor of Mirrors

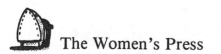 The Women's Press

First published by The Women's Press Limited
A member of the Namara Group
34 Great Sutton Street, London EC1V 0DX

British Library Cataloguing in Publication Data

Manning, Rosemary
  Corridor of mirrors.
  1. Manning, Rosemary—Biography
  2. Authors, English—20th century—
Biography
  I. Title
  823'.914   PR6063.A385Z/

  ISBN 0-7043-4054-2

Typeset by Boldface Typesetters, London EC1
Printed and bound by Hazell Watson & Viney Ltd,
Aylesbury, Bucks.

For Jan

Contents

And identity is funny being yourself is funny as you are never yourself to yourself except as you remember yourself and then of course you do not believe yourself. That is really the trouble with an autobiography you do not of course you do not really believe yourself why should you, you know so well so very well that it is not yourself, it could not be yourself because you cannot remember right and if you do remember right it does not sound right and of course it does not sound right because it is not right. You are of course never yourself.

– from *Everybody's Autobiography* by Gertrude Stein

1
Truth Will Out

To come out at the age of seventy . . . to come out of what, I ask myself? A cave? Old prejudices? An outworn carapace? Perhaps that is the best word for it. I had kept my lesbianism a secret all my life. I had not even spoken of it to more than one or two close friends, though it must have been known to most of my circle. This secrecy was made necessary by the hostile climate of opinion that obtained throughout so much of this century. Lesbians were not actively persecuted when I was a young woman, but they were sneered at and derided. With the opposite sex it was best to pretend to be shy, or unwilling to go too far, usually to find oneself jollied along by men. Incredulous, uncomprehending and of course entrenched in their masculine attitudes of superiority and irresistible charm, they were apt to exclaim: 'Aw, come on! Try it with me and you'll soon get over it!' It – that secret preference disguised as shy reluctance – might have been a cold in the head. Try a couple of aspirins and you'll soon feel better. 'Better' was indeed the operative word, for lesbianism was widely believed to be a disease. However, there were other reasons for my silence than the climate of opinion as it affected my personal relationships. There was my upbringing in an overwhelmingly masculine family, and there was my career.

Though lesbians suffered no legal penalties as male homosexuals did, there was a strong prejudice against them when I was growing up in the thirties and forties, and an active unwritten law against their holding posts which brought them into contact with children and young people: it was generally believed (and this is so today) that most gay people are pederasts.

Hysterical reaction by the public to any news involving lesbians reveals at once the deep-seated prejudices that many people experience against those they suspect, uneasily, of being different. It also reveals a sickening prurience on the part of some who could perhaps accept situations of gay love and partnership if they were better informed about them. But the job of the journalist in the popular press is not to inform but to titillate, arouse prejudice, and set up witch-hunts. Cases where lesbian mothers appear in court over disputed custody of children are rarely treated without moral opprobrium and ignorant prejudice. A case of lesbian violence is pure jam to the press. Such a case was given the full treatment in the summer of 1986. Few journalists would be rewarded for informing the public about the pressures under which gay people live. It is convenient to forget the violence in some heterosexual partnerships, and to ignore the obvious fact that the socially imposed secrecy behind which so many lesbian relationships still exist may produce a claustrophobic atmosphere in which quarrels and bitterness erupt. Talking over emotional problems with friends and relations – a way of releasing tensions – is usually denied to closet lesbians.

I could write more on this theme, but this is an autobiography not a polemic. It is time to make the personal point that I became a teacher in my late twenties and a headmistress in my thirties. It was essential for me to keep my lesbianism under covers. I have to add this rider: it would be just as necessary for me to remain in the closet if I were a headmistress today, some forty years later. Much of the public prejudice had grown up after the publications of such writers as Krafft-Ebing and Havelock Ellis. I don't think that I had even heard of these sexologists when I was growing up, and perhaps it was as well that I did not study their work. Havelock Ellis followed Krafft-Ebing's theory that lesbianism was due to 'cerebral anomalies', and the sign of 'an *inherited disease* of the central nervous system' (my italics). If I had read these bizarre opinions, I think I should have been frightened into believing them and become even more disturbed and distressed than I already was. It is fair to say that such writers were carrying the debate about the origins of homosexuality away from moral sin into the medical field, but as Jane Rule writes: 'They could not foresee that translating contempt into pity, punishment into treatment would finally not increase social acceptance for homosexuals but sidetrack scientific investigation for generations. To try to cure what is not an illness in the first place is like trying to weed a field without knowing the nature of the crop.' (*Lesbian Images,* Doubleday, 1975).

'Sickness', 'inverted', '*per*verted', 'abnormal': all were labels emanating from such writers as Havelock Ellis (much of whose work was based on minimal research), and labels are quickly seized upon by those who do not want to think for themselves. A strong whiff of these malodorous views hung in the air during the first twenty or thirty years of this century, emerging often in half-baked form here and there in the press, in novels, in overheard, half-understood conversations. Ignorant though I was of the sexologists' writings, I grew up with unexpressed fears derived from them, a dread lest these labels should be applied to myself, though mercifully I did not till much later meet the most monstrous theory emanating from the pundits: that lesbianism frequently ends in madness and suicide.

I knew something of Freud, but I was so antipathetic to the little that I knew that I made almost no effort to furnish my ignorant mind by reading more than two or three of his books. I was repelled by a theory that has become a psychological cliché: that neuroses and indeed character traits in general are rooted entirely in our infant life, in the treatment that we received from parents, siblings, nurses, teachers. I chose to ignore the partial truth of this, finding it repugnant to my pride. My upbringing and still more my wide reading in the English classics and Latin authors taught me that gentlemen don't whine about their unhappy childhoods, or blame them for their later sorrows and misdeeds. They remember them through gritted teeth – and was not I one of the chaps? A public-school stoic? Indeed I was. The classical ethos which informed the English middle-class educational system was also exemplified in much of our literature (rather more in that written by men than by women, but I had not then worked this out). It was something I never questioned. I, too, studied Latin and loved and venerated the heroes of the stoic pantheon who committed suicide rather than suffer dishonour. I was the captain of my soul and I rejected totally the idea that I was a victim of my upbringing, still more that I was a stereotype in some psychological theory.

Captain of my soul I may have felt secretly, but it did not give me much public courage. How could it, when my own assessment of my sexuality was so ambivalent and so fearful? When to find one's own identity was so difficult amid the pressures put upon one to accept society's norm in every field: dress, behaviour, speech, tastes?

The habit of secrecy has remained with me all my life. It persisted throughout the seventies, even after I retired from teaching. I could not entirely shake it off even after I had come out as a lesbian on an ITV programme early in 1980. Coming out gives one the chance to be honest; indeed, it imposes the burden of honesty and it is a heavy burden to take up. The years of dishonesty had formed a hard shell and I continually found myself moving back under its protection, as a prisoner sometimes comes to love his gaoler. Or perhaps I was playing a game, like a child crying out to her companions or to the grown-ups around her: 'I'm invisible! You can't see me!'

The ITV programme was the first in a series of late-night programmes about the gay scene. To hell with it, I thought, when I was invited to take part. Why not? I felt an enormous load fall from my back. I was a lesbian. Let the world know it. At least, this was my first reaction, but freedom from the past does not come all that easily. Shall I ever be liberated from its shackles?

'Coming out' on that TV programme proclaimed me a lesbian but little more. Today it appears to have no depth. It is no more true than the various photographs of me: the one on my passport (unrecognisable), on my British Library ticket (where I look like a butch prison officer), the portrait on the jacket of my 1983 novel, *Open the Door*, which shows me in my serious, thoughtful persona. I will say that it is a good likeness. Or do I admire it because it makes me look almost handsome and interesting?

That label 'lesbian' has its importance but leaves out the rest of what makes up my personality. At last my sexual proclivities, which I had had to suppress for so long, were out in the open. This was significant to me not so much as a truth revealed to the world but as an inner tension relaxed, a deception laid aside. But, I feel justified in asking, would a heterosexual person feel elevated, released, vindicated or anything else if her heterosexuality were to be publicly acknowledged on a TV programme? The notion is absurd. In so far as homosexuality has presented me with a problem in the past, that problem ceased to exist for my inner self once I had discovered my own sexual tastes and felt sure about them and found love through them. That the problem continued to exist was the fault of social, heterosexual *mores* and prejudices. Subject to these I have had to live, and this has in the past severely affected my lifestyle, but not the inner truth of my life, once I had escaped from the brainwashed years of establishing my own identity. These lasted a long time, until I was at least forty, and to a lesser degree beyond that. I am not of course unique. I am one of many – far more than our heterosexual society is willing to admit.

When I was in my forties I at last acknowledged the truth to myself. Thirty years later, I proclaimed it.

2
When I Reflect, Brother Toby

Unhappiness is a bad habit. A fat, slow fish lurking in muddy waters and weed-rooted depths. And it is a gross feeder. It can be caught by someone sufficiently patient, skilled and determined, brought to the bank and knocked on the head. Or it can be hooked and played with: its life is apparently everlasting. Depression is then its name and you will be cunning if you land that one. It will slip off the hook again and again and elude you by diving into its restorative slime. Throughout my life I have been so unskilful an angler that it would be ludicrous and boring to attempt to describe at any length my sad, rainsodden excursions with rod and line.

Until comparatively late in my life I have accepted unhappiness and depression as my lot, almost without question. Yet I am capable of immense joy. It is this capacity which has no doubt given me a circle of lasting friends, who have supported me through so much that it may seem churlish that the only book I have ever dedicated to them is a children's book. Churlish, that is, to outsiders. I value my books for children, however, and this particular one,* with its dedication 'To my friends young and old', meant much to me in the writing, and my friends can read into it the tribute to friendship that is its key.

I find that to acknowledge how far unhappiness can be simply a bad habit does not free me from it, but it does make me unwilling to accept it as readily as I have in the past, and I have made the discovery that this obscene fish can be kept skulking in its murky depths by the company of friends, by music and by books.

In the privacy of my study, my bed, my walks, my restless driving about the countryside, when friends are far off (and one should not demand too much in any case), certain authors have sustained me.

---

* *Dragon in the Harbour* (Kestrel, 1980; Puffin Books, 1982)

This goes back to my childhood when I spent hours by myself, often lonely and unhappy as many children are, reading and rereading Thomas Hardy's novels. His pessimism chimed in with my own dark view of life and indeed reinforced it, and his descriptive writing transported me back to the Dorset hills and valleys that I had left when I was ten years old.

But I have not always sought out writers of an unhappy cast of mind; rather those whose philosophy is one of survival in the face of loss and despair, like Montaigne and Sterne. I know nothing of the latter's private life or how far he wrote to dispel his doubts in the essential goodness of man, but for me, whose conviction about this is decidedly shaky, he is a most sustaining author:

> When I reflect, brother Toby, upon MAN; and take a view of that dark side of him which represents his life as open to so many causes of trouble . . . the catalogue of all the crossreckonings and sorrowful Items with which the heart of man is overcharg'd, 'tis wonderful by what hidden resource it is enabled to stand out, and bear itself up.

This paragraph lifts my spirits whenever I read it and it urges me to turn to my own inner resources. They do not always prove reliable but they are the only safety net of my own that I have. Cheered almost to optimism by rereading *Tristram Shandy*, I wonder at my repeated readiness to admit unhappiness, as though it were a sullen bailiff arrived to distrain my humour, my love of friends and all my other assets. But this is absurd of me, for I live in the second half of the twentieth century when far more than personal unhappiness (which belongs to no century) weighs upon my spirits.

I live in a world of nuclear threat, of starvation and extreme poverty cheek by jowl with Western greed and crapulence. Material advantage has always made wealthy countries reluctant to put pressure upon South Africa to abandon the apartheid system, and no country has been more reluctant than Great Britain. Cash is more important than human lives. I suppose that a disregard for the value of life, the treatment of inferiors as objects is hardly new, but it is now very sophisticated and wider in scope. If one condemns apartheid in South Africa, what is one to say of Russia's treatment of Jews or the Indonesian oppression of East Timor and Iriane (West Papua)? Are these not forms of apartheid?

Shandean hope in the resources of the human spirit or in the recuperative powers of our mutilated planet and its starving and abused peoples is waning within me. Would Mr Shandy be so sanguine today, as he conversed with brother Toby?

Whether or no he would be, at least the small world he created in the face of despair, cosmic or personal, is one that can be visited and revisited in his pages, which fortify the reader with a reminder that perhaps not all is lost, that the holiness of the heart's affections, the values of truth and toleration, are still valid and to be pursued doggedly, that some faint hope remains of stemming the tide of evil.

I have deliberately cut out of this book many of the literary allusions dear to me and many of the quotations which the rough draft contained, but it would give a false picture of myself if I omitted the powerful influence of certain authors upon me and the part they have played in the personal survival course I have pursued throughout so much of my life. I support my delight in quotation with Montaigne's words – and few authors are so quotable – 'When I quote others I do so in order to express my own ideas more clearly.'

Montaigne and Thomas Hardy are not so much pessimistic as clearsighted, both of them expressing that uncompromising vision: 'If way to the better there be, It demands a full look at the worst.' Whatever I may think about the world I live in, and they are often sombre thoughts, fundamentally I have sought happiness. The habit of pessimism sprang perhaps from a conflict within me between hope and clear observation that the odds are too often stacked against it. It was to fortify my essentially life-loving inner self that I drew so deeply upon a cherished group of writers. Sterne's humanity can still lift my spirits today as it did in my fifties when I was going through a severe crisis. The loss of my lover had led me to attempt suicide. As I pulled myself up from the depths, Laurence Sterne came to my aid and, being at the time peculiarly isolated, it was natural to me to turn to books.

There was another writer, the poet Rilke, more important to me than any other during my middle years, for he spoke directly to my creative self and reminded me that I had the means of survival within myself through writing. His poetry had already had an inspiring influence upon me some ten years before this, when I first discovered it in my forties. As I shall be explaining in the chapters on writing, his *Duino Elegies* had at that time released my imagination. I began to write seriously and with concentration and produced several novels

within a few years. I was just fifty. *In extremis*, I turned again to Rilke
to fortify me and stimulate me into beginning a new book, and in the
writing of it to make sense of what I had done.

By a strange coincidence Rilke has again acted as a catalyst in the
best sense of the word. Fairly recently I found some verses by him
which I had never read before. They surprised me with their angry
impatience, their severe castigation of writers who wilfully neglect the
material they have within themselves:

> O ancient curse of poets!
> being sorry for themselves instead of saying,
> forever passing judgement on their feeling
> instead of shaping it . . .
> > invalids,
> using a language full of woefulness
> to tell us where it hurts, instead of sternly transforming
> into words those selves of theirs,
> as imperturbable cathedral carvers
> transposed themselves into the constant stone.

'Transforming into words those selves of theirs . . . ' When I copied
those words into my journal I added this: 'A poem to be set before
myself when I come to write this new autobiography.' All that Rilke
had meant to me in my forties and fifties flooded back into my mind
with new force and understanding, and once again my creative self
responded.

The central themes of this book will be my inner imaginative life,
and two major experiences of love. Both of these ended in separation
and loss. I have attempted to analyse the totally different ways in
which I rebuilt my life after these two cataclysms, which occurred
relatively late in my life, in my forties and sixties. I believe that it is
what we make of events rather than the events themselves which is
worth recording, for it is our reactions to experience that proclaim
what we are.

I hope that in a broader sense this book will be regarded as a contribution to the body of women's experience during this century, limited
though it is of course by my class and colour. Perhaps what I have
written will reach out beyond its personal bounds and afford confidence and reassurance to women as confused and unhappy as I have
been at times during my seventy-odd years.

In the OED definition, an autobiography is 'the writing of one's own history'. This definition is better applied to a memoir. The most typical parts of such a work usually derive from the notable personalities whom the author has met and from such aspects of her/his life as travel, politics, career. There is nothing like that in this book. Its truth must derive from my ability to capture as faithfully as I can and interpret the lives I have lived, and I, the writer who looks back upon those earlier selves, am a multiple personality created by them, incorporating their essences, often metamorphosed and, in some cases, long suppressed. I am not painting a static portrait. I am, rather, walking along a corridor of mirrors in which I observe myself at different stages of my life.

The book is a dialectic between old and present selves. When I have finished it, I shall expect to have changed still further. The present self who writes this page cannot stand still. To a great extent I have written my fiction to discover who I am, what I think, how to live my life. In this respect the present book differs from my novels only in setting me free from the demands of fiction to walk down this corridor and to examine and record what I see as truthfully as I can. 'Escape oblivion,' wrote George Sand. 'Write your own history, all of you who have understood your life and sounded your heart.'

In these first two chapters I stand as it were at the head of the stairs, a woman in my early seventies. As I begin to walk along the passage before me, I see myself first in a series of small mirrors, hanging close together, for in memory childhood is telescoped. You do not see the years spread out but clustered together in a tight pattern, very like an apple-wood picture frame I still possess, carved by my father and holding five tiny round photographs. In the centre is my father's face. My three schoolboy brothers surround him, Tom smiling and handsome in a sailor suit, Roger fat and genial, Bob with his serious face above a stiff collar and tie; and the last tiny picture – they are only half an inch across – is of myself, a round-faced baby a few months old. Who is absent?

As I begin to walk down the corridor, there I am at various stages: beginning to walk, sitting looking up at my father, wearing a blue dressing gown with a peaked hood that I remember well; and there are my brothers and my father and my mother. Although my father did not include her in the apple-wood frame (but was not this for symmetry's sake, for it is shaped like a four-leaved clover?), my mother was the dominant influence in my family. It is time to introduce her.

3
Home, Sweet Home

My mother was a late-nineteenth-century career woman.
Perhaps she should never have married. She was born in 1869. Her
father was an officer in the Bombay Staff Corps and her twenty-one-
year-old mother died giving birth to her daughter in an Indian hill
station with, no doubt, little skilled medical attention. Curiously
enough, my mother was not brought up by either paternal or
maternal grandparents, or even by relatives. She was sent back to
England at a few months old and cared for by a family whose name
she never told me. Even more curious, to my mind, is the fact that she
was incorrect about her mother's name. I have a sepia photograph of
this pitifully young grandmother, and on the back of it in my
mother's hand are the words: 'My mother Mary Ann Curgenven,
aged 19'. It is this surname that appears in the family tree drawn up
by my father, so the story must have been given to him. I later
discovered that my grandmother's name was Mary Ann Marshall.
One of the two witnesses to her wedding to Lieutenant Coles in 1866
bears the Cornish name of Curgenven, but whether he was a relative
or not I have no idea. As her own father lived until Mother was in her
teens it seems odd that she never learned her mother's correct name,
and that no relative, Curgenven or Marshall, appears to have played
any part in her life. My father lost both parents when he was ten, and
my brothers and I grew up never knowing our grandparents on either
side and singularly short of relatives of any degree.

Mother was given a meagre education at a Tunbridge Wells school
for the daughters of gentlemen. Her father returned from India and
remarried when she was a small child, choosing a strong-minded
woman against whom my mother had to struggle to win her independence later on. After nursing her father when she was in her teens and
seeing him die in a diabetic coma, she determined upon a career in

nursing, but her stepmother forbade this. She wanted no career but marriage for her young and eligible stepdaughter.

However, my mother was resolved to escape from home – home being a stifling provincial town, Malvern Wells. She might have married early, for in her late teens she fell in love with a handsome young man whose father was the incumbent of a small parish near Ross-on-Wye, not far from Malvern. This sweetheart, as Mother always called him, died very suddenly in his early twenties. Fifty years later, when I was taking my mother for a tour through Somerset and Gloucestershire, she suddenly asked me to take her to a village near Ross-on-Wye. When we entered the churchyard she crossed it with unerring precision, and found the young man's nearly overgrown grave with its lichened headstone. As we stood there in the late spring sunshine, my mother said: 'He was the most beautiful and lovable man I have ever known.' Her marriage to my father, her children, her long years of loneliness, fell away before this enduring memory of first love.

Perhaps it was her grief at this loss that stiffened her resolve to leave home. Unable to enter the nursing profession immediately, she answered the advertisement of a London clergyman who was seeking young gentlewomen to assist him in his social work in an East End parish. It was 'good works', so it passed muster with her stepmother. Mary Ann Coles escaped to London and concealed the fact that her social work was among fallen women. I think this odd experience probably laid the foundation for her enduring love for East End Londoners and later drew her to that area as a hospital nurse.

The 'good works' fell under suspicion when the clergyman became enamoured of my mother, a strikingly beautiful girl with dark hair and large pure grey eyes. The parson began holding love-feasts of a dubious nature and finally departed for Devonshire and a more secluded spot for his agapes, asking Mother to accompany him as his 'little helpmeet', to quote Mother, who told this story with relish. At this point Stepmother tumbled to the situation and whisked the girl back to Malvern, probably with some justification.

Again Mother escaped, this time to train as a nurse at Shadwell Children's Hospital in the heart of dockland, and close to the Ratcliffe Highway, locale of Jack the Ripper. It was not long before Stepmother made an attempt to get her home. She staged a nervous condition and demanded Mother's presence. If she wanted to nurse, let her do it at home, she suggested. Deceived, my mother hurried home, decided briskly that there was nothing whatever the matter with her stepmother, and returned to Shadwell where she worked for several years, to become the youngest sister in the nursing profession.

She loved Whitechapel, the Mile End Road, the docks, and the people who lived there. Many of her young patients were suffering from malnutrition and food-poisoning after eating the rotten fruit and decaying bread from the gutters of the local street markets. Fifty years later she could speak of this with undiminished feeling. I have two professional photographs of my mother, standing in a Shadwell ward, an upright, small figure in a stiff cap, unsmiling (but that must have been due to nerves for she had a strong sense of humour). She stands beside two little children who share an iron hospital bed; an aspidistra decorates the mantelpiece above the open fire, and an oleograph of 'The Good Shepherd' hangs on the wall.

I wish that my mother had written a book about her hospital experiences, for my memory has mislaid many of the stories she told me. One, however, I do recall vividly. In her Shadwell ward she nursed a little boy of whom she became very fond. She also came to love and respect his parents. His father was a woodman working in Epping Forest and he and his wife travelled all the way to the hospital in dockland to visit their dying child. When the little boy eventually died my mother was unable to go to his funeral but, knowing the cemetery to which he had been taken, she decided to visit his grave on her half day and put some flowers on it. She set off down what must have been the Mile End Road, I suppose, and asked the cemetery porter for the position of the grave. He consulted the records and gave the young nurse a strange look. 'I'd better take you there, miss,' he said. He led my unsuspecting, innocent mother through the cemetery to a huge open grave for paupers, where lay dozens of coffins side by side, lighly sprinkled with yellow, clayey earth. 'He's somewhere down there,' said the porter laconically. Appalled, my mother dropped her flowers into the common grave and departed weeping. She never forgot the scene.

When she was about twenty-six she obtained a post at Great Ormond Street Hospital for Sick Children. I've no doubt she would have ended up as matron of it, but her promising career was again interrupted. A friend of hers who had become matron of a large Hampshire hospital asked her to join her staff and help her pull up its standards. It was in a rundown inefficient state. One of its inadequacies, I remember, was that the canvas baths on wheels in which sick children were given their weekly ablutions were used at other times as receptacles for dirty diphtheria swabs and other infected detrita.

Her stay at this hospital was short, for she had become alarmingly anaemic. The medical cure prescribed for her condition was an immediate return to India, the land of her birth. She sailed east, therefore, to stay with her late father's Indian Civil Service and Army relatives and friends, and on board ship she met the ship's doctor who was my father, out to see the world. He went on to China and Japan. He wrote her ardent letters, begging her to return with him to England and marry him. She met him in Bombay and travelled back with him. On this romantic voyage across the Indian Ocean, up the Red Sea and through the exotic Mediterranean, she succumbed to his persistent wooing and became engaged to him.

Stepmother, now remarried and with two little boys of her own, Carl and Harry, was incensed at the idea of her stepdaughter, with her Indian Army connections, throwing herself away on a mere apothecary – this was in 1896 – and at once forbade the marriage. However, my mother was not only in love. She must have realised that her nursing career could not be resumed, for her visit to India, hardly surprisingly, had not cured her anaemia. She became obstinate. Eventually her stepmother capitulated – my father had great charm, and enough capital to buy a practice. Thomas Davys Manning and Mary Ann Coles, known as Molly or May, were married on 1 September 1897. They honeymooned – my father was one of the most romantic men I have ever known – at the New Inn, halfway down the cobbled street of Clovelly in north Devon. My eldest brother, Tom, was born in the late summer of the following year. My mother was still in poor health and the baby, she once told me, was like a little wax doll.

Roger and Humphrey (known as Bob) were born in 1901 and 1903. I was born late in the marriage when my mother was forty-four, nearly ten years after my brothers. She once told me that she couldn't think how it happened. 'I thought all that sort of thing was over,' she added, a trifle smugly. If this had always been her attitude to sex – 'all that sort of thing' – it is easy to understand my father's later discontent and restlessness. Or was it that he had not proved a very sensitive lover and had made sex repugnant to her? These are things that can never be known now. My mother's real passion, I believe, was not for my father but for the career she had lost.

I have in my possession still a touching memento of my parents' romanticism in the early days of their marriage: a large handsome volume, inscribed in gilt lettering amid scrolls of flowers:

THE LOG BOOK OF MAY AND DAVYS

The first item mounted within it shows that even a voyage to India and the glamour of her engagement had not dimmed my mother's loyalty to her beloved East End of London. It is a notice of the White-chapel Fine Art Exhibition, Easter 1897, at St Jude's School-house, Commercial Street, E. A charming floral device occupies the left-hand side of the advertisement and under it are printed some words of Ruskin: 'Life without industry is guilt, and industry without Art is Brutality.' Mother would have approved of that sentiment. She had a taste for Ruskin, Morris and Browning. My parents went to the Exhibition on Sunday 2 May, my mother's writing tells me.

The rest of the scrapbook is of little interest beyond my own family. It is a curiosity compounded of pressed flowers, theatre programmes (Daly's Theatre and the Savoy, what else?), cards and faded photographs, and what appears to be the newly wedded couple's first grocery bill, containing items 'BOUGHT of Geo. Paulin on Sept. 10th 1897'. It adds up to £4. 1*d*., of which a half-pound of butter at 7½*d* must be the most nostalgic item for most of us today.

My father's family is said to have come from Saxony in pre-Conquest times and settled in East Anglia, the surname persisting in a few place-names. Later, some of the Mannings seem to have moved to the richer pastures of Somerset and eventually settled in the Black-down Hills south of Taunton. By the eighteenth century they were yeoman farmers, prosperous enough to provide higher education for their sons. My grandfather, Thomas Davys Manning, left the Black-downs for Yeovil, where he set up a chemist's shop and left enough money to send his sons to Bruton, a respected West Country public school, and then into professions. History does not relate what the single girl, Christabel, was given in the way of education. The eldest son, Owen, became an engineer; the youngest, Ralph, went into the Merchant Navy. My father took a degree at King's College, London University, and then went on to Guy's Hospital to qualify as a doctor. The family had been brought up all through their teens by two maiden cousins living near Montacute in Somerset, both their parents having died within a week of each other, of the measles. Neither of my parents, therefore, had the experience of the usual Victorian home with a mother and a father, an important factor in their later married lives, perhaps – certainly in my father's.

On two occasions in the last two hundred years the family's sober

Saxon blood has been leavened and invigorated by a Celtic infusion. It was not infrequent, and this may be true today, for Welsh and Somerset families to marry. In the eighteenth century a Manning yeoman farmer married the daughter of a Welshman, Thomas Davys, and christened their eldest son Thomas Davys Manning. I possess the long, elegant tablespoon that his grandfather gave the child as a christening present, engraved: 'From TD to TDM 1798'. The eldest son of the family was named Thomas Davys for four generations in all, my father being the third and my brother Tom the fourth and last. The second Welsh woman to enter the Manning family was my great-grandmother, Mary Owen, whose surname was again taken over as a Christian name in the family. My mother, even if she was not the daughter of a Cornish Curgenven, as she persistently stated, certainly had something of the Celt in her. Her mother's real name of Marshall is common in Cornwall, and her maternal grandfather was called Voyle and came from Tenby in South Wales.

After my father finished his training at Guy's Hospital, he worked as a junior doctor in a Reigate practice, going on his rounds on horseback, and on dark nights feeling his way along the hedgerows with his whip, he once told me. He then travelled to the East as a ship's doctor and met my mother on board, as I have described.

When my father married, he bought his own practice in Hoddesdon, Hertfordshire, then a pretty market town. The doctor's house was a Queen Anne town house of dark-red brick in the High Street, with a walled garden. I assume that his chemist father must have done well and left all three sons money. My father was the first man in Hoddesdon to own a car, a de Dion Bouton. One wealthy patient refused his medical attention on the ground that his predecessor had always driven up to her house in a pony and trap and she was not going to entrust herself to a doctor who drove about in one of these newfangled machines with their disgusting smell and vulgar noisiness. Other residents wagged their heads over his poor pregnant wife, who would undoubtedly give birth to a stillborn child, or worse, a monster, if her husband persisted in driving her at breakneck speed through the Hertfordshire lanes, elegant motoring veil and protective goggles notwithstanding.

However, the three sons were born safely and only the firstborn gave any cause for anxiesty, and that was due to Mother's anaemia. This disappeared soon after Tom's birth, whether from the wholesome country air, the exciting drives in the de Dion Bouton, or my father's passion for feeding her upon fresh fruit and vegetables in a dangerously modern fashion, I don't know. All the same, Tom remained obstinately delicate and it was decided that sea air was necessary for him. My father chose to move to Weymouth in Dorset, delighted to return to his native West Country after the foggy fields and lanes of Hertfordshire – a county that his daughter was later condemned to live in for some five years and loathed more than any other part of England.

The three little boys were still small when the family moved. There were excursions to the beach, endless picnics and drives through the beautiful Dorset countryside. For the parents on their own there were holidays in Fowey and in Clovelly. The practice prospered. There were servants, a new Ford car, rounds of dinner parties. Living in this pleasant, carefree ambience, and ruling her household of boys with nursemaids to do the really taxing work, my mother and father were, I imagine, still riding on a crest of romantic happiness. A cottage in Clovelly, Number 73 in the High Street, was rented in about 1911 or 1912 and remained the chief place for family holidays until about 1922. I was born in 1911 and was taken to Clovelly with my brothers. I remember it very clearly. On the seaward side of the cottage was a low wall and a bench. Here the old fishermen would sit or lean, looking down over the precipitous street, the grey roofs of the cottages tumbling below them like a pack of cards to the half-moon of a harbour, and beyond it the glittering waters of the Bristol Channel. We knew all the old men and called them collectively 'the leaners', a term I used for similar harbourside folk in a children's book sixty years later.

The cottage was rented unfurnished for twenty pounds a year from the Hamlyns of Clovelly Court, who owned the whole village and would never sell any of its cottages. Our furniture came down the High Street on sledges drawn by donkeys which wore metal headbands with their names painted on them. In those days, the Clovelly people, or the children at least, wore boots with shining studs on the soles which struck sparks as they clattered up and down the cobbles. They ring in my ears still. Number 73 was simple, with two biggish rooms on the ground floor and a kitchen and, as far as I recollect, three bedrooms above. There must have been a WC, but no bathroom, of course, only an enamel hip-bath that stood in one of the low-ceilinged bedrooms, the window sills of which were almost level with the sloping floors. The hip-bath remains indelibly impressed on my mind, for under its rim lurked cockroaches. Even Mother, strong-minded woman though she was, was afraid of the cockroaches.

By the time I was five or six I had acquired several pseudo-brothers, boys whose parents were abroad or who required a family home for some reason. There were Pat and Vernon, whose parents were in Africa, and Chan, a Siamese boy, who took me out on the sands and taught me to sing 'If you were the only girl in the world', and there was George, who became a permanency. His mother had appeared on the doorstep of our house on the Weymouth esplanade one day, dragging a pale-faced, undersized little boy behind her. She really must put George into some nice household, she said, as he didn't get on at all with her pet monkey. Mother at once took him in. He attached himself to my youngest brother and remained devoted to him and indeed to the family for the rest of his life. These four boys were roughly contemporaries of my three brothers and therefore some nine or ten years older than I was.

They shared our life completely. Brothers, co-brothers, friends and cousins all came to Clovelly and we overflowed from Number 73 into cottages around us. My mother was in her element, organising their pleasures, cooking meals in the primitive kitchen (perhaps she should have been a missionary's wife), providing endless picnics, reading aloud in the evening. We seldom stayed in during the day. The chara-bancs and the little Ilfracombe steamer debouched hordes of trippers each morning and we went out in the Ford, sitting on the open hood, standing on the running-boards. Packed among the pairs of legs were piled the baskets of food and drink, sketching materials for Dad, a book for Mother, and bathing gear if we were going near a beach. More often than going to the sea, we walked across Clovelly Park to the winged shelter or to Gallantry Bower, where an unhappy lover once jumped to his death, or drove through the Hobby Drive, or westwards to Mouth Mills or Hartland Point. Here the parents would leave us, to walk out as far as was possible and stand, their arms clasped in each other's, united in their passion for the towering seas that reared their immense crests against the rocks.

A golden time for me, it might be thought, but I don't remember that I myself enjoyed it much. Clovelly is not ideal for a child of six or seven.

We went there often, for my father had acquired a partner and in those leisurely days it was easy for him to leave the practice and take a long weekend off or even a week. We would pack into the Ford and depart, taking the switchback coast road through Bridport to Devon — one of the most lovely roads in England — and always halting at Moore's bakery at Morecambe Lake near Charmouth, where the rich odour of hot bread hung in the air round the low white building. We carried the aroma of hot loaves and warm fruitcake and Knob biscuits with us to the car. Number 73 Clovelly High Street was never without Moore's succulent cakes and tins of the buttery, golden knobs to eat with Cheddar cheese and Dorset Blue Vinny, the delicious, dry, crumbly cheese, nothing like the greasy 'Dorset Blue' sold in local shops today. Blue Vinny was a farmworker's cheese, made of skim milk and costing a few pence a pound before the Great War, and not more than a shilling or two after it. The call at Moore's bakery was a ritual with my father, as was his much-admired way with a Knob biscuit. He cracked it in half in the palm of his broad hand, while the rest of us fumbled with our knives and left a mass of yellow crumbs on our plates.

How good it sounds. Descriptions of food usually evoke a sense of well-being and induce me to take a backward look on what seems a perpetual game of Happy Families at Number 73 Clovelly High Street. Indeed, we did play cards in the evening, Racing Demon and Cooncan, which I think was the precursor of the more exciting Rummy. Dad played his two invariable games of Patience (with two packs, of course): Les Huits and Senior Wrangler, while mother knitted or sewed or read aloud. The more energetic brothers and cousins and friends went out again, swimming in the evening light off the end of the quay, or mackerel-fishing in the bay with one or two of the 'leaners'.

I was so much younger than the boys, and the walks were so long and arduous that one of the brothers usually had to bring me home sitting on his shoulder. My memories of the place, like so much of my childhood, have come down to me filtered through the memories of others. There must have been many moments of happiness. I remember wandering in the deep, ferny lanes and playing with village children in the cobbled back alleys or on the beach. Above all, I remember the pervasive smell of woodsmoke in the air. Even now, more than sixty years later, that smell instantly recalls Clovelly, always sunlit, with shady stone walls and banks of wild garlic, thin wreaths of smoke in the lanes and heavy, nodding hydrangeas outside the cottages. And I have one more private and specific memory.

When I went down the cobbled street to the quay one morning, I saw two women diving off the end of the quay into deep water. One of them was thin and enormously tall. I thought her the most beautiful creature I had ever seen, a dark-haired mermaid, as she flashed in and out of the blue water and at last climbed up the iron ladder to the end of the quay where I was sitting.

'What's your name?' I asked boldly.

'Iris,' she replied, and we sat down on the wet flagstones and exchanged information about each other. She and her friend worked in London and were having a fortnight's holiday in Clovelly. I told her about my family and insisted that she and her friend, whose name I cannot remember, must come and meet them. They demurred at first, but I was determined. I had discovered a marvellous, hardly human creature who bathed from the quay every morning and I wanted to share her with my family, I who had so little usually to contribute.

I had not misjudged the effect that Iris Blaikie was going to have. My father and mother were enchanted with her and she and her friend were soon coming to meals, going out for walks and drives and picnics with us. Later on, my brothers fell in love with her one after the other. Tom's affair was the briefest, for he did not live in London and had little chance of seeing her. Roger had a more substantial relationship with her, but he was soon to go abroad. Bob embarked on a long friendship with her which somehow never bloomed into a love affair. It is sad, looking back on it, for Iris would have been a lovely wife for him. I certainly thought this at the time and had also worked out that as Bob was just over six foot tall, Iris would find her own height no embarrassment. Alas, Bob was very shy. Nothing came of the affair, if affair it was, and Iris Blaikie went out of our lives, but I have never forgotten her and her kindness to me when I was a small child and 'odd man out' in the family life at Clovelly.

Now that I am for the first time in my writing life returning to my childhood, my parents and siblings, with serious scrutiny, I have to build up my material, contained fragmentarily in such images as 'Iris diving off the quay', into a coherent narrative, rather as an archaeologist deduces an historical account from the finds on a dig. Owing to the ten-year gap between myself and my youngest brother, few of these memories have been actually shared between me and my siblings, and perhaps they are more like those tales that have travelled far and doubtless been much altered in the telling.

4
A Union of Souls

My father was a restless man, as those who pursue the
elusive flare of happiness over the marshes usually are. He uprooted
his family several times during the twenty years they lived at Weymouth, perhaps searching for a substitute for the house that had held
their happiness at Hoddesdon. I believe there were two or three terrace houses, discarded one after the other, and then, after three years
at Rodwell Lodge on the heights above the harbour, the house where
I was born in 1911, he moved down to the esplanade. I spent most of
my childhood, from a few months old to seven years, in the late Georgian house of great charm and distinction in the centre of the esplanade,
Number 2 Gloucester Row. This building and two others of the row of
four, the finest houses along the front, have been allowed by the philis-
tines of the local Council planners to be turned into amusement
arcades. The beautiful, dark-red brick elevations have been murder-
ously cemented from top to bottom, and even the historic name
Gloucester Row has been obliterated. The four houses built between
the Royal Hotel and the Gloucester have become just numbers on the
esplanade. Here my three brothers were brought up as they came into
their teens and went to the local public school, Weymouth College, as
day boys. Here, too, lived the extra brothers, George, Pat, Vernon
and Chan.

I suppose that it was on one of my almost daily visits to the sands
opposite our windows that, carefully nurtured as I was, I escaped my
nanny's hand and made friends with a little boy who lived in one of
the back streets behind Gloucester Row. 'My parents kept me from
children that were rough' but somehow this urchin – I'll call him
Cyril for I forget his name – managed to persuade me round to his
house to play. There we concocted a splendid scheme for getting
money. I think it must have been my idea, inspired by the chapter

called 'The Conscience Pudding' in E. Nesbit's novel, *The New Trea-sure Seekers*, a chapter which Mother read aloud to the family every Christmas. The poor-but-honest Bastables, alone for Christmas, decide to make a festal pudding, clubbing their money together to buy the ingredients. When they discover that H.O., the youngest, has raised his contribution by begging on the pavement for pennies for poor children, they righteously go out and try to give away the pud-ding to the deserving poor.

Cyril and I stood begging on a windy corner near our house, that is what I remember: the wind cutting at my bare legs under my cotton frock, the inshore wind off the sea that always seemed to sweep relent-lessly down those little streets behind the esplanade. And I recall too the brightly coloured tin that we held out for pennies. It was a cigarette or tobacco tin that I had retrieved from my father's study waste-paper basket. We went back to Cyril's front parlour, a stuffy little room that I can recollect with curious clarity, and counted our ill-gotten gains. Someone, I think it was my mother, arrived like an avenging angel to sweep me away, never to see Cyril again. She, of course, blamed Cyril for this wickedness but all the time the idea was mine, and inspired by one of the family's favourite books, and I don't suppose I had the courage to say so. I was brought up on E. Nesbit, whose novels had been coming out when my brothers were children. I still have some of the early, indeed first editions of them, and gladly admit to her influence upon my writing in my children's books.

Number 2 Gloucester Row was built around a square central yard. The living rooms were in front: my father's consulting room on the ground floor, the drawing room above it. The long french windows, overlooking the bay, opened on to a graceful iron balcony. The dining room was at the back of this room, its windows looking inwards on to the yard and across to the first-floor kitchen opposite, for the old basement kitchen quarters had been abandoned. The domestics had to bring the crockery and food along the passage that ran down the third side of the square, the fourth side being the wall of the next-door house. This long walk seemed to my father hard on both the servants and the food. He built a kind of wooden ark, a substantial cupboard with gabled roof, suspended on pulley-wheels on a stout cable slung across the yard from the dining-room window to the kitchen opposite. Into the ark went the food and the hot plates. The parlourmaid waited for it in the dining room and it arrived on our plates hot and, I am sure, nourishing, for my father was curiously modern in his attitude to diet. He had fed the little boys, when they were babies at the outset of the century, upon sieved vegetables like carrots and spinach, arousing in many of his patients the gloomy conviction that he would kill the three of them, as they had already predicted that his poor young wife would suffer from her drives in the open de Dion Bouton.

Under the kitchen at the back of the house was the garage, once a coach house and stable, opening on to a lane. A stray cat made her home in the garage, and was known to the family as 'Caretaker'. On one occasion she had her kittens in the hood of the car, conveniently folded down to form a cosy maternity couch. My father never had the hood up except in very severe weather. He drove on his rounds like a blazing sun, his cheeks red with sea-wind, his curly brown hair, which he wore unfashionably long, blowing about under the rim of his hat – a trilby with a rolled brim as curly as his hair – his dog beside him stern and erect on the seat, guarding the car at every house he visited.

Below the ground-floor study and waiting room were the old basement quarters, rooms leading off a stone-flagged, beetle-infested passage. The biggest room seems vast as I remember it. It was used as a lumber room and in it were stored tennis posts, croquet mallets, balls and hoops in a long coffin-like box, and the garden tools from Rodwell Lodge, for my father hoped to move yet again, this time to a house with a garden. Dominating this room was a splendid rocking-horse. My imagination endowed him with breath and I rode him with a heightened sense of adventure to do battle with foes I did not identify. Perhaps I elevated the cockroaches into enemy hordes.

Less attractive but always the most powerful object in that old kitchen was the calefactor. This was a gas water-boiler fastened to the wall several feet above the floor. There it hung, infested with dirt and black loops of cobweb, grunting and chortling and hissing like a living monster. I cannot think why I was not terrified of it. Perhaps I was. There are some fears that are enjoyable in childhood. Anyhow, I braved it and drowned its savage growls with the squeak of the rockers as I rode my way, always to victory. I believe that the calefactor – the word had a wonderful resonance that has remained with me for over sixty years – blew itself up ignominiously in the end. The whole scene disappears. When we left Gloucester Row to live in a house by the harbour, the croquet mallets and tennis posts went with us. The rocking-horse did not.

The esplanade today is still very much as it was in my childhood, with its Victorian shelters and the jaunty Jubilee clock, though the lovely sweep of the promenade was ruined years ago by the building out of an ugly skating-rink pier just adjacent to one of Weymouth's most elegant rows of Georgian houses, Brunswick Terrace. At the other end of the front, the charming Edwardian pavilion, where I once danced the Teddy Bears' Picnic in Miss de Vos's dancing class, was burnt down after the last war and replaced by something that hardly deserves the title of 'building'. Now, behind it, the pier has been extended to take the lorries rolling off the Channel boats. They pound along the esplanade and eventually no doubt much of what is left of old Weymouth, which suffered enough destruction in the last war, will be sacrificed to accommodate them. This is the age of the juggernaut and Weymouth Council loves them.

While we were living at 2 Gloucester Row on the esplanade, the 1914 war broke out. My nanny walked with me in the wind, sheltered me from rain in the cheerful Victorian shelters, gave me donkey rides and jaunts in goat-carriages and we both gazed with wonder at the elaborate sandcastles built by 'sand artists', seldom seen today. Or we would wander round the Alexandra Gardens, then graced by an iron-and-glass wintergarden theatre, its delightful structure now completely obliterated by wooden boarding, and its interior used as a bingo hall. The gardens themselves are vulgarised by ugly ice-cream parlours, and the rustic shelters have gone – small huts with pointed roofs, dark and smelling strongly of the ivy that encased them, full of spiders in black corners and sour smells that I could not identify and that often overpowered the bitter but clean scent of ivy. It was more pleasant to sit outside on a wooden seat while my nanny chatted with the boys in blue from the hospital, many of them on crutches. I, too, talked to the soldiers. Weymouth was full of Anzacs and I was intrigued by their broad-brimmed hats, which they wore with one side flap pinned up by the 'rising sun' badge.

'Why do you wear your hat that way?' I asked, aged four.

I can see the man now, lean, clean-shaven and hard-featured. He took off his hat, stared at it for a moment, and then unpinned the badge and replaced the hat on his head with the brim turned down all round.

'That better?' he asked.

I nodded.

'Here, the badge is for you,' he went on, putting the 'rising sun' into my hand.

I had strayed away from my nanny but she came round at last from her idyll with a wounded soldier, searched for me and found me collecting more badges and admiration from homesick Aussies. She whisked me away firmly, but I kept the badges for years.

During my first seven years, our hospitable and apparently elastic Georgian house on the esplanade welcomed a succession of women visitors. They were introduced into the ménage by Father, who loved to have pretty girls around him. Most of them were, I think, nurses from the local hospitals, army nurses often far from their homes. The most loved was Nora, who married an army doctor whom she nursed. The wedding was given from our house and the newly wed couple honeymooned at Number 73 Clovelly. Nora became my godmother and was an amusing and delightful person much loved by all our family, and after the war endlessly hospitable to us all in her beautiful house on Mount Sion in Tunbridge Wells.

Three sons and several surrogates may have given my mother a career of sorts, a substitute for her abandoned nursing life. With hindsight I believe that she found their masculinity gratifying mainly because it was unthreatening. She could rule them, mould them, amuse them, be their confidante. Probably they were all half in love with her, for she was still very attractive. My eldest brother, Tom, certainly was. These boys formed a band of escorts, a little court of admirers, and there was, mercifully, no danger of their turning into husbands.

Perhaps my father hoped that the surrogate sons would give Mother something that he had failed to establish within his marriage, an absorbing interest, a purpose beyond giving birth to and bringing up children. But she needed something more. She found it in the young women that he invited to the house, on his part out of genuine kindness and also, I think now, because of his own need for a response to his warmth and his romanticism, a response which Mother no longer gave him. He did not obtain what he longed for. She was more fortunate. She wanted a soulmate and above all with Nora she found what she sought. They remained close friends for the rest of their lives. Fervent friendship blossomed in the lofty, panelled drawing room, with its balcony overlooking the bay of Weymouth, that romantic English Naples. There were picnics in bluebell woods beside the winding Frome, or on beaches in secluded bays along the coast, not then ruined by caravan sites, or enclosed in barbed wire by army authorities.

Of course, my father must have enjoyed a great deal of this gallivanting, especially at first. He adored 'outings' and picnics and showing people the many beauties of his beloved Dorset. He had a *tendresse* for the pretty nurses but he was not seeking soulmates. Though I think he was a faithful husband in the exact sense, he enjoyed being gallant with the girls, putting his arm round their plump shoulders, kissing them, if no more than paternally, giving them small presents. He did not understand why Mother liked doing the same. It made him uneasy. As time went on he became jealous and ill-tempered, though his blustering had a pathetic side to it that moved me even when I was a small child. Mother was so much cleverer than he was, her wit was barbed. She could plant a cruel blade in his ill-fitting armour. It put me forever on his side. I suppose that in the end he came to accept that if he wanted pretty girls around him, they would fall in love with Mother rather than with him. He put up with this but he never, I believe, understood it or accepted it wholly.

I don't think that my mother's affairs were of a sexual nature, or at least not explicitly so even if they were sexual in origin. Like so many eighteenth- and nineteenth-century women who embarked upon romantic friendships with members of their own sex, often for life, my mother was probably relieved that sex was left out of it. She was imprisoned within a Victorian marriage. It is well proven now that the overall picture of Victorian women shrinking from the nastiness of sex is much exaggerated, and that many wives enjoyed a full and happy sexual life with their partners. My father's romanticism was undoubtedly reciprocated in the early years of their marriage and his sexual passion may also have been. But I believe that there may have been too much romanticism, that the fantasy was not lived through into reality. In my mother's case it degenerated into sentimentality, in my father's into bitterness.

Another factor in the marriage was that my mother was not a woman who could have easily accepted the role of inferior partner, of banishment to nursery and kitchen, after being in a position of authority in a hospital long before her marriage. In most ways my father was far more Victorian than she was, and saw nothing wrong with the restrictions he placed upon such things as the household budget and with his embargo against his capable wife sharing, still less organising, the business side of the practice. He was later to refuse me my wish to be a doctor. He did not approve of women doctors. 'Why not be a nurse?' he suggested with total lack of comprehension.

My mother never once suggested nursing to me, which rather surprises me. She talked to me about her experiences often and I am sure that her own dedication to her profession had not been superseded entirely by married life and children. She was the type who, had she continued in her career and not married, might well have set up house with a woman friend. In the circumstances of home, however, the fervency of her female friendships were difficult for the family to come to terms with, and must have made my father uneasy at the least. Dressed and breakfasted for his early surgery and morning round, he left his wife still abed, and there Nora (or some other one) would join her for delicious talk, a shared pillow, shared embraces.

This century has heard so much of words like 'pervert', 'deviant' and 'abnormal' that one has to cut away a forest of misapprehension and downright untruths. In earlier centuries men's innate sense of superiority usually made it easy for them to tolerate women's love for each other, often simply as an analogue of their own male friendships and as a preparation for the 'real thing' – marriage. Sex, of course, was regarded as beyond the capacity of two females except in rare cases, and then obviously inferior and probably only possible at all with the use of a phallus-substitute.

However, not all women's friendships were belittled as sentimental and inferior. The Ladies of Llangollen were widely admired, and women of the seventeenth and eighteenth centuries had entered the world of poetry and drama to an extent which, though accepted at the time, was not allowed to become part of the canon of literature. Most of it sank into obscurity until recent research brought it to light.

In the nineteenth century women acquired higher education and embarked upon careers in schools and colleges. The numbers were, of course, tiny in comparison with the vast majority who became wives and mothers, and the not insignificant number whose spinsterhood and lack of qualifications or ability doomed them to lives of poverty and hardship, usually as governesses and nursemaids. But there were some women who rose to high positions in education, particularly in America, becoming headmistresses and college principals. Nursing and social welfare also offered careers regarded as specially suited to women. And it was seen as perfectly acceptable that women in professional positions should up to a point adopt the appearance, almost the lifestyle, of the males whose jobs they were usurping. Hence the severe tailor-made skirts and jackets, the mannish hats and ties and shoes. It was certainly taken for granted that no husband would agree to being subordinate to his wife in their household. On the other hand, a woman was not blamed for a reluctance to live alone. After all, she belonged to the weaker sex. She needed the support of a close companion and it was suitable for her to share her home with another woman. In the United States 'Boston marriages' were widely accepted and were indeed celebrated in Henry James' novel, *The Bostonians* (1885), where Olive Chancellor (note the masculine connotation of the surname), a wealthy feminist, trains a charismatic and beautiful young woman, Verena Tarrant, to speak at her meetings. Verena is the person Olive 'had been looking for for so long – a friend of her own sex with whom she might have a union of souls'. Two interesting points: sex is kept discreetly out of sight, and Olive Chancellor's appearance and behaviour are a deliberate reflection of the masculine, for how else could a capable woman of strong, modern ideas be regarded except as a man in petticoats?

My mother never achieved the career for which her abilities fitted her. She was forced to create what career she could out of the sons and extra-family boys whom she brought up, young people for whom she had in fact less responsibility than she would have done had they been patients in her own ward or hospital. This is not to say that my mother had not wanted children or failed to create a happy home for them. My brothers always spoke with deep affection of her and of their home in Hoddesdon, and later Weymouth. In a way, the rift was made manifest by my late birth, ten years after the others. Dad picked Christmas roses for my mother the morning I was born in December, and hung flags from the windows of the house to declare his joy in having a daughter. But it was too late. I could not bring them together. There was too little to hold them.

My father must have had his losses, too. I think that he had been deeply in love with my beautiful mother. It must be speculation; I can only draw inferences from later remarks made by my mother, which give me the idea that, at least after the first few years, she had little pleasure in the sexual side of her marriage. Dad's upbringing was not of a kind to prepare him for adult relationships, as I have said in a previous chapter, and it also is true that my mother's childhood years were unlikely to have left her well equipped for the married life. In the matter of their tastes one would not expect them to share more than a few, but it seems to me, looking back, that my mother had a limiting effect upon my father's expansiveness and even his talents. The move to Weymouth gave him the opportunity to exploit his love of the sea. One of his first acts was to buy a sailing boat. But my mother was afraid of the sea and made such an unending fuss about the trips that my father made that he hardly used it and finally laid it up on the edge of the harbour, where it rotted away.

The boat was symbolic of the limitations of my parents' married life. My father was well off in Weymouth, where he was one of the leading doctors in the town. He and mother could have travelled yet they never went abroad once. Presumably this was partly because of my mother's alleged hatred of the sea, though she loved to watch even the wildest storms from the safety of the land. Of course they had the Clovelly cottage, a sentimental anchor and remembrance of their honeymoon. They shared a love for walking and they enjoyed short holidays in Devon and Cornwall. They never went to London, however, to visit a concert hall or a theatre and they made no effort to go further afield than the West Country.

Not only my mother's involvement with her woman friends, but the gravitation of the boys towards her and away from my father widened the rift from the hair-crack that was probably there from the outset of the marriage. Then there was my father's inventiveness. Maybe it was a very minor talent but it was there. The ark across the yard was derided as though he was playing a rather silly game, but more damaging was her discouragement of his talents when they were turned to the invention of useful medical gadgets, for the dispensary for instance. There was an imaginative side to my father which I think was the basis of his outstanding feature as a doctor: his flair for diagnosis. Talents are too often misdirected or not fully developed. Diagnosis, yes, but the medical gadgets seem to me little more than toys of an inventive mind that might with encouragement have developed more substance. Sadly, the intuition that he brought to his medical profession was not exercised when it came to his relationships with his wife and family. His life was compartmentalised. Equally, my mother's capacity for organisation, which must have been considerable, was gradually eroded through having so little to organise. She became like a high-powered engine running noisily at high speed, unconnected to anything.

But the worst effects of the rift – the open rows and bitterness – were still in the future while we were at Weymouth. I return to the subject of my mother's women friends. They stayed at the house sometimes for weeks and were also, especially Nora, taken to the Clovelly cottage, for there was one taste that certainly united my parents: a love of giving hospitality. I have no means of knowing how much my father at this time longed to indulge in sexual affairs outside his marriage. Was his gallantry, his mild flirtatiousness with young women a safety valve for him? How far did it increase the tensions within the marriage? I came to know my mother so much better than I ever knew my father. I don't think she minded his behaviour. After all, most of the girls gravitated towards her in the end and she would have seen her husband's behaviour as natural and forgivable in a poor benighted male and a welcome sublimation of his unwelcome sexual urges.

I have written much of this chapter about my mother's women friends as a novelist for, with the exception of Nora whom I knew for the rest of her life, I do not remember them clearly. I have had to recreate the situation in which they played a part in my life. I knew them all as aunts, except Nora, to whom I gave the nickname Norraine. But memory provides me with a scene I do not have to tinker with. It is a scene recurring year after year, always bathed in a delight of fresh green leaves, a running stream, and the whole family united in giving each other pleasure.

June the second was my mother's birthday and always there was a grand picnic in a copse beside the river Frome, where it crosses Hardy's Egdon Heath near the village of Moreton. The river is fairly wide. Hazels and willows overhang its banks. In a small clearing rugs are spread out over the dry leaves; sandwiches, cold chicken, thermoses of tea stand ready; the three boys and I, and no doubt some of the extra brothers and women friends, sit laughing and talking and teasing Mother, while the whole picnic is held up by Dad's absence. He appears at last triumphant, in his hand a small spray of wild roses, for he never fails to find some to give Mother on her birthday.

The spot was known to us as the 'birthday wood' and I pass it sometimes, but have never stopped the car and tried to find the actual place by the river where we sat, for once a united family — united by an occasion when most of those present (but not myself) must have felt beneath the sentimentality of it all a genuine love, a genuine bond, going back to earlier days before I was even born.

Did I feel myself an outsider then, as I do now, peering in upon a group of total strangers belonging to a past I never knew?

5
Designs of Childhood

When I was about seven we left the house on the esplanade and moved to a tall, bow-windowed house right on the edge of the harbour. I loved that part of Weymouth: the endless traffic of the boats – the fishing fleet, sailing dinghies and paddle-steamers; the Channel boats and even some cargo vessels in those days. I snuffed up with pleasure the sweet smell of the hops from the breweries near by, redeemed from sickliness by a sharp infusion of salty harbour smells. There were small shops along the quay, many of which one stepped down into as into a cave full of fascinating merchandise, from licorice bootlaces and peppermint gobstoppers to fishing-tackle and live bait. Cousins came to stay, and boys from my brother Tom's school, and I was old enough now to accompany them on blue days, prowling round the harbour, crossing it in the twopenny ferry, going out on mackerel-fishing trips in the bay, and playing heaven knows what games up and down the stone-flagged alleyways. Ten years ago I bought one of the small houses along the harbourside. Standing on the quay outside its door, looking down to the Town Bridge and across to the Victorian seamen's mission in variegated brickwork, hearing the railway train running along the quayside opposite from the station to the Channel ferries, smelling the breweries in Hope Square just behind the house and occasionally being awoken by the maroon at the nearby lifeboat station – all this gave me a sense of returning home.

My ten years of childhood at Weymouth gave me some unforgettable memories 'felt in the blood and felt along the heart', but not all are welcome to me, in particular those experiences which left me with a lifelong fear of being lost in a strange place. Those who have never suffered from this burden may not realise what misery it causes and what a handicap it is. My parents delighted in taking short, unexpected holidays, driving off to some favourite West Country spot for a few days. The boys were left to look after themselves, but once my nanny had left when I was five or six, they disposed of me by farming me out for the duration of their jaunts, usually in the house of some patient or other of Dad's. On one occasion I was taken to the Clovelly cottage for a week by a Mrs Smith, a near neighbour whom I loathed and whose affectionate and whimsical attempts to play with me I found nauseating and embarrassing. 'Let's play tickletoes!' she would exclaim with a roguish look and plunge her bony ice-cold fingers under the bedclothes, to seize upon my squirming feet.

A more traumatic occasion was a stay with patients on the island of Portland. I can still remember the garden, white with stone-dust, and the hot, drystone walls around the solid grey cottage. The people I cannot remember at all. Portland impressed its grim bleak image indelibly upon my mind. It was not entirely unknown to me, for my father loved it and every time his rounds took him to a Portland patient, he would cry: 'Come on, Molly, a picnic! Make us a picnic! We're going over to Portland!' Off we would go, and the car would crawl up the steep hill above the village of Chiswell to stop on the edge of the West Weare which overlooked the Chesil Beach and the distant cliffs along the coast, as far as Start Point on a clear day.

The sea heaved below us, often rough with snarling white crests above vast dark-green troughs of water. It rolled into the bay with relentless power and, as I remember it, the Chesil Bank was seldom without some wreck or wrecks stranded upon it or breaking up among the huge rocks below our feet. My father would sit upon the very edge of the cliff, his feet dangling over the precipice – samphire grows on those cliffs – his face glowing, his farsighted blue eyes gazing down the coast he so much loved, his long curly hair blowing in the gusty wind, while Mother and I cowered some way behind him, both of us subject to a dread of heights, both of us loathing the fierce incessant wind that carried stone-dust into our eyes and hair and into the sandwiches.

Those expeditions and the week's stay with the patients on Portland gave me such a fear of the island that I never returned to it for some forty years. When I wrote a novel called *Look, Stranger* and gave it a Portland setting, even then I did not revisit the island. I recreated it from memory and imagination. I described a baroque church standing alone, empty and boarded up, surrounded by a graveyard where most of the headstones had fallen askew or backwards, lying as though tossed about by the Channel gales. There, I wrote, the wife of one of the chief characters sits on a fallen tombstone in the long, coarse grass, grieving for the loss of a young man with whom she fancied she was in love. He had just drowned himself, persecuted because he was a homosexual, and there she sat, the silly woman, reading 'Adonais' and crying, and I really thought I had created the whole scene, church and all. When I went back to the island later, there was the baroque church, Renforne, still boarded up and decaying. There were the tombstones lying in a careless disarray around it, and the wind in the brownish grass. I felt like a *revenant*.

I cannot think of the first ten years of my life as either happy or unhappy. Perhaps I was happier than I now think I was. Perhaps I was a little spoilt and expected too much. I was certainly increasingly lonely as the gulf between myself and the brothers widened. Did I know what I wanted? Undoubtedly not, though I think I must have known what I did *not* want – these elderly parents and overgrown schoolboy brothers, to whom I was alternately a plaything or a nuisance.

I was happiest at my small day school, where I had two inseparable companions, Eric, a fat little boy, and Paul, a small thin one with large searching brown eyes. Our games were very innocent and highly imaginative and bloodthirsty, with much capturing of pirates on the high seas, much sleighting of forts and towns and putting the inhabitants to the sword. The word 'town' reminds me that the most creative of our games was the construction of an elaborate, imaginary town within the brick foundations of a demolished greenhouse in a corner of the school garden. We never actually built its walls or gave it a name. We simply laid it out with lines on the ground, marking the streets and houses. The lines were made with bits of brick and pieces of broken china which abounded in the debris, with sticks and fragments of mortar. The fascination of those pieces of broken china depicting blue flowers and trees and birds must have been strong, for often when I am walking my stick turns up a little piece of glazed pottery, the remains of a kitchen jug or cup, perhaps, and I am taken back in an instant to the derelict greenhouse and the lay-out of that imaginary town.

As I have said, we never actually built it. In our vivid imaginations, the walls and houses, churches and shops were there, above the rudimentary foundations. What form did our play take? My recollection falters here. Perhaps all that mattered to us was the construction of those imagined buildings as we grovelled in the dusty ruins of the greenhouse. It was a secret world. So little of it was seen by the curious, so much was in our minds, that it remained entirely private to the three of us, our own domain.

I do not remember playing with any other children at that little school in the Dorchester Road, only with Eric and Paul. Eric was sometimes invited home to tea and I to his home in Chickerell, but Paul never. Paul's father kept a grocer's shop in a small town a few miles away from Weymouth. My father would not have cared about this but my mother certainly did. Besides, she wanted me to have nice girl friends, not boys, and she provided a fairly wide selection. I hated them all as I hated anything soft and sweet. I disappointed my mother and her friends not only in my dislike of the little girls ('Mummy, when are these horrid children going away?') whom she invited to come to tea and play with me, but by my refusal to eat chocolate éclairs in Bennett's tea rooms and monotonously demanding plain bread and butter.

Cousins (despite lack of uncles and aunts, there were a couple of step-cousins) came to stay, but the house by the harbour has a more potent memory for me of a fully realised loneliness. I slept at the very top of the building and felt very remote and often full of fears. I had a deep-rooted hatred of the dark which has never altogether left me. The only room near my own was Tom's den but he was seldom there. He was serving in the Royal Naval Air Service from 1917 on. The other two brothers were still at school and preoccupied with their own concerns. I don't remember where they slept. I only remember the sensation of being utterly remote from the rest of the family when I went to bed. I used to bury myself under the bedclothes to shut out creaks and tapping and other nameless terrors. When I was smaller, at 2 Gloucester Row, it was lions under the bed that I feared. Nothing so specific launched me into frightened misery at Trinity Road, but I have never forgotten the nameless terrors, at last mitigated when I was given a black kitten with two white toes on each paw and a white bib. She became my closest companion and comforted me for many years.

The long drawing room ran from the front of the house to the back on the first storey, with large windows at each end. Here I would sit, reading my brothers' bound copies of the *Boy's Own Paper* and the novels of Henty, and wishing that I was a boy and could have such adventures. There was a gramophone with a horn, and on it I played the records that Tom brought home when he was on leave, mostly songs from the music halls and shows he saw in London. I never remember sharing this musical feast with a friend, not even Eric when he was invited to tea, and certainly not with the silly girls who consumed mounds of jam and cakes while I looked glumly on, chewing my bread and butter and listening to the condemnatory remarks of the grown-ups: 'What an odd little girl!' The seeds of my otherness were probably sown on the laden plates of the mahogany dumb-waiter.

The records were my solitary passion and my happiness. I sang the songs over and over again. I danced to them up and down the long drawing room. I can sing many of them now:

> Everybody calls me Teddy,
>   T-E-double D-Y,
> Yanky, swanky,
> Full of hanky-panky,
> With the RSVP eye,
> All day long my telephone
> Keeps repeating hard:
>   Are you there,
>   Little Teddy-bear?
>   Naughty naughty one Gerard!

The American artist Teddy Gerard sang this engaging song in *Bric-à-Brac*, which also contained such gems as 'Chalk Farm to Camberwell Green all on a summer's day' ('But *I* wasn't Camberwell Green by a very . . . long . . . chalk'), and 'Neville was a Devil'. I could write many nostalgic pages threaded along the tunes and words of the songs I knew and sang from *The Bing Boys, Chu Chin Chow* and *The Maid of the Mountains*. Unhappily, memory is unselective and irresponsible. I am also fated to remember the words of a popular song so awful that I am hoping to exorcise it now by bringing it out into the open from its dark lair in my mind:

> O little Jammy-face,
>   I love you so!
> I wish I were your sweetheart
>   Or your Mammy!
> O little Jammy-face,
>   I love you so!
> I love you 'cos your little face
>   Is ja-a-am-my!

I can sing that one too, and sometimes wonder, with an unwilling nod to Freud, whether it contributed to my revulsion from small children whose general messiness has no maternal appeal for me.

At Trinity Road life changed in many ways. My mother's friends and confidantes no longer came so frequently and I don't think that there were any new ones. My brothers were growing up and my father became increasingly distanced from them. He had never been at ease with Tom, though he was proud of him when he joined up as an ordinary seaman in 1917, and later became an officer in the RNAS. But Tom's close relationship with Mother made him increasingly intolerant of Dad, especially towards the end of our Weymouth life when the marriage was showing signs of strain. The time was to come when Tom would hardly be on speaking terms with his father. To Mother he remained devoted all his life, writing to her every week and addressing her as 'Darling Bird'. Dad was attached to his youngest son, Bob, but had little use for Roger. This middle son was too like himself in temperament and appearance and it is usually a likeness to our least desirable qualities that stands out and causes offence, distorting the image we have built up of ourselves.

Soon after we moved to the harbour, Bob started at Birmingham University, and was at home only during vacations. He was subsequently to become a civil engineer. Tom had become a teacher when he was demobbed from the RNAS. He was offered a place at Oxford like many young men coming back from the war, but my father advised him not to take it up. 'My friend Hawkins has a prep school in Sussex,' he said. 'He's told me there's a place for you on his staff and you don't need a degree to teach little boys.' It may appear crass of my father to have prevented Tom from going to Oxford, but I don't imagine that Tom himself was keen to go. He had been independent since he was seventeen and now wanted to get a job. He joined the RNVR at once and devoted his school holidays to it for the rest of his life, combining two careers. He liked teaching and was good at it, bringing a fresh breeze of originality and eccentricity into the conventional form rooms of a boys' prep school. His naval interests led him to write a history of British ship names. He was called up in the Second World War and had a distinguished career in the Volunteer Reserve.

Roger's career was more troublesome both for him and his father. He had expressed a desire to travel, which was enough to induce my father to conjure up another useful friend, a tea planter in Java. This man gave Roger a job in the company but this was far from a success.

Growing tea on plantations worked by ill-paid native labour was not what Roger meant by travel. Possibly it was his Javan experience that turned his mind towards politics, for a few years later he became a confirmed Communist. Not only had he loathed his life in the Far East; he contracted malaria and came home, now determined to be an artist. This my father regarded as no career at all. He was nonplussed by his unsatisfactory second son, but he let him live at home for a while and take a correspondence course in cartoon drawing, again hardly what Roger meant by training as an artist. Since my father and his brothers had been to universities or an equivalent form of specialist training, it is hard to see why he sent only one of his sons to college when he was by no means short of money, at least at that time.

However, shortage of money was soon to come, and our circumstances changed in a drastic manner which I shall describe in the next chapter. Roger was quite good at drawing but probably not good enough to make a career of it. My father, pressed for ready cash, found another friend, this time the brother of an old school friend of my mother's. He was a well-established architect. 'After all, if the boy can draw, he might as well be an architect,' was the argument used. So Roger departed for London to work in an office and get his qualifications in evening classes. He was kept extremely short of cash but he hardly minded. He took to architecture, loved his London life, and was engaged to a delightful girl whom he loved devotedly for four years. He had no hope of marrying her until he qualified. She wearied of the situation at last and left Roger to marry an old flame. I don't think Roger ever got over this rejection. All of us lacked resilience in the face of loss of happiness. Except Tom, who had escaped from home when he was seventeen and in a way had escaped from his family well before that, for he had never as a boy had anything to do with his brothers, even walking to school on the opposite side of the road from Roger and Bob. I think that except for Tom we were like half-grown trees, not deeply rooted or well nourished enough to shoot up strongly or to withstand the mutilations inflicted by storm and flood. Despite a strong stoic element in most of the Manning family, reinforced in my case by boarding school and family pressure to keep a stiff upper lip, at least two of us, Roger and myself, always tended to take things very hard and — perhaps in reaction against the stoic ethics of our youth — often showed our feelings too readily, and had difficulty in restraining immediate responses from showing, such as anger, despondency and unreasonable argumentativeness, all employed in a dramatic overreaction to events.

Tom forged his own career and with it his personality. It was to the latter that he devoted the creative side of himself, producing a character who could make friends and earn the respect of a wide range of people, from the small boys he taught to the ratings he commanded on board ship and the upper-class parents who patronised the school. Many of these were service people and it might be supposed that a man who was only the 'wavy navy', as the R N V R was called, would not be much respected, but Tom made himself an expert in navigation and other essentials of good seamanship. It was not till what remained of his family attended his memorial service that we learned that during the war between Italy and Abyssinia he had been called up and sent to the Mediterranean in command of a fleet of minesweepers, Merchant Navy ships manned of course by men who had little use for regular Navy officers and still less for R N V R men. Yet, we were told, he won their affection and respect and this would have been first of all through his expertise, any defect in which those horny-handed Merchant Navy men would have been quick to discover.

Tom also had a charm of manner and was strikingly handsome, the only one of us to have a strong likeness to my mother. He never married, though he was in his young days much pursued. He told me once that he nearly succumbed to the advances of a rich widow, but when he found that she kept her dead husband's ashes in a vase on the mantelpiece in her sitting room, it was too much for him and he quickly extricated himself from the situation.

Roger suffered from the way his father interfered with his life during his formative years. He was given nothing substantial on which to build his life and my father often treated this middle son, so like himself, dismissively and even with contempt – 'How like Roger!' and 'What can you expect from Roger?' were the kind of phrases he used and they are hardly forgivable. Although Roger qualified as an architect he lacked confidence, and the abrupt end to his long love affair and his sense of being the least wanted in the family turned him into a man with a chip on his shoulder. He not only became a Party member. He also became a trouble-maker, which virtually destroyed his career in public service. It is easy to say that he ruined his own career but this is a facile judgment. My sympathies lay very much with Roger, especially in my later years when I got to know him well.

In some ways we were alike, both immature, both ignorant and inexpert over healing our wounds, both devoid of worldly wisdom and equally lacking in self-knowledge. We both felt adrift in our lives and allowed currents to carry us into foolish decisions and in directions that ultimately proved disastrous. Outwardly, we were both aggressive, positive, decisive. Inwardly, Roger and I were the least confident members of the family and the most self-destructive. The main difference between us is that I am still alive.

I can't leave my brother Roger without paying a tribute to his charm as a companion, which for me outweighed in the end his arrogance and other undesirable qualities. It was he who introduced me to London when I was in my late teens, but at this moment I recall the many hours I spent with him after he lost his wife, exploring English towns and villages and going abroad several times: to Yugoslavia, Venice and Paris, where as a single companion he could be sensitive and enthusiastic, attributes that made me forget the fact that he found it almost impossible to get on with his fellows in an office, quickly becoming critical, pig-headed and given to writing lengthy, abusive letters.

Roger had a proselytising streak rather like mine, and a passion for sharing his enthusiasms, especially over a new record he had bought, or a book he had just read. A small vignette retains for me the essence of this often difficult and unsuccessful brother: we went together to Milton Abbey to hear a magnificent concert, one of the best I have ever heard outside London. As we came out of the abbey into the night, our senses were ravished again. Roger stopped dead in his tracks and looked up at a sky thick with brilliant stars. 'God, what a sky!' he exclaimed, but it's not the words I remember, but his large, bulky frame standing like a rock outside the abbey doorway, his eyes gazing upwards with a childlike wonder, and a crowd pressing behind him to get past him to their cars.

My third brother, Bob, became an eminent civil engineer. He was a shy and somewhat silent man, but he had a highly successful career, indeed the most successful perhaps in the family. Gifted but modest, tactful and humorous, he survived a painfully unhappy marriage by devoting himself quietly to his career and to his passion for sailing. The most self-contained of us, Bob never admitted to unhappiness, but at odd times, usually on my birthday, he would send me strange, wry poems which often revealed things about himself and his life. When he remarried in his early seventies, all his reserves of warmth and his capacity for friendship and social life, his enjoyment of theatre and music, were released by his happiness with his delightful new wife. He even began to wear fancy waistcoats. Nine years older than myself, he was the brother closest to me in my early teens and his caring companionship then was a source of strength to me that I do not forget.

The fact that my three brothers were so much older than myself, the youngest nine years ahead of me, meant that when I was ten, the last year we were at Weymouth, I was beginning to see less and less of them. I have said something of their careers, but what does it matter what they did in the world? What did these three men mean personally, to me? During the years when I was at college and then working in London, I virtually never saw them. Tom was in Sussex, Bob and Roger married and had children. The gap between us became wider and wider. It was only when I grew older, really older in my fifties, that the gap began to close and I found myself beginning to love them as I never had when I was a child, except perhaps for Bob. I remember only isolated episodes. I have to sift my memory as one would sift gravel, hoping to catch one or two tiny grains of gold. It is on these minute particles that one could construct a novel. Indeed, this whole book could be regarded as a body of notes for a series of novels.

Bob, the last to die, was my companion at a time when I was intensely lonely, when we had just left Weymouth and moved to Sandhurst. Bob took me away for two holidays. The first was for about ten days when we explored the Cotswolds on bicycles, and went on across the Forest of Dean to Ross-on-Wye. It helped to lay the foundations of my love for that part of England, but my only vivid memory is a scene in a cheap pub in Ross where Bob and I ate an extremely poor supper and afterwards were afflicted by the unsavoury presence of the landlady, who invaded the seedy little parlour where we were sitting, leaned against the door and entered into a rambling monologue. She was drunk and at thirteen I hadn't a clue how to deal with this disagreeable situation. Neither had my strong and silent brother, for Bob at twenty-two was not only shy but unworldly and inexperienced. He was also weighed down by his responsibility for his young sister.

The landlady maundered on, asking questions, relating inconclusive anecdotes. Bob answered her in a few monosyllables. I was tongue-tied. The room was dank and smelly and I longed for bed. Whether she thought we were not brother and sister (for I was a tall, well-developed child) and entertained more lively and reprehensible thoughts about us that doubtless she would relate to the bar customers, I have no idea. Only the acute discomfort and embarrassment of my fresh-faced, innocent, sternly puritanical brother remains. And one other thing; a bug in my bed. I had never seen such a thing before and called Bob in to look at it.

'I think it's a bed-bug,' he faltered, after an appalled scrutiny of the creature. 'I will deal with it.' He took it up in his handkerchief and despatched it through the window.

'We'd better see if there are any more,' he suggested. We pulled the bed to pieces but there were no more of them and, like most resilient teenagers, I'm sure I slept well, healthily worn out by the long day's cycling to Ross.

A year later Bob bought a tiny car called a Clyno and took me away in it for a brief tour of Dorset. For him the few days we had there were a return to the country places and the coast which he had known and explored with Roger in his boyhood and for which he felt an unexpressed nostalgia. Both these brothers never lost their love for Dorset and both returned to live there in later life. For me that brief holiday was to crystallise my vague bitterness at being torn away from Weymouth into a positive passion for Dorset. I went back to it all through my life until I finally built the house which looks across the Blackmore Vale to Hambledon. Though I have only indistinct memories of the actual holiday and the places we visited, it was a key to much of my future. Some of the emotions we have felt in the past, perhaps incoherently, live on and grow to maturity in our hearts, tranformed and certainly more clearly understood. So it has been with my lifelong love affair with Dorset.

6
Scenes in the Conifer Country of Surrey

The affair which led to our leaving Weymouth as abruptly as we did was not clear or comprehensible to me, aged then nearly ten. As far as I have since discovered, my father, deprived of his pretty nurses, had turned his mildly amorous attentions to his dispenser. I do not think he was a man who would have been unfaithful to my mother, at least not then. He was gallant by nature and loved to give attractive girls the kind of attention he thought they deserved and appreciated and which my mother had ceased to inspire in him. This kind of attention could justly be regarded as sexual harassment, especially when directed to his young dispenser, and I cannot defend my father on this issue. It had moreover disastrous consequences which affected the whole family. I suppose I should feel angry with him, but built into me is a love which accepts faults that to an outsider will seem less forgivable.

A new partner had been taken on, a young man. Catching my father in a compromising situation with his arm round the dispenser's shoulders and a light in his blue eye that this young Dr Montague distrusted, he created a scene and he had a right to, though it is now only a matter of conjecture what actually happened. I have no doubt that my father regarded Dr Montague's intervention as obtrusive if not impertinent. If he had been a less choleric man and a less fundamentally moral one he would not have felt a mixture of fury and guilt. If he had not been proud and pig-headed maybe the matter could have blown over, but instead of keeping calm and riding the storm, no, Dr Manning shouted: 'Be damned to you! [or so I imagine] I won't stay here to be criticised and insulted!' And before the family had time to reason with him – if indeed they could have done so – he had resigned from the practice and uprooted us all from Weymouth.

It is possible that more pressure was put upon him than I know, that his partner, Dr Hethcott, was brought into the business and urged him to go. Indeed, Dad's behaviour to the dispenser may not have been quite the innocent gallantry I have assumed. But whatever the truth, the result was that he walked out of an excellent, long-established practice, thus denying to the family, most of all myself, the opportunity to grow up in a pleasant town and countryside where all of us had made friends and where my mother enjoyed an agreeable social circle. We were transported through his impulsive action to one of the nastiest overgrown villages in England: Sandhurst, near Camberley in Surrey. He selected this unlikeable place simply because he found there a small house with two acres of largely neglected garden and woodland, and seized the chance to make practical use of his creative talent and to assuage his hunger for a garden, which he had not had for over ten years at Weymouth. Perhaps he hoped, too, that designing and planting the two acres with my mother's help – for she was as keen a gardener as he was – might repair the damage of the dispenser incident and recall the old happy days of Hoddesdon and Rodwell Lodge, both of which had substantial gardens.

The house – it was a redbrick villa originally built for the curate – stood above the village in a quiet lane. Opposite was a large larch wood, part of the property, and behind the house itself a long, narrow garden, ending in a little fir-crowned tump. Along the hedge that bordered one side of the property stood six tall silver birch trees – one for each member of the family, Mother used to say hopefully. But it was never to be a family home in the sense that the Weymouth houses had been. We all hated it. In any case, the three boys were no longer living at home. And the practice was a wretched one, run down by the previous doctor, and worth only about £200 a year.

'Didn't you examine Dr Smith's books?' asked my practical mother.

'My dear, the man's a gentleman. Of course I couldn't ask to see his books.'

It was the beginning of the end, of the downward spiral from a lively, well-to-do life in congenial surroundings to a mean, straggling village, where my father's gift for diagnosis and his expertise with women's and children's complaints could be exercised only upon a tiny number of patients; where money was increasingly short and he himself became despondent and seedy, overweight, smoking too much. He withdrew more and more to his study into the company of his grey African parrot, Jacko, who sat on his shoulder and reached round to kiss him at intervals. Jacko also tore the backs off the medical books while Dad slept in his chair, and he slept a great deal. There was so little work to do. Perhaps Jacko provided a symbol of the virtual end of my father's career as a doctor. Unfortunately, at ten years old, I had not built up that reserve of security which might have supported me in the growing crisis at home.

The move from Weymouth was regarded by all of us as a total disaster. My father confided to no one the financial straits that he was now in, except incidentally, usually in the form of protests against expenditure. At first he behaved as though he were still earning a substantial income, spending money on the garden, giving lavish hospitality to our cousins as before. We were deceived, but the rot soon set in.

We moved to Sandhurst in a warm sunny April and the early days there have a bright clarity rather like a pre-Raphaelite painting. For a child a move is usually exciting and at first I was eager to explore my new surroundings, so different from Weymouth but not disagreeable, for we were surrounded by woodlands. We were not at first in the new house but stayed further up the hill in a small cottage belonging to a Mrs Wombwell, and I enjoyed her meals – country meals in which bacon, suet dumplings and apple pies played a large part.

In my memory it is always April. The air is cool with primroses. The windows of the new house are wide open – french windows in the drawing room that bring you out into the garden under a pergola covered with greening sweetbriar. The family are in the house, cleaning, painting, unpacking, and on the light wind there come to my ears the strains of 'Gipsy Love', played over and over again on a ten-inch, plum-label H M V record. It is one of mother's favourites and mine. When my brother Roger comes down from London, the record is usually one of *his* prevailing passions, 'Valencia' ('If you have not heard "Valencia",' he exclaims, 'you have not lived.') – or 'Kitten on the Keys', and my father remarks that if this is jazz, it's damned clever and he likes it. He does not, however, like 'Tiger Rag'.

And still it is April, no matter what followed. The larch wood opposite the house has been planted on a gentle upward slope and hangs towards the road like a pale-green drape. In my memory the vivid green of it has never darkened. But when we lived there I never wanted to explore it even though it belonged to the house. It was alien to me and so was the wooded hill on which the house stood. Once the excitement of the move was over I began to pine for the open downs, the cloud-shadowed sea.

There are trees all around the new house: the lane up to it is like a pleached alley. Bordering our garden are two great estates: Forest Dean is mostly pine, very black and forbidding. The other, King's Stag House, is green and romantic, with wide lawns and groups of chestnut, oak and sycamore, screening a huge, eccentric redbrick Victorian house, turreted and pinnacled in Scottish-baronial style. Its boundary, which I pass every time I walk to and from Mrs Wombwell's cottage about a quarter of a mile further up the hill, is a high bank on top of which sprawls a tangled mass of rhododendrons, hazels and holly. I always turn my eyes towards this pleasant sea-green wilderness on my right, to avoid looking into the firs of Forest Dean, ranked behind gaunt, spiked iron railings, a dense sombre estate in the depths of which there stands a house inhabited by a very old lady. *Noli me tangere*, the forbidding fence says.

If I recall Sandhurst as perpetually clothed in April viridian, it is certainly not because the human elements in the scene are hopeful. We were looking away, we were looking back, all of us I think, and did not feel at home there. Father and Mother were full of desperate plans for the derelict garden and seedy house, plans that were their private line of defence against an encroaching past.

The scene of preparation remains for me more vivid than any other of the eight or nine years we lived there. We unpack our furniture and possessions, slowly and untidily with no clear picture of where the things are to go. Roger is singing (he hopes like Jack Buchanan) 'And her mother came too', and foxtrotting about the room with a pile of cushions in his arms. Father leaves it all to Mother, who then finds herself entirely in the wrong when he returns from his rounds. 'Oh, Lord, Molly, you can't think I'd want *that* in the drawing room? Of all places! No, no, put it in the dining room. The patients can sit on it. I thought we'd agreed . . . I thought we'd discussed . . . I thought you all had more sense . . . '

And then he rushes out of the house and stalks about the neglected garden, and sees it all in his mind's eye as it is going to be: the lawns rolled flat and closely mown, and his croquet hoops in position; that hideous cypress hedge ('Who could have planted such a monstrosity?') rooted out; the kitchen garden full of fruit and vegetables. There will be loganberries and a long asparagus bed. He will plant a couple of medlar trees. He will set half a dozen quinces down the side of the lawn. He dreams of these uncommon trees, for they grew in the walled garden of the Hoddesdon house where they lived in the early days of their marriage. And Mother is drawn into the same dream: 'It'll be like it was at Hoddesdon,' she says to me, trying to shield me from the present by a curtain of old order and beauty which I never knew.

The Hoddesdon house had been left to Mother in the will that Father has never altered. But he has secretly sold the house. He would like to forget this but it invades his mind often in those early days at Sandhurst, when the happiness has long since leached away and money is short and children unloving and critical. To reconstruct the garden is the only creative work left to him. Before we have been in Sandhurst a month, the parents have been to Wisley more than once and come back laden with new plants which are heeled in among Mrs Wombwell's cabbages up the hill.

Tom arrived at the end of his school term, after we had been in Sandhurst for little more than a week. He looked at the house we were going to move into with scornful amazement which changed to active condemnation after he had examined the bathroom, the earth-closets (one up, one down and difficult to say which was the most unsavoury), the kitchen, scullery and larder. His comment upon these stone-floored domestic quarters was damning: 'Might be a morgue,' he observed morosely.

He was equally appalled at the grubby little cottage up the hill where we were camping out while the builders were in our house. They were, however, only renovating the living rooms. Nothing was apparently to be done to the kitchen quarters. Dad liked his food but could not see why any convenience was necessary for its preparation. It was part of the good old days that he was going to miss more and more, those happy times of black-leaded ranges and antiquated kitchens from which were produced succulent meals, presided over by Mother in a tight-waisted dress and her hair piled on top of her head, looking very beautiful and (from the photographs I have of her) quite unapproachable, and as cold as the stone flags beneath her elegant feet. *Noli me tangere*, in fact.

Tom refused to stay with us. He took a room in a thatched cottage owned by a decrepit retired actress. This was where he stayed all the time we lived in Sandhurst, on the occasions when he arrived to see Mother and support her with his unvarying affection. Tom is her confidant and she is his. They share a secret past. When Tom was ten years old he had a mysterious illness which kept him on his back for a year. Mother devoted all her skill and art to keeping him amused, reading aloud to him, playing cards and other games. Now she is middle aged but Tom is still her champion. He comes from another world where they still wear bright armour and carry a lady's favour in their helmets. But things will change. At the end of our unhappy stay at Sandhurst, Tom will bring his weapons up to date and we shall be recruited into his New Model Army against Father.

Tom was always very fond of me, far fonder than of his brothers, but I never really got to know him well and when I was a child he seemed to me remote. He had already in his twenties adopted certain habits which set him apart. He even smoked in a peculiar way, screwing the tobacco into a little circle of paper and then inserting it into his pipe bowl. But it was most of all his lifestyle which was so remote from us. Despite being a schoolmaster, his naval life was what gave him most of his extensive circle of friends, his senior service manner, his reputation, and none of this was shared with his family. He might have lived on another planet. Tom was rather like the larch wood opposite the house: beautiful to look at, part of the estate legally, but quite separate from it and daunting in its unexplored and pathless interior.

The move was undoubtedly worse for my mother than anyone else. She lost her friends and her Weymouth interests and occupations, and at the very time when her family had left home except for myself, and when Dad was becoming estranged from her. I was little support to her. I was too unhappy and disorientated, for once the spring had passed and we were settled uncomfortably into the curate's villa, I woke up from the anaesthetised state induced by the move. I, too, I realised, had lost my friends. I should never see Eric or Paul again. Sandhurst had few children of my own age and the two schools I went to for short periods did not provide me with companions. I was miserable there, especially at the first one, adrift and uncertain of myself, conscious now of my loathing for the village of Sandhurst, for the mean little house and the surrounding countryside of sandy heathland and pine woods, so forbidding, so secretive compared with the clean, open bare lines of the chalk downs and the white cliffs surrounding Weymouth bay. Only one aspect of Sandhurst, an area beyond the village itself, gave me a little pleasure – perhaps because it reminded me of the fields and copses along the Frome, where the 'birthday wood' was situated. Sandhurst had a river too, running through water meadows and alder copses, full of aconites and, later in the spring, bluebells. The fields were yellow with buttercups and cows stood munching in the lush grass. It was an oasis and here I walked with Bob, endlessly kind and companionable to me. An even dearer and closer friend of my secret hours alone was my cat, Panna, whom I had brought from Weymouth. When, after a few years, she had to be put down, I was desolate with the kind of all-consuming misery that children experience, for they are without philosophy or any weapon to combat agony of heart. I remember the kindness of the vet, who took me aside and told me that animals had their heaven. It said so in the Hindu writings. He lent me a copy of a book called *The Light of Asia*. I don't think I got very far with it, but his words gave me some comfort.

I was too self-absorbed to see what my mother was going through. Her health was beginning to react to her mental and emotional anxieties. She looked much older. Her figure was no longer elegant and, because she was short, gave her a dumpy appearance. Her hair was greying and her face showing deeper lines, especially around her down-drawn mouth. Domestic help was now short and the house was difficult to run, with its big gloomy kitchen and two murderous, battered stone steps down into the flagged scullery and larder. It was bitterly cold in these quarters, facing north and further darkened by trees outside growing far too close to the house. But my father never cut down trees if he could help it. The drawing room and the parents' bedroom had been properly redecorated and were both charming rooms, but the rest of the house was frankly awful, with mean rooms and small windows. My father employed a chauffeur-handyman and a gardener, but Mother had to make do with a daily woman whose ministrations generally left much to be desired.

I had to go to school, of course. Looking back, I am grateful for the excellent grounding and imaginative freedom of my Dorchester Road school, for I learned almost nothing from the age of ten to twelve, when I went to boarding school. While we were still settling in at Sandhurst, I was sent to a nearby school as a weekly boarder, a situation that gives a child the worst of both worlds. At this quite large, very respectable and much respected school in Camberley, I was bullied ruthlessly. I was a tall, strong child and my brothers had taught me never to cry. This often invites bullying. My attraction for the sadists was that my strength gave me endurance and my upbringing in a masculine family had made me early on a stoic, which is jam to the bully.

I never told my parents, still less my brothers, what was going on, but I suppose my fears and misery became obvious and I was taken away after a term and sent to a quite pleasant school some six miles away as a day girl. My father drove me there before surgery and fetched me every afternoon. These journeys and the walks we began taking together drew us close. For two or three years I was more of a companion to him and he to me than I had ever been or should be again. I didn't see his faults. I loved him and admired him, and longed to be what he was, a general practitioner, kindly and patient, welcome in people's homes.

The day school was an unexciting but I think a fairly happy place, full of moral platitudes and uplift.

> Bright and joyous the world around us
> Every day . . .

we sang in the school song. I did find the world of nature bright and joyous but not much else. School songs of the twenties and thirties often retained the belligerent clichés that had sent 'our boys' to their deaths in the trenches. This particular specimen extolled 'brotherhood' (not sisterhood, you will note), 'courage' and that overworked moral commodity, 'honour', and referred to life as 'a glorious fray'. Such expressions are absorbed all too easily into youthful minds and become part of the mental furniture of adults. It is not only wars that are won on the playing fields of Eton, or Roedean either. Attitudes and values are established all too firmly. School songs are often imbued with a militaristic jargon and an aggressiveness which is difficult to discard when as grown-ups we try to adopt more reasonable and agreeable stances.

A study of school songs would provide an interesting gloss on the immature masculine ethos which makes a virtue of lack of tenderness and warmth in domestic relations. This may well be partly responsible for the positive male hatred of women that surfaces at times, and also for the attitude that turns war and many other aspects of life into competitive games.

The songs of girls' schools can be just as influential and are often imitations of the male patterns. At my later boarding school I remember that we always sang 'Forty Years On', that Harrovian celebration of toughness and sentimentality, at the end of the summer term Games Supper. For those unfamiliar with this footballing song, I must add that the refrain goes: 'Till the field rings again and again/ With the tramp of the twenty-two men.' Headmistress and staff saw no incongruity in this and I have since discovered that many girls' schools sing 'Forty Years On', equally oblivious of this idiocy. Girls' school songs are amusingly, affectionately, but not very critically dealt with by Celia Haddon in *Great Days and Jolly Days* (Hodder and Stoughton, 1971), but she does make the point that the education of girls was usually modelled on that of boys. I find it extraordinary, all the same, that the founders of the early establishments had not the critical acumen to examine the male values of the boys' schools nor the confidence and courage to reject at least the worst of them.

To return to this day school where we sang so enthusiastically of brotherhood and honour, there was an episode during my time there which, though it may not seem to a reader as serious as the sadistic bullying I suffered as a weekly boarder in the previous establishment, was, I believe, morally far worse. Trivial in itself, it was not treated as such. A childish peccadillo was elevated into an act of the deepest moral turpitude and the episode ended in a betrayal of trust by the grown-ups involved. The story is this: I formed a friendship with a rather feeble little girl whose name I have long forgotten. I suggested to her that we should filch things like pens and india-rubbers from other children, hide them under a loose floorboard that I had discovered and then produce them later as gifts to our form mates. It was a simple Robin Hood scheme, designed selfishly on my part to ingratiate myself with my fellows. Being without any talent for games or indeed anything else at that time, I was cutting no ice with them and this damaged my growing ego. Our thefts were discovered by an older girl and reported to the Headmistress, Miss Blake. As a punishment we were to be arraigned in our wickedness before the whole school the following morning. I don't think I cared a pin, though my fellow thief wept copiously. I probably welcomed the publicity, but I did want to spare my parents the revelation that I was a thief. Miss Blake promised solemnly that she would not tell our parents, but the next day my father opened a letter from her at breakfast, setting out the whole story. As I feared, my mother and father were hurt and humiliated and I felt betrayed.

Betrayal was to become a major factor, far beyond that trivial episode, when I was in my teens, and something that undermined even my stoicism. 'In trust I have found treason,' said Queen Elizabeth the First to her parliament, and the Virgin Queen was a major heroine of my youth and in many ways still is. The foundations of my admiration were laid at the boarding school I was soon to go to, where the Head was an enthusiast for the verse plays of Clemence Dane, then a much-admired writer. She was never tired of quoting Queen Elizabeth's long speech in that somewhat lush poetic drama, *Will Shakespeare*, using it to reinforce the stoic code I was to adopt so enthusiastically in my teens. It was a code that would have bored her (and us, no doubt) if it had been presented in philosophical terms, but which carried immense weight in the language of Clemence Dane's poetry:

> I'll not bow
> To the gentle Jesus of the women, I –
> But to the man who hung 'twixt earth and heaven
> Six mortal hours.

I was later to find betrayal a theme dwelt upon by many of the authors I most admired in my adult years, like Conrad and Flaubert. I was to find it in film and theatre and in the political world around me, where in the thirties and forties betrayal became almost a way of life . . . the Spanish Civil War, Nazi Germany, Stalin's Russia.

But it was personal betrayal that set the pattern early in my life and led me thirty years later to make it a central issue in more than one of my novels. It began at school, in that stupid, blown-up incident that I have just described. It was to occur again when I went to boarding school, the subject of the next chapter. In the earlier incident, the important element was that the betrayal was committed by my headmistress, who broke her promise not to tell my parents, and I find it unforgivable for grown-ups to break promises to children. At Bampfield, my boarding school, it was my love and trust in my housemistress that was destroyed by her act of denial. This was a far deeper personal wound and it was the climax of a novel I wrote in my forties called *The Chinese Garden*.

Having spent two years at these fairly local schools, I was eventually to go, aged eleven, to a West Country boarding school. I now see that this was an attempt on my parents' part to get me away from home and the growing dissension within their marriage. What they failed to see was the effect upon me of cutting me off from the family and from the place we lived in, however disagreeable it was. And there were two long summer holidays spent away from home with my godmother, one before and one after I had gone to boarding school, both of which contributed to my growing isolation. Even before this, it had proved hard for me to find friends of my own age and tastes in Sandhurst, with its wide gap between working and upper classes, into which our family fitted so uneasily on the periphery of the middle class. The upper crust, moneyed and military rather than aristocratic, lived in large houses or on extensive estates of many acres like the two or three that surrounded our own small villa. I was cut off from their children, if any, for they went to fashionable and younger doctors in nearby Camberley for the most part. The incompetence and laziness of Dad's predecessor in Sandhurst had, of course, contributed much to this. There was no longer money to entertain and the Clovelly cottage had been given up when we moved from Weymouth.

To give me some compensation for this, my godmother, Nora, stepped into the breach, inviting me to stay with her in Tunbridge Wells. I loved Nora but unfortunately I did not like the young people I met in her house. She gave a home, rather as my mother had, to children whose parents were abroad. For two or three years she looked after a Scots family, two boys in their early teens and a girl, Alison, the same age as myself. Alison was red-haired, extrovert and indecently happy. I spent two long summer holidays with them and was bitterly unhappy and homesick on both occasions.

I went further and further into retreat, concentrating my love upon my black-and-white cat, Panna, whom I felt to be my only true friend. Whenever I could, I escaped from the house to the top of the garden among the pine trees. Though I hated them as trees, they attracted me because they stood on a small rise which formed a lookout, and from there I could see a blue distance of fields and woods. The sun poured on to the sandy bank where I sat among gorse smelling of burnt almonds, and dry, resinous pine needles. Here I began to build up that sense of possession that would later become a provider and sustainer. I was monarch of all I surveyed. I was stout Cortés. I was a noble savage in my own demesne. I could dream and fantasise and achieve a kind of remote happiness.

My first holiday with Nora was at Praa Sands in Cornwall. I was already a bookish, solitary child and not only was I bad at games, but I hated and feared them. No one had ever taught me to throw a ball or hit one with any form of bat. Alison and I slept in the same room and I had to stifle my tears, which she would have scorned. It was the same a year or two later when we went to Wales. All three children were hearty, open-air types, big-boned and athletic. They had no interest whatever in books or in the birds and butterflies that I was trying to persuade myself I ought to study now that I was living in the country. They wanted endless ball games on the beach, and were, of course, expert at throwing and catching. Not only was I a duffer at these boring sports, but I had been brought up to put games at a low value compared with books and such individual skills as rowing. My father had taught me to row, both on the sea and on a river, and I was rather good at it, even at feathering. But these children weren't interested in a boat unless it had a motor in it and made a noise. Nor did they think of a bicycle as anything but an inferior mode of transport, whereas I had been given one and was taking pleasure in long cycle rides that were a mixture of delight and endurance, but essentially solitary as yet and certainly not competitive. Alison and her two brothers made a competition of every activity.

With this family I felt an utter outsider, though I don't think that they were actually unkind to me. Probably only patronising and impatiently patient. I blamed my parents for their unthinking cruelty in sending me away and I built up a store of resentment. I did not know how poor we were now and how relieved they felt that I could have with my godmother the holidays that they could no longer provide. But I think that I may well have connected these trips to Cornwall and Wales, even if unconsciously, with those earlier occasions when Mother and Dad went off to Clovelly or Fowey and parked me out with patients.

By a curious coincidence, my godmother's Scottish family was all too similar to another that I saw frequently as soon as we had arrived in Sandhurst. My parents then discovered that friends of their Hoddesdon days were living only about twenty miles away. In fact they were the grown-up children of Hoddesdon friends, rather younger than my parents, and they had a family of three teenage sons and a daughter, Marian, of exactly my age. While the grown-ups reminisced about the old Hoddesdon days, I went through the purgatory of ferocious ball games, always played with a hard cricket ball. Marian was a very sporting type and quite as good as her brothers in these terrifying games. At least in Cornwall and later Wales there were a few other occupations and my dear godmother was there to talk to. Now I was really thrown to the wolves and I found the afternoons and evenings spent with this family pure hell.

My father was very struck with their description of the boarding school they had chosen for Marian. It was in the West Country, which strongly appealed to him, and he and Mother went to see it in the summer of 1924. It was inexpensive, uncompromisingly dedicated to open windows and cold water, and the Headmistress was persuasive. I was sent there in September that year with Marian, just before I was twelve. I doubt if she and I spoke more than half a dozen sentences to each other the whole six years we were there.

7

The Chinese Garden

We all lead several lives. Routes of discovery in our youth, undivulged to grown-ups and often kept hidden through deceit, and habitual role-playing as we get older. In childhood prevarication is a necessity. How otherwise could we survive the terrible claustrophobia of family and home life, or keep our sanity in the madhouse of school? But how truthful will be the backward glances and present assessment of those years? How much of the essential underground where we lived our real lives, where we fashioned our survival kit for our twenties and after, will be recalled when we are middle aged, when we are old?

When I wrote *The Chinese Garden*,* an account of one year out of the six that I spent at that West Country boarding school, I gave it as title the secret centre of that world, a place known to hardly anyone but myself. I was a conspirator, sharing with only one companion the deserted pagoda and its weedy lakes, that private Xanadu which glowed for me with pure poetry. What did we actually talk about as we sat on the crumbling steps? Was it so poetical? I doubt it. We were sixteen-year-old rebels, scribbling scurrilous verses and rebellious articles for a magazine which we wrote almost entirely ourselves and circulated among our friends. Yet there were other lives we led, both of us, and hidden from each other. Like Mrs Ramsay, when I look back I see words 'like little shaded lights' flickering in the corner of my mind; and there in the half-dark, are

> All the lives we ever lived
> And all the lives to be,

---

* Published by Jonathan Cape, 1962; republished by Brilliance Books in 1984 with an Introduction by Alison Hennegan.

for the Chinese garden was to grow within my life and spread its branches, like a tree thrusting its way up through the broken floor of an empty house.

The novel with this title, *The Chinese Garden*, was my second to be published. It was autobiographical, the most truthful book I have ever written about myself. It is difficult for me to go over the same ground here, yet I cannot omit that year or indeed the whole experience of six years spent at the school I called Bampfield. I have to view them from a new perspective, by-pass the novel and take a fresh look at my teenage self in this corridor of mirrors. In my mind's gallery still hangs a vivid picture of weedy pools framed in dense green undergrowth beneath their fringe of willows, and at the heart of the silent, sweet especial scene stands the Chinese pagoda, with its painted eaves, its tiny bells and, to either side of it, two tiny bridges. In this picture it is perfect, as fresh as it was when first created at the end of the eighteenth century, but in my novel I faithfully described its decay, for its rotten floorboards and broken roof were part of the corruption of Bampfield as a whole.

At Bampfield I discovered a new world which held much of what I longed for and lacked at home: I was protected (at least at first) by certainties and absolutes; I had the stimulus of companions of my own age and found friends as I had not done since leaving Weymouth; I was surrounded by a natural world which I could explore and make my own. Although it was not my beloved Dorset but the very different and far softer landscape of Devon, it had for me that inexpressible quality of the West Country that comes to me whenever I travel westwards. At Bampfield I was hardly aware of anything at first but the negative side of this. At last I was out of that hateful and hated conifer country of Surrey. Unconsciously, during those six years there grew up my strong feeling for place, an empathy with landscape and the physical image which I was to find ready to my hand when I later began to write.

Bampfield was founded by a remarkable woman just after the First World War, with the express ideal of turning out officers and gentlemen of the female sex. Discipline was strict, even military, with a great deal of marching and countermarching in all weathers. Surnames were used generally instead of Christian names. A spartan regime of wide-open windows, cold washing water and dreadful food was elevated into a virtue. So there I stand in the mirror, stiff as a ramrod, stern-faced, resolved to do or die like those brave lads so recently in the trenches. The enemy was now not the Boche – though we were still singing, 'Clang, clang, clang! on the anvil – There are steel ships wanted on the sea!' The foe was now a deplorable character defect designated as 'slackness' or 'slooming', a uniquely apt word invented by Chief, as we called the Headmistress.

I have to admit at once that I loved the discipline and was smarter than most on the march. It upheld me like a brace and I also loved it, paradoxically, as something absurd, irrational, even at times repugnant, something against which I could and did rebel whenever I felt like it, especially in the company of my boon-companion, Margaret, with whom I edited the anti-establishment magazine when I was sixteen. I don't think it is a bad thing for children to have something to sharpen their claws on. The illogicality about so much of the regime delighted my fundamentally nonconformist heart, even while the uncertainties and fears of my inner self compelled me to clasp it eagerly. Moreover, Chief herself liked to overturn it at times, to introduce wild schemes, bizarre alternatives to the ordinary business of lessons. No doubt this was deliberate and a part of her belief that school must prepare us for any situation we might meet in life. It was also an expression of the absolute power she wielded. And the rigidity of the regime could be bent at times – but not too often – not only by Chief herself, but by some outlandish and unorthodox suggestion on a child's part. A flu epidemic among the school laundrymaids took my own class off lessons for about a fortnight to work all day in the laundry. It made me fairly expert with an iron but I loathe ironing to this day. It was a form of education a little too reminiscent of Mr Squeers' principles: 'Spell winder: W-I-N-D-E-R. Now go and clean 'em.' But Chief was no Squeers. It was all part of the practical versatility which she saw as lamentably absent in middle-class girls. She had met incompetence and lack of leadership among the V A D s she had commanded in the Great War. She was determined that Bampfield girls would be turned out differently.

I do not regret the various talents I acquired during my six years, though at the time their chief virtue lay for me in getting away from lessons or, most worthwhile of all, off the games field. Opportunities were so rare that my friends and I had to invent our own. A well-placed criticism of the state of the gravel paths in the pleasure gardens, for instance, led to three of us being given permission to miss games periods for a whole blessed term, while we cleared them in a leisurely way with plenty of idle conversation and smoking, out of sight in the surrounding shrubberies. A random observation about the sad number of fallen trees in the neglected park, made as I strolled with Chief down the cricket pitch in amiable conversation, her arm about my shoulders, led to my being seconded to the bailiff's department where I was taught to swing an axe and work at one end of a two-handed saw, when I was not spending idyllic hours with a garden boy and a horse and cart, collecting fallen boughs and bringing them back into the sweet-smelling woodsheds. All valuable experience. I don't know many women among my friends and acquaintances who can swing an axe accurately.

In a sense, these sudden variations in the otherwise rigid structure of the Bampfield regime were a certainty in themselves. I came to realise that it was the imaginative, the inventive, that appealed to Chief so strongly. And I was very inventive. Yet I had to learn as I grew older that there were limits and that Chief was no pipe to be played upon. She made me a house captain when I was seventeen, but I was passed over for head girl. She said, frankly: 'You are too unreliable, Manning.' She was never one to hold back criticism. 'You're a person who rushes in where fools fear to tread.' I can see the words now, written at the bottom of a school report in her large, sprawling hand.

I stand at another mirror and see myself with Margaret, creeping about in the vast cellars under the house like a pair of Guy Fawkes, torches in our hands; or sitting side by side in the soft bins of chicken-meal in an outhouse – Bampfield offered many secluded spots to conspirators like us – with notebooks in hand, shaping a leader or some scurrilous verses against Chief, the staff, the regime and all its works. Smoking cigarettes, of course. We bribed servants to smuggle them in for us. Bampfield was above all a place of double standards. As long as these were my own, even if unrecognised, they did little harm to me, arising as they did mostly from my ambivalent attitudes to the regime. All children of any spirit indulge in them. The double standards of Chief and the staff were another matter and were to involve Margaret and myself in a nearly disastrous situation.

Surprising aspects of my character emerged at Bampfield that I did not know I had. I learned to be a clown among my contemporaries and even among the staff, or at least those who tolerated and were amused by my exhibitions. I found that I could make witty speeches off the cuff and write crude but effective parodies. More seriously, I wrote and produced plays adapted from novels and short stories, and

I was encouraged to do so. I learned to read music and hold an alto part, which laid the foundation of my career in amateur music. I found myself popular in most quarters in spite of being a total (and wilful) duffer at all games, and this in a school which prided itself on high standards in sport, especially in the manly game of cricket. I learned to read widely. There was a good if quirky library which was strong on Victoriana and weak on the moderns, and members of staff were often willing to lend from their in some cases extensive collections. Not only Chief, but two of the three housemistresses often kept open house in the evenings. One could turn up in their rooms and talk, or listen to them reading poetry or short stories aloud. The field was not all that wide. Much of the poetry was drawn from anthologies of Georgian verse, lyrics by Noyes, Drinkwater, Masefield, Frances Cornford, Henry Newbolt, but there were sometimes more exciting poets on the agenda: Tennyson, Francis Thompson, James Elroy Flecker. The most extensively read, both in prose and poetry, was Rudyard Kipling. I came to know most of his stories and an immense amount of his poetry and never have I heard his work so finely read and his verbal expertise so relished as it was by the elderly, eccentric teacher we knew as Punch. She inhabited a kind of den at the top of the Tudor turret staircase. Its windows were never opened and its worn floor-covering smelt strongly of ancient fishlike dog, but to me it was a haven. My knowledge of the Old Testament, too, became extensive, especially in those books which have a poetic flavour. Chief had once been an actress and read passages like the Song of Deborah with fine histrionic panache at prayers and in chapel.

> Thus sang Deborah and Barak . . . Praise ye the Lord for the avenging of Israel, when the people willingly offered themselves . . .
> Awake, awake, Deborah: awake, awake, utter a song, arise, Barak, and lead thy captivity captive, thou son of Abinoam . . .
>   The kings came and fought, then fought the kings of Canaan in Tanaach by the waters of Megiddo; they took no gain of money. They fought from heaven; the stars in their courses fought against Sisera. The river of Kishon swept them away, that ancient river, the river Kishon. O my soul, thou hast trodden down strength. Then were the horsehoofs broken by the means of the pransings, the pransings of their mighty ones.

I can hear the splendid poetry reverberating down the chapel as Chief read it. And then came the climax, always given a bloodthirsty relish:

He asked for water, and she gave him milk; she brought forth butter in a lordly dish. She put her hand to the nail, and her right hand
to the workmen's hammer; and with the hammer she smote Sisera
... At her feet he bowed, he fell, he lay down; at her feet he
bowed, he fell: where he bowed, there he fell down dead.

Chapters from the New Testament were not as favoured except as
texts upon which she could expatiate when extolling the virtues of self-
control, leadership and willpower, the Triple Alliance on which the
school's morality was founded and which was cunningly extracted
from such chapters as the Sermon on the Mount. The last days of
Jesus' life were, of course, a pure gift. My upbringing and education
had strongly reinforced the ethic of strength of mind, even within the
weak body of Woman. Not that my body was particularly weak.
When I was a child, my three brothers had much of my mother's
attention, and though she loved me and was in many ways a good
mother to me in a conventional sense, pressures from the brothers
and the extra-brothers implanted in me the deplorable masculine
ideal of the stiff upper lip. It was contemptible to cry, at least in front
of anyone. All my life I have found it difficult to weep except when I
am alone, and I remain stony-eyed at, say, a film, when others
around me are in tears. The stiff-upper-lip attitude was strongly reinforced by the spartan ethic of Bampfield. A poem which the Head
often quoted was one by Galsworthy, the salient verse of which I can
remember to this day:

> If on a Spring night I went by
> And God was standing there,
> What is the prayer that I would cry
> To Him? This is the prayer:
> O God of Courage grave,
> O Master of this night of Spring!
> Make firm in me a heart too brave
> To ask Thee anything.

I seem to remember that the heroines upon whom we were exhorted
to model ourselves were Nurse Cavell and that Deborah in the Book
of Judges whose hymn is a glorious burst of poetry to celebrate the
driving of a nail through the head of Sisera, an act hardly admirable
by most moral standards. Jezebel may have been held up to us as a
martyr, but I would not swear to this now.

There was much to deplore in the Bampfield regime and, from what I have observed, many of its worst aspects still prevail in the dwindling number of girls' boarding schools even today. I grew up a spartan and a stoic who never left a morsel on the side of her plate, however beastly. I was taught to love formality overmuch, to adopt meaningless military punctiliousness in behaviour and dress. I had later to unlearn much, free myself from much. I have not wholly succeeded even now. But it is fair to say that some of the best elements stayed with me for life and were to prove the foundation of more agreeable aspects of my personality and tastes.

I learned to love Latin with passion while I was at Bampfield, and this took me to the university. I read poetry with pleasure and was encouraged to write it myself. And I took away with me something which was to infuse much of my writing: a commitment to the English countryside so strong that I am sometimes forced to recognise that I have loved certain places more than I have loved people. I also carried away with me the burden of a flawed and immature personality.

Bampfield was a large, square late-eighteenth-century mansion, with pillared portico and cream stucco walls, topped by a parapet. It incorporated in one corner a wing of the Tudor house it had replaced. My first form room, when I was coming up to twelve years old, was in this wing: an immense salon, where rows of inked and mutilated desks were ranged beneath a gorgeously rich plaster ceiling; where doors were adorned by swags of carved wooden fruit and leaves, reputed to be by Grinling Gibbons. There were heavy wooden shutters at each side of the deep window embrasures and an elegant marble mantelpiece, put in two centuries later than the room itself. Just outside the form room was a circular stone staircase with a handsome wooden handrail, the Tudor turret staircase already mentioned. This led first to Chief's sitting room, a Tudor salon of similar proportions and plaster ceiling. Above that, it took you to the warren of small rooms on the second storey, inhabited mostly by the servants, but also where Punch of the Kipling stories had her quarters.

The house stood in a deer park. The herd came up to the house at night and their antlers clashed beneath our dormitory windows, their hoofs scuffed the loose flint of the carriage sweep in front of the classical portico. At the back of the house were extensive pleasure gardens with shrubberies and flowerbeds, now overgrown; a centre path a quarter of a mile long, cut through once-shaven lawns planted with exotic trees like eucalyptus and cork. Golden pheasants could be glimpsed under their shade, relics of the now ruined aviaries where chickens scratched on bare earth. The long gardens were flanked by two handsome lime avenues, the grassy verges a mass of primroses in spring. In the house, several of the rooms where we slept or worked were papered with eighteenth-century wallpapers in the taste for chinoiserie of that time: the Parrot Room and the Pheasant Room were two of the most beautiful. But the *chef d'oeuvre* of the eighteenth-century owners must have been the creation of a Chinese garden.

Here I prefer to quote from the novel, first explaining that a stream ran across the park, at one point disappearing into a sizeable circular plantation of azaleas, rhododendrons and willows. I gave myself the name of Rachel in the book, and described my first sight of the garden, which was strictly out of bounds, and which I only found after fighting my way through a strong fence and a mass of bramble, nettle and elder.

> Through this she [Rachel] pushed her way with some difficulty, drawn towards the centre of the plantation only by her sense of direction . . . She emerged into a strange, secret world, a clear blue sky above, willows, a lake, a coloured pagoda, and a tiny bridge – the world of a willow-pattern plate.
>
> The park stream ran right through the centre of the large plantation and in the heart of it had been created two pools big enough to sail a boat on, and indeed the poor relic of a punt still lay rotting in the boat-house. The pools lay close together and the stream that joined them had been divided into two courses, making a tiny, almost circular island between the lakes. Here stood a summerhouse, built like a Chinese pagoda, and reached by two bridges, one over each stream, highly ornamented in the oriental style.

The garden, like everything at Bampfield, was derelict, the pagoda's paint peeling, its woodwork eaten away, the bridges rotten. It shared with the house, the park and the pleasure gardens the corruption of the regime and those who administered it. The word 'corruption' appears several times in *The Chinese Garden*. When I wrote the book in my late forties, I made its main theme the betrayal of a child's trust in an adult. I recalled in every detail the landscape so beautiful and so decayed, and recognised that the whole regime had been built upon double standards and reflected the same soft corruption, the same fall from grace, as the physical world around it.

It had taken me some thirty-five years to come to terms with my experience at Bampfield. Clearly, I cannot spell out here the climax of the novel, since it has so recently been republished, but I feel it necessary to state briefly events which marked me deeply – otherwise there would be a gap in this autobiography, as though one of those mirrors I have used as symbols had been taken down from the walls.

When I was sixteen I fell deeply in love with my housemistress, whom I call Georgie Murrill. Chief herself was a lesbian and was having affairs with several members of the staff, some concurrently. Those she cast off stayed on, a little army of devotees. Georgie Murrill was one of them. It was my misfortune that I should have felt for her far more than the usual schoolgirl 'crush'. Or perhaps that was all it was until she made use of it for her own ends.

It was unfortunate for me for two reasons: firstly because Georgie Murrill's mind was trivial and narrow. Intellectually she hardly extended me at all. She taught me a wretchedly restricted form of history. Secondly, and far more importantly, she exploited me sexually. Again, she did not educate me, she did not expand my experience. I was woefully ignorant about sex and certainly far from being aware of my lesbian leanings. She subscribed to the general double standards of Bampfield whereby the pretence was kept up that every member of the staff was 'normal' and if there were virtually no men in evidence, this was because potential sweethearts and husbands had been killed in the war. Georgie Murrill *did* boast of having a young man. At one moment she was pulling me into bed with her, and at the next she was extolling the pleasures of her affair with Chief's red-headed nephew. Although I am now persuaded that this was a pure fabrication, it was at the time more than a little confusing for me.

This was a crucial affair and one from which I could have learned so much if Georgie Murrill had been motivated by less selfish feelings and by a desire to help me to understand my own. She was in fact using me to provide her with some of the sexual excitement she had lost when Chief jettisoned her. Physically, I have to say that we did not get much further than cuddling and petting (in *her* bed, of course, well away from the dormitories), but this aroused feelings I could not fully understand. It would have been better if she had gone the whole way and given me some experience of sex as enjoyable and productive of happiness, instead of behaving in a way that left me still ignorant, frightened of my overwhelming sensations, and burdened with inhibitions and fears which were to last me half a lifetime.

My affair with Georgie Murrill was very damaging and I have no forgiveness for her whatever. For this essentially untrustworthy, mean little personality I reserved one of the only bitter remarks in the novel: 'Her cowardly desire to appear on the side of the angels led her to jettison the child she should have protected. I think it is for the Georgie Murrills of this world that the millstones have been reserved.'

The betrayal of trust came about briefly in this way: my friendship with the clever, iconoclastic rebel, Margaret, was disapproved of and we kept it under covers. I was too ignorant, or perhaps I quelled my own uneasy suspicions about the relationship which Margaret was having with a dark, sinuously pretty girl called Rena, a girl whom I greatly disliked. We never therefore made a trio and Margaret rarely spoke to me of Rena. The girls were discovered to be having a lesbian affair and were expelled. Their parents alleged that both of them, but Margaret in particular, referred to me as 'the one person at Bampfield who wouldn't condemn them, who understood them', and so forth. Eager to find a scapegoat, the parents accused me of complicity. There were talks of a legal action. I was, of course, interviewed by Chief, who I think now was just and intelligent about it. If I were more cynical I should say that she was merely trying to save her own skin, but I did not think that at the time, nor do I feel this now with any certainty. She did not accuse me. She simply told me of the accusation, and asked me to think about it for two or three days and then come and see her again. When I did this and said that I was not guilty, she believed me and never said another word on the matter.

In the meanwhile, however, I had gone to Georgie Murrill's room, I suppose for help, comfort, advice. An 'ENGAGED' notice was hanging from her doorhandle. I ignored this and knocked. She opened the door a little way and spoke a few words, angry and accusatory. I felt myself prejudged and my trust in her betrayed. Had I been older and wiser I would have known that she was badly frightened.

I went up to my study where I made a somewhat ludicrous, ham-fisted attempt to kill myself, so ludicrous indeed that I almost wept with laughter over it. I told no one and once I had cleared myself with Chief, Georgie Murrill accepted my innocence and took me back into favour. It is not at all to my credit that I was too dependent upon her to hate her and escape from her influence. I needed the caustic comments of Margaret, but Margaret had gone. Perhaps through *her* agency – she was far maturer than I was – I might have come to terms with the episode, from which I only freed myself when I wrote *The Chinese Garden* in my forties. And did I free myself even then?

8
The Hunt Is Up

Six years at boarding school gave me only a third of the year at home but it was more than enough. Increasingly I used to long for the holidays to end. I saw less and less of my brothers. Tom appeared usually in the school holidays and took his room in the thatched cottage near by. He enjoyed the company of the aged actress who lived there, a bright parakeet of a woman who adored him, told him endless stories and much scandal about the stage world, spoiled him and flirted with him. I hardly remember his visits having any impact upon me.

My mother's health was deteriorating. Friction between her and my father was growing with the steady downward spiral of the practice. This gave Dad less and less work and allowed him too much time to moon about the garden and snooze over sandwiches in his study with Jacko. He was out for part of every day on his rounds but I think he spent longer and longer over cups of coffee and tea in his patients' houses, where his once genial spirits recovered a little, where he felt himself valued and, finally, loved. He had a surgery at our house and two others in neighbouring villages, and he and a surgeon friend more or less ran the local cottage hospital. Why was he not more successful in building up the practice? I can only surmise that he had lost heart, that for him, too, the move from Weymouth had been traumatic. I must add that I believe his own high-handed treatment of his three sons was coming home to roost. They gave him no support or encouragement, and indeed, as far as I can remember, criticised him and overtly took Mother's side against him.

In my teens I witnessed in my own home the truth that men are given, and consequently are brought up to expect, support and love and understanding from women. Girls are trained to give that support and, in a limited way, I think I tried to give it to my father. But the dependency needs of the girls are for the most part ignored. By a curious topsy-turvy reasoning, men are held up to be the independent, strong sex and take their nurturing for granted. Women are regarded as the soft, dependent sex, but are expected to suppress their own needs in this direction and prop up their men. A minstering angel, thou, indeed.

In the case of my brother Tom, his devotion to my mother made him her constant champion. Roger never showed any such devotion to her, but on an occasion when he was deeply unhappy he turned at once to her for comfort. This was when his girlfriend broke off her engagement after they had been together for four years. In those days Roger and Maud would never have thought of living together, though they occupied rooms in the same London digs, which must have put a strain upon them and have made the parting more painful. Roger went to pieces. My mother dropped everything and went to London to stay with him. She remained there for about three weeks and once told me that the two of them tramped the streets until far into the night, talking about the wretched affair. She would not have done this for me, I believe. But then – I admit that I never gave her the chance: I never confided in her all my life.

I cannot, on the other hand, recall feeling left out or jealous on the score that my brothers had so much more of my mother's attention than me. I had been brought up to accept that men should have the lion's share of everything. That *I* might have had an overwhelming need for support, encouragement or emotional tenderness never occurred to any member of the family except to my father, who loved me so much more than any of his other children, but was too inarticulate to say or do much about it.

In Georgie Murrill I may have been looking for a mother, and I suppose to a certain extent she fulfilled this need in that she gave me emotional warmth and she was someone I could confide in. But it was at a cost. It may well be that her ultimate betrayal of me was an act I regarded unconsciously as the withdrawal of motherly sustenance and protection. I am not sure that I want to stress this Freudian idea, however.

The experience at Bampfield was, I am certain, a major factor in my failure to find my sexual identity. At home I was always under pressure to get married, like a nice normal girl. This, and Georgie Murrill's spineless pretence that she herself was really heterosexual, deepened my conviction that in loving her I was an outsider and a 'deviant', as we were called in those days. Despite gay phone-lines, occasional T V programmes, and much franker discussion in public about homosexuality, many young people today feel amost as totally isolated as I did in my twenties and thirties. When you are young, it is all too easy to think that you are the only person in the world who has acne, who stammers, who suffers from constipation. I did not have these disabilities, but I did have the lonely conviction that I belonged to a tiny minority of women called deviant or queer, who loved their own sex and had no right to do so. There was the rider, that still seems to persist, that one would grow out of it, like spots or excess fat.

At last, about this time, I found a friend in Sandhurst. He was the only child of wealthy parents. My mother, I am sure, called them *nouveaux riches*. They owned a large pig farm. At the time I met Pat I was a rather overgrown tomboy, endeavouring to mitigate the awfulness of home life by solitary ramblings and fantasies of living rough in the woods. Perhaps the big spinney of larches opposite the house fostered these dreams, or maybe they were more inspired by Seton Thompson's novel *Two Little Savages*, a book I read over and over again.

When Pat's mother first suggested that I should come round to their house in the summer holidays, I was delighted. Here was a companion at last, I hoped. I thought of the woodland pleasures of the two little savages, and even of the milder romantic dream of a willow cabin down by the river, for *Twelfth Night* had cast its spell over me. But Pat wasn't given to fantasies. He was a solid, foursquare boy whose chief delight was going for long bike rides with me, sometimes taking food and spending the whole day out. This was a physical exercise that I was good at and thoroughly enjoyed. When we were not out in the countryside, we played rough and exhilarating games of bicycle polo on his parents' lawn, using croquet mallets and hoops and balls.

I began to spend most of my time with Pat and if further crises were building up at home, I did not notice them. Mother suspected him of having designs upon me. She asked me stupid, circumlocutory questions which I hardly understood and barely listened to, anyway, the burden of them being: 'Is Pat a *nice* boy?' Well, of course he was, in my eyes, or I wouldn't have spent so much of my time with him. 'Yes, but is he ... ' and her voice would mumble words I couldn't hear properly and though I really knew what she was getting at (or knew vaguely), I refused to help her out. I had become very anti-parent. I left her stuck on her sandspit of 'nice' with the tide of my relationship with Pat washing over her ineffectual shores.

Pat and I went out for hours on our bikes and I tasted the joys of free-wheeling very fast down hills, riding across the rough turf of fields, and at last stretching out, sweaty and agreeably tired, chewing stalks of long grass while we told each other about our schools and what daft things we had to do. I kept silent about troubles at home that I was becoming more and more aware of. I wanted to escape from them into a different world where they could be obliterated from my mind. Pat provided this, and without any strings. I don't know what *he* was escaping from but we built a friendship on easy surface terms, oddly free from adolescent hang-ups, perhaps because each of us wanted precisely this and no more.

At first, when I arrived home after a day out on my bike with Pat, the family were quite solicitous. Was I tired? Had I had a decent lunch? – presumably they thought I ate at his parents' house. They circled round me with enquiring eyes but they did not invite me into their closed club. So it was that I didn't learn what was really going on at home for months, maybe over a year. During that time, Pat and I met every holidays and spent most of our time careering through the lanes all over the river valley. He shared my passion for the river, but his was a practical interest. He tried to build a boat and spent several days on it. It didn't keep afloat but we had fun experimenting with it and getting soaked in the process. And Pat cured me of birdwatching, I think for life.

One day I took my logbook to the river with me and pulled it out of my pocket to log a yellow water-wagtail.

'What's that you've got?' Pat asked, lazily.

'It's a bird logbook,' I explained rather pompously. 'That bird there's a yellow wagtail. I'm awfully keen on birds.' Even as I said the words, they sounded fatuous.

'Why?' asked Pat, chewing a long feathery stalk and speaking through his teeth.

'Why? Well, birds are interesting.'

'I don't see it.' He spat out the stem of grass and half sat up, leaning on his elbow. 'Okay. You've seen a yellow wagtail or whatever. But in fact I watched it for far longer than you did because you were so busy scribbling in your silly book.'

'It's not silly.'

'Yes it is. When will you ever look at it again?'

'Well, next year, I suppose. Then I'll look back to see what I logged this year.'

Pat lay back and laughed aloud. 'I must try a logbook. September the third: saw a black raincloud. September the fourth: felt rain. September the fifth: in bed with a cold. I think you're daft.' He rolled over suddenly towards me and grabbed the logbook out of my hand.

'You're wasting your time,' he insisted, getting up and standing over me, a bulky figure against the pale-blue April sky. 'Come on. It's me or the logbook. Which d'you want?'

And of course I leapt up and grappled with him and he threw the logbook into the river. We had a sharp and angry fight and he came off victorious.

When we sat down again, panting, he said: 'I'm sorry about that. It was a bit mean of me to throw the bloody thing away like that. Shall I dive in and rescue it or buy you another?'

'No, Pat, it's all right. Honestly, I don't enjoy birdwatching terribly.'

'Good,' he said, approvingly. 'Look here. I'll never mind watching an *interesting* bird, just for a bit. As long as you don't start writing about it in some old book. In fact, I'd quite like to do a bit of birdwatching if there were any rare birds about. We'll need binoculars.' He waxed enthusiastic. 'I think Dad would lend me his and we could take them with us sometimes. But forget all this logging tripe, see?'

One day we had cycled into the country beyond the river to find the source of a tributary into the main stream. We had to leave our bikes for the going was rough. At last we found the tiny spring on a rock-strewn hillside and fell upon it gladly, scooping up water in our grimy hands, drinking it, pouring it over our sweaty cheeks and necks. Then we lay down exhausted. We had no food, for it was in our saddlebags and we had abandoned our bikes some way off at the bottom of the hill. Pat produced a bar of rather soft chocolate and gave me half. 'Iron rations,' he observed. 'Lucky I had it with me.'

We ate it slowly and washed it down with spring water.

'Okay?' he asked, wiping the chocolate off his mouth with the back of his hand. 'Not too whacked, are you?'

'Of course not,' I answered stoutly.

He sucked the remains of silver paper for a lingering scrap of chocolate, and said thoughtfully: 'I like a girl who's one of the chaps. The only girls I've known have been sisters of fellows at school. I don't like 'em much. I've stayed with one or two fellows and their sisters

give me the creeps. They don't want to do the kind of things I like
doing. Like finding the source of this stream, f'r instance.'

I made no comment, but wetted my handkerchief and, after mop-
ping my own face with it, offered it to Pat.

'You're definitely a chap,' he said, handing it back.

I was too pleased to say anything but applied the now dung-coloured
handkerchief to my brow and mopped assiduously.

'Mother likes you,' he went on. 'That's because she's not afraid of
you. We're rich' – he said it artlessly, without offence – 'and she's
always afraid people only like us for our money. I suppose it's pretty
obvious, really. That's why Dad married her. *She*'d got the money,
you see. And now – well, he doesn't seem to have much use for her.
Lord, I don't ever want to marry. What about you?' He rolled over
and lay on his stomach, staring at me with his dark eyes, his hair mat-
ted in strands over his forehead.

I wasn't prepared for this question and started to mumble, but he
cut me short with: 'Oh, you must know what I'm getting at. You and
me, we've seen marriage at close quarters. It's like a prison. I bet Dad
would get away if he could, but there's Mum with her hands grasping
the purse strings, and then your parents – well, I don't really know
them, of course, but they're so old – '

'I was born long after my brothers,' I said defensively.

'Yes, maybe,' said Pat impatiently. 'That's not the point. I meant
– getting old, and – and having to stay together whether you like it or
not, because society says so, or because you haven't got the money to
get free or something like that. I intend to be free all my life.'

Yes, it was what I wanted and I had written a fierce play about Cly-
temnestra, condemning the married state. Very cogent I thought it
was, but I didn't tell Pat about it. I had enough sense to understand
that playwriting might seem worse to him than birdwatching.

I found myself saying hotly that nothing would make me marry
and, as I said it, I knew it was the truth. Thinking of my parents, it
seemed a rotten way to live, and hadn't I written this play? But I
didn't feel that I wanted to talk much to Pat about what I vaguely
sensed was going on. I was too much of a stoic.

Childhood spirals around me like smoke. I cannot see myself clearly
in the glass. And there are no records, no letters, no one now with
whom I could recover past happenings. I cannot remember exactly
when I first met Pat or how long our friendship lasted. It returns to
me in scents and sounds: in the cold delight of spring water on a warm

April day – but it could have been August; in the hot greedy pleasure of lying under laden redcurrant bushes and stringing the fruit through my teeth – but in whose garden? I can see the dusty unmetalled road below my front wheel and a fine powder of dust on my shabby black toecaps, like icing-sugar on the little chocolate cakes that my mother cooked for my father's tea.

Pain always returns too easily, even in its trivial forms. I hurt my mother by refusing to eat the goodies she made. Food is the old temptation as far back as Eve's apple. I saw Mother's attempts to win me as a threat, as a preliminary to talk that I did not wish to hear. So it was only the wounded look in her face that I registered, the turning away in tears, the disappointment. These remain like thorns in my heart. Only once do I remember her confiding in me the reason for her tears. She was cooking and I was leaning against the kitchen table. She turned round to get some ingredient and I saw that her face was distorted with grief. The whole scene is absolutely clear: the grimy kitchen, darkened by the huge black fir tree just outside the window, the sour smell of the scullery adjoining. I put my arms round her and asked her what the matter was.

'I had a letter this morning,' she said. 'A letter from Yorkshire. My old friend Emmie Harrop is dead. I haven't seen her for so long. And now she's dead. As you grow old, they die, your friends, the people you have loved. You are left alone.'

She had no escape. The inexorable loneliness of old age was closing in upon her and though she had the support of her three sons, this was in a sense political. Their defence of her was really an attack upon their father, especially on the part of Tom and Roger. The hunt was up and they would drive him to make his escape. That is how someone outside the family saw the situation, but I think he needed little driving. And I, too, was in flight, escaping from the impending pain of losing him. There had been so little time with him, since I was away for two-thirds of the year. Memory is fragmented, carried to me now in a few sensations: the bell-like sound of wood on wood, when I found myself playing croquet the other day and couldn't remember the rules. My mind suddenly filled up like a bucket with water, brimming with memories of summer days playing croquet with Dad; walking with him on wintry afternoons with his stick ringing against the ground at every other step; playing piquet with him in the evenings. This companionship with my father: so infrequent, its pleasures unexpressed and undervalued, and with it a growing sense of threat –

to him, to myself. The family drew round my mother like a praetorian guard. I was an onlooker. So I spent hours I might have spent with him coursing over the countryside with Pat.

What happened to Pat? I never knew. For when the news that Dad was 'carrying on', as they put it, with a woman who was not only his patient, but – probably worse in their eyes – a Eurasian, a despised half-caste, Sandhurst society turned their backs on us. That included Pat's parents. The details have gone and all that remains of Pat and our friendship returns to me borne on river scents and felt in the jolt of a bicycle wheel on a rough road. Did I really get up at dawn and go to a meet with him, I who had been brought up to hate hunting? Certainly I went to a meet once: it could only have been with Pat.

The alarm woke me and I rolled out of bed. It was cold and when I went to the window, I found that I could hardly see any distance for the September mist. The pine wood at the top of the garden was invisible, the lawn a silvery velvet beaded with dew. Excited by the mystery of a time of day I had rarely seen before, I dressed quickly. When I looked out again just before going downstairs, there was a glow in the sky to the east. Pulling on a thick sweater, I went quietly down the stairs. Then I remembered the previous night, the recriminations and angry voices in my parents' room, so familiar now and so painful, and the sound of Dad's footsteps clumping down the stairs.

I assumed that he must have come up again after I had gone to sleep, but some curiosity impelled me to stand outside his study for a few seconds, wondering whether to go in or not. The need to hurry made up my mind for me. I couldn't bear to leave the house without knowing so I opened the door. He was sitting in his old, shabby armchair, his head lying back against one 'ear' of it. On his shoulder was Jacko, his beloved African parrot, fast asleep on one leg. I think I was never so physically stricken with pain as at that moment. Not, that is, till I was almost in middle age. It paralysed me. If he had awoken, I could not have said a word. That he should be lying there, still in his clothes in the early light, the only creature to share his loneliness and despair a grey parrot. I took a step towards him, my throat tight with misery. But I was on my way to the meet. If I stopped now and woke him up I should stay with him, perhaps for an hour or more, and Pat would never understand why I stayed. So I left him sleeping at what could have been the most intimate moment of our lives, and stole out of the house into the September mist.

Pat ran down the steps from his front door almost as I arrived at

the foot of them on my bike, and braked hard on the gravel. 'Good
timing!' he announced with approval. 'I've got the food here' – he
patted the saddlebag of his bike. 'Let's get going! Isn't it jolly being
out so early?'

It was. As we free-wheeled down the hill into the village, the sun
was coming up over the hills on the far side of the river valley. We
rode through the birdsong of the lanes without speaking. The mist
had left the hills but was still hanging like white seafoam over the valley itself, and when we rode into it, it was cold and mysterious. At
last, however, we came into Yockley village in golden light, and there
were the hounds, filling the green like swaying wheat, and men and
women on horseback and a few people on foot. It was after half-past
six and Pat undid the saddlebag and handed me a huge ham sandwich. We were just starting on the apples, when the hunt moved off.

'Come on!' shouted Pat. 'Eat your apple as you go along.'

So we wobbled slowly along behind the hunt, chewing our apples
and trying to avoid running down those on foot, until the houses of
the village were left behind. The hounds swept round through a farm
and out on to the open fields. The pace quickened. Pat and I had to
dismount. There was no track across the field ahead of us, and after
watching the hounds for a few minutes, Pat said: 'I think they're running towards Polstock. Let's ride round by the road and catch up
with them. There must be some lanes going in their direction.'

We pedalled like maniacs through a network of narrow lanes. For-
tunately we knew the country pretty well from our expeditions and
needed no map. No one else was about except a car that overtook us,
full of hunt followers who shouted encouragement and disappeared
down a road to the left.

'If they're going that way, we'd better go too,' shouted Pat, so we
rode down between hedges thick with blackberries, clouded still with
dew, while the sun rose over the trees in the fields. Ahead of us we
soon saw the car party who had taken to their feet. The footpath was
fairly dry, so we took our bikes through the gate and rode them.

'Keep going!' the party shouted, and 'Tantivy! Tantivy!' and 'Give
us a ride, will yer?' and similar witticisms.

The footpath ran along the edge of a couple of fields and then we
were in a wood and the going became too soft for the wheels. We
pushed our bikes through the undergrowth and suddenly heard cries
and shouts, and the baying of hounds over on our right. 'This way!'
cried Pat and struck out into the brambles. We tore our way through

them, oblivious of cuts and scratches, and emerged on the boundary of the copse, to see the hunt in full cry crossing a wide, grassy parkland.

'It's Hayward House,' panted my companion, as we lifted our bikes over barbed wire.

We were now on higher ground than the hunt and could see what was happening pretty clearly. We sat down and ate the last sandwich, and took swigs alternately at a bottle of milk. There was a sudden flurry of excitement, cries and the sound of horns, as the pack gathered speed and veered round to flash down the slope of the hill towards the river. A moment later we saw the fox ahead of them, a streak of russet on the green. I had thought cubbing was different from an ordinary hunt, and Pat shouted: 'They've picked up an old fox! Wonder if they'll call off the hounds or let them go after him.'

It seemed that this was what they were doing. We leapt on our bikes and rode down the field. We came to another lane at the bottom, which helped, for it was going in the right direction and looked as if it might be heading for the riverside copses. It was, but we lost the hunt on the way. The hounds must have reached the river a fair way further downstream, for we couldn't see or even hear them.

We stopped and drew breath. 'What do we do now?' I asked.

'Difficult to say,' answered Pat. 'If the fox gets to the river and across it, he'll throw them off the scent. Then they might come back over the fields, towards us. You never know. Wish we could see them.'

'Well, we could if we got higher up the hill.'

'It's a bit of a sweat, but – okay, up we go.'

So we pushed our bikes, which now seemed far heavier, up the side of the nearby slopes. At last we found a gate. Pat threw down his bike and climbed on to it to scan the view.

'There they are!' he shouted. 'They're a bit far off but I can see some horses – can't see the hounds though. Wait a mo'! Yes, I can!'

I was beside him now, and we were hanging on to each other, balanced precariously on the gate. 'There! There!' He pointed. 'Gosh! They're swinging round in our direction!' He threw out his free arm to point, but the gesture was our undoing. We both swayed for a moment and then I fell off the gate and dragged Pat on top of me. I thought I'd broken my leg, but I was determined to get to my feet. I struggled up and limped round in a circle, fighting to keep my tears back.

'Where does it hurt?' asked Pat, with concern.

'Everywhere – my shin, my knee,' I groaned.

'Here, lie down a mo',' he commanded, pushing me on to the grass.

'Let me have a go,' and he seized my leg and massaged it fiercely for a few minutes.

'I don't think you've broken anything, actually. Any better?'

'I think so,' I wavered, secretly convinced that he had made it far worse.

'Good! I'll leave it alone, then, until we've had something to eat. That's probably the best cure. Let's eat some of the biscuits.'

They proved to be a delicious and expensive assortment, and by the time I'd eaten half a dozen and drunk the rest of the milk, the pain seemed to be abating. I moved my leg about cautiously. No, there didn't seem to be anything broken. Only then did I recollect that I hadn't asked Pat if *he* was hurt.

'I'm okay,' he said with a grin. 'You only stepped on my hand pretty heavily.' He held out his left hand and I saw that the skin was bruised and actually broken in one place and oozing blood.

'I'm terribly sorry,' I said. 'Ought we to tie it up? My hanky's fairly clean.'

'Oh, God, no! Come on, we must get going – a bit higher up, I should think, so that we can keep them in view, if possible.'

We started off, still on a slope – and a steepening one, but the hedge was now lower and it was clear from what we could see that the hunt was coming our way.

'I say,' observed Pat as we sweated on under the increasing warmth of the sun, 'I say, you were quite a chap just now. Over that fall, I mean.'

I couldn't speak for pride. And at that moment – I didn't understand why – the hunt was blacked out and I saw with painful clarity my father asleep in his chair, with Jacko on his shoulder, and the first light of dawn coming in through the undrawn curtains of his study. I could feel tears coming hot to my eyes and dashed them away with my hand, remarking brusquely: 'Still hurts a bit.' But Pat hadn't noticed anyway. He was tramping across the field just ahead of me to see if there was a gate higher up before we reached the copse which crowned the hill, beech, hornbeam and alder glowing as the sun touched leaves already beginning to turn to autumn colours.

There was another gate at the top just under the copse, and we paused at it to draw breath. We were leaning on it together, not speaking, welcoming the wind on our sweaty backs, when we saw the fox. It was running fairly fast across the stubble about three fields away, making straight for our gate, or so I thought. Then it checked and lifted its muzzle.

'It's scented us,' whispered Pat. 'Don't move.'

After a few uncertain steps the fox veered away, still heading for the wood, but further over towards the far side of the hill. We then noticed that it had a limp.

'Oh, marvellous!' cried Pat. 'Let's get into the wood here and we might pick up the hunt on the other side of it.'

We could hear the hounds now and faint horns and men's cries. We scrambled through the barbed wire and along the edge of the wood. Gaps in the trees gave us glimpses of the riders galloping across the fields with the hounds like a golden skein unravelling ahead of them. It was slow going through the wood. 'Why on earth didn't we stay in the field?' I complained. My leg was still rather painful.

'We might have got ahead of the hounds if we had,' answered Pat. 'If you do that you don't half get cursed at.'

So we fought on through brambles until we could hear the hounds, much closer now and crashing about in the undergrowth. There were yelps and shouts.

'Probably going to earth,' panted Pat. 'But they'll have stopped it.' Suddenly he started to run. 'I believe they've got him!' he shouted. We'd abandoned our bikes at the edge of the wood, of course, but the undergrowth was thinning out. We saw several hounds ahead of us, noses to the ground. A few minutes later we were on the edge of a wide clearing, and there was the fox rolling over and over, snapping at the first hounds that had reached him. Within seconds, a flood of brown and yellow backs engulfed him. Then the huntsmen rode into the clearing, the Master drove his horse among the pack and amid the baying and snarling, the hounds parted a little. The Master stooped for a moment and then held up the fox's dead body, the fur muddy and red-stained at the throat. We were only a few feet away.

'That's not a cub, is it, sir?' shouted Pat.

'That it's not, young man,' cried the Master, turning towards us. 'It's an old dog fox. We've been after him more than once before and more credit to these young hounds that they've killed him.'

I wanted to cry. I wouldn't have minded a cub, but I couldn't bear it that after his long years of freedom the old dog fox had been caught at last by these eager young hounds. The excitement of the hunt and the kill drained away in despairing pity that the fox would never feel the September sun on his back again, or breathe in the warm smells of his earth in the high wood in winter's season. I turned away from the gathering throng of horses and people and stumbled back through the trees to the edge of the woods to pick up my bike. Pat never even noticed my going.

9
Through the Looking Glass

If I had been the marrying kind I should have wanted a large family – say, five children very close together. In fact, not only have I never wanted to marry; I have never felt the faintest sentimental, maternal or biological urge to have children. No doubt the somewhat ridiculous statement that I have occasionally harboured secret thoughts of a jolly close-knit family is simply a reaction against my own fragmented, dislocated sibling group. As for my parents, I know that so far I have done little more than portray their relationships with their sons, but not with myself. I have described my mother's early career, my father's behaviour. I have used them, in fact, like a novelist. They might not be my parents at all. In the mirror, the self-image stands in the way. Their shadowy figures are just visible behind me, and even further back, even more insubstantial, are the grandparents whom I never knew but who contributed to my character and, I am certain, to my creative talent: the Owens and Davyses, the Trenchards and Voyles and Coleses, their lives entirely sealed up from me, their voices silent, and all the little things – the drawers and cupboards of their living ways and their loves – scattered and gone to dust. At last the mirror clears and I stand alone before its reflections, knowing so little why I am here, what chance meetings, fugitive or lasting loves, ended in the woman before my eyes. Outward forms . . . perhaps one should start with these. Perhaps that is all I shall ever really know of my parents.

My father was a tall, heavily built man with a ruddy complexion, veined and weather-beaten, his hair long and curly, and when young a reddish gold, still apparent in his moustache when I knew him. My mother had a thick tress of it, a memento of his early years, tied up in creased, yellowing tissue paper. He had slim, well-shaped ankles and smallish feet of which he was rather vain. He wore well-polished shoes and in winter grey spats over them. His temper was good-humoured and genial. I can never forget his frequent bursts of song from a wide repertoire of music-hall ditties, musical comedy and Gilbert and Sullivan. One of his favourites was a temperance song:

> *Oh* . . . I love to drink of a social glass
>   But it must be filled with water,
> It makes the time so pleasantly pass
>   For every son and daughter.
>   But sad is the fix
>   If the liquor you mix,
>   I never do that! Oh no! Oh no!

It was my father who introduced me to the delights of the theatre and I have my happiest memories of him in those visits to London shows at the end of my school life and the beginning of my university career. It was mostly to the Lyric Theatre in Hammersmith that he escorted me. He parked the car at Normands' Garage (still there), and then took me by bus to central London where we ate at *Le Diner Français* in Old Compton Street. My father loved to pore over the menu, relishing the foreign dishes – this elderly man who read so many travel books and who had longed all his life to see the world but had never gone abroad once since his marriage. He pronounced the French execrably but held the waiters in his hand by his natural unaffected manner, his keen interest in the ingredients of different dishes, his enthusiastic sampling of them when they arrived on the table. It was only a cheap, unpretentious little restaurant of a respectability that made it ideal for a gauche, ill-dressed teenage daughter alone with her father, but it might have been Maxim's.

We took the bus back to Hammersmith and the seats were always, I think, in the dress circle of the Lyric, that charming theatre with all the atmosphere that for me is part of theatrical experience. Again, he was a delightful companion, eager and relaxed. For him it was a brief taste of freedom and a nostalgic trip into his youth of theatre-going when he was a student at King's College in the Strand, and later at Guy's Hospital. Forgotten were the worries of his Sandhurst practice, the unpleasant letters from the bank manager, the growing dissensions with my mother, the alienation from his sons. It was *our* evening. He gave everything an air, a flourish, even to the buying of the programmes. I have most of them still. They laid the foundation of a huge programme collection that goes back to 1926 or 1927, when

I was taken to the Playhouse Theatre to see *The Rose and the Ring*, performed by a starry cast: John Mott, Elsie French, Frederick Ranalow, Laurence Baskcomb, Vivienne Chatterton.

Recently I was going through the collection and found a curious gap in theatre and opera programmes between 1966 and 1968. It took me several days to realise why there was not a single programme from those years. When a love affair broke up in about 1966 I lived bleakly without hope that I would even find love again. I had a sudden destructive urge. I could envisage no future for myself and saw no point in the past I had lived. I decided to destroy my diaries (though my writer's cunning made me type out any material that might be of use), and with the programmes I worked backwards, destroying those of 1968, 1967 and 1966. At that point I stopped, my destructive passions appeased. The creative passion of love took hold of me and moved into the centre of my life. I am glad the bulldozing went no further.

I single out from those shows of the late twenties and early thirties *The Beggar's Opera, The Co-Optimists* and *Riverside Nights.* There was more notably my first experience of classical plays like *The Country Wife* and *The Old Bachelor*. One evening stands out with never-to-be-forgotten vividness. The play was Congreve's *Way of the World* and the Millamant was Edith Evans. I see that I was already such a hardened playgoer that I had seen her in a small part in *The Old Bachelor* – as Fondlewife's spouse, Laetitia. That production also introduced me to such players as Eric Portman, Miles Malleson and Diana Wynyard. But *The Old Bachelor* was a far cry, as a play, from the glories of Millamant and Lady Wishfort. I can to this day recall the very sound of Edith Evans' voice drawling the words: 'Shall I have him? Or . . . not? . . . I think . . . I will have him!' With her in the cast was Peggy Ashcroft playing the part of Betty, 'servant wench to the Chocolate House'. These two Congreve plays were also my first introduction to bawdy, which no doubt my father thought I shouldn't understand. I doubt if I did but I was alive even then to the language and to the wit. One of the greatest pleasures of Restoration comedy and the later plays of Sheridan is the perfect balance of the sentences, the joyful exploitation of the riches of the English language. It is too seldom heard in the theatre today, even less in the media.

Years after my parents separated, I read Montaigne's *Essays,* using my father's little leatherbound copies. They were heavily underlined, marked and annotated, often very personally in his unmistakable handwriting. It shed such an unexpected light upon his character and ideas about life that for some time I seriously contemplated using him as the central character of a novel called *The Man Who Loved Montaigne*. Perhaps I will write it yet.

But there were no confidences between my father and me. By the time I left school, I did realise that things were going very wrong at home, and I think it must have been the long vacation before I went to the university in October that I was at last let into the secret that had been going on behind my back.

Two Eurasian sisters had come to live at Sandhurst. This heavily military village, full of red-faced, white moustachioed retired colonels and majors, was not the best place for them to have chosen. Angry at the way they were cold-shouldered by Sandhurst society, Mother and Dad were for a time drawn together by a desire to show them kindness. The two ladies were asked to tea, taken for drives and picnics, an echo of the old days when the parents kept open house at Weymouth and entertained the young women in the Great War. Now it was a different situation. One of the Eurasian sisters was often ill, it seemed, for my father was called in frequently and stayed at the house for long periods. At last my mother pulled the whole matter out in the open. Tom came home and summoned the other two brothers. Arrangements were made for my father to have a long break, some four or five weeks, with my mother. Nostalgically they chose to go to Fowey, but when they returned things were no better. My father wanted to have his freedom.

Tom ranged his brothers in defence of Mother, and actually went with them to see the lady concerned in an effort to persuade her to leave Sandhurst and give up my father. Heaven knows how the three of them conversed with her on the subject. I only know that it was entirely unsuccessful. It was clear that something decisive had to be done, for rumours were rife in Sandhurst and Dad could easily have been struck off the register. At last my mother urged him to go and the practice was put up for sale. The would-be purchaser was soon told of the affair, and put pressure upon my father to go quickly and for a far lower purchase price than he was asking. It was a *fait accompli*. As for me, I was just at the end of my first year at college. I was loaned my fees for my remaining two years, and a tiny cottage in Devon was to provide myself and Mother with a home, through the kind offices of Chief at Bampfield.

I see my father as he was in my late teens, when I came closer to him than I ever had before, except perhaps for the winter evenings when we first came to Sandhurst, and he spent much of his leisure time teaching me to rig a model sailing-boat and later to sail it on local lakes. And there were walks with him, and days when I worked at his accounts, a dismal business, for they were confused and ill-kept. One thing emerged which explained in part our growing penury: he charged his few upper-class patients high fees but was often not paid. His working-class patients either paid him nothing or very little or were on the 'panel'. This brought him ten shillings a year per patient at that time, if I remember rightly. There were not many people on the 'panel', for agricultural labourers were not included in the scheme and most of the male population of Sandhurst worked as gardeners or farm labourers.

Mrs Wombwell up the hill, in whose cottage we had camped out in 1922, had a tubercular family of various ages, some living in huts in the garden. She supplied us with eggs and I found that my father was paying her for them. I was indignant. 'You're always up there, attending to them *free,*' I protested.

'My dear,' answered my father mildly, 'if I didn't pay her for the eggs she couldn't keep the chickens. Don't equate my medical attendance on her children with your breakfast boiled eggs.' I felt exasperated, ashamed and overwhelmed with unexpressed affection.

To the end, despite the lack of money, he remained a bit of a dandy, and here I will quote a short passage from *A Time and a Time*, an autobiography I wrote in the sixties,* which brings him vividly before me:

[His] bow-ties always seemed to me to mark him off from other men. The ties themselves were different from the few I have encountered since. They were generous, plump bow-ties, loosely knotted and winged like gulls. The collar which they adorned was in my recollection not very high – an absolutely straight band of starched linen, the front edges of which were not turned sharply back but curved gently outwards beneath my father's double chin, suiting their contours to the contours of his ample neck. The ties were always black or grey, and spotted or otherwise decorated with small mullets or roundels or other devices. They were gay despite their sombre colouring, and set off the redness of my father's cheeks.

---

*Published in a new edition by Marion Boyars in September 1986, under my own name, with an introduction by myself.

When my parents finally separated in 1931, I was cut off from my father with dramatic finality. At the outbreak of war in 1939 he at once joined up as ship's doctor. Alas, he fell ill on his troopship sailing along the African coast, and was put ashore at Durban, his brief war career ended. He died soon afterwards, in January 1943, of a series of strokes. He was seventy-five.

My brothers Bob and Roger – Tom was on war service – took my mother and me down to the village in the New Forest where my father's lady companion – what am I to call her? – flung open the door and cried in heart-broken tones: 'He's just gone! Come and feel him – he's still warm!'

My mother – and this gives a wonderful picture of her enduring strength of character – turned to the three of us, her face stricken, her tiny figure shrunken in upon itself. 'I don't wish you to come in,' she said, firmly. 'Please wait outside in the garden. I'll join you in a few minutes.'

We walked glumly and in silence up and down the bedraggled wintry garden among brown-leaved chrysanthemums and mildewed Michaelmas daisies. My mother emerged and we drove into Bournemouth. We stayed at an almost empty, vast hotel, drinking rum, the only spirits they could provide. In a few days, my father's cremation took place. Mother did not attend it.

I recently found some instructions he had left, one of only two things in his handwriting that I still possess, with its old-fashioned βs for double s, which used to delight me on the envelopes that arrived at boarding school – Miβ Rosemary Manning:

IT IS MY WISH after due consideration that after my death my body shall be cremated and the ashes scattered to the four winds.

It is also my desire that this shall be done as economically as possible – the coffin or casket shall be as cheap as may be consistent with efficiency.

Flowers are not to be wasted on me, but if anyone feels an urge to offer up sacrifice of thanksgiving for my attention, may it be given to the nearest hospital.

No one is to be invited to my funeral – no mourning is to be worn.

It is a matter of indifference to me whether there is a religious service or not – that is to be as my surviving relatives wish.

I desire that no memorial of any kind be put up or record of my existence beyond any kindly memory which may remain in the heart of anyone whom by a lucky chance I have befriended.

Thos. D. Manning.

With it were a couple of loose pages, pulled out of what looks like one of the notebooks he used for his rounds. Only the first page has been used, written over in pencil in small close writing, rather different from his usual hand. The date is June 1938, years after he left us. Was his mistress religious? It sounds as if she was and that he found her religiosity trying. My father had no use for religion whatever. This is what is written:

Doctrine of salvation/justification by confession is rotten unless accompanied by true penitence and *effort at reformation*. To indulge one's temper & speak cruelly is never justifiable – To do so and then by confession with or without sincere regret may justify in eyes of a priest (especially + alms) justify him in excusing it but the key of sit^n is 'Go & sin no mre.' Often abuse and reprobation arise from the knowledge that retaliation is difficult or impossible therefore recipient is (1) in no position to retaliate or (2) does not care to do so i.e. feels that abuse is weak – ill & that the abuse does not really truthfully represent the abuser's feeling towards the abused – or maybe abused feels that the abuser is really ill and lacking in self-control. But does that justify? No. Nothing does so. Nothing can justify *refusal* to look at the abused one's point of view tho' there may be something to be said for inability to appreciate it. No one can help being a fool – we all are that is to say our intelligence is allways more or less variably limited. But if the question is approached goodtemperedly – generously – then you will always find there is something to be said on the other side.

What was the pain that produced this rather tortuous outburst? I look at the date again: 1938. He had been living with her for seven years and, yes, he was dependent upon her. He had no money of his own at all. It is the word 'dependent' that gives the game away.

His cremation ended in a way I think would have heartily amused my father. As Roger, Bob and I walked silently down the drive of the crematorium in the January frost a Dickensian figure with dripping nose emerged from the porter's lodge and held out a sheaf of papers to Bob, who no doubt looked the most responsible of the trio.

'You'll be wanting something to put the gentleman's ashes into, sir,' he snuffled. 'Now, 'ere we 'ave a nurn, price thirty-three pounds, and 'ere we 'ave –'

My brother Bob drew himself up to his over six feet and looked down his long Wellingtonian nose at the snuffler. 'My father would not care,' he said in measured tones, 'if his ashes were put in a tobacco tin. Put them in whatever you like. I'll collect them later.'

Bob did this alone. He drove to Swyre Head on the Dorset coast near Corfe Castle, where we had so often picnicked when we lived at Weymouth. Among my mother's papers I found this letter which Bob had written to her at the time – actually just after he had scattered the ashes, for he was still on the headland when he wrote it.

Swyre Head. 17.11.43

Dear Missus,

I am sitting on the little hillock at the end of the Head. It is just getting dusk but I can see very faintly the outline of Portland and St Alban's Head stands up like a rocky castle to my left.

I am glad I managed to get up here – a wonderful spot.

It has been a clear, frosty day and now a very still grey evening with a faint orange glow here & there. I shall try to find a few little sprigs to send you with this but there is very little but a sort of heather – mostly dried up – is it ling?

I cannot add anything to what we have already said of Deeds (my father's family nickname) – I have the happiest memories of him.

Best love,
Bobby

And now it is over forty years ago, about half my lifetime, and I, too, have the happiest memories of him. It seems that memory can sometimes be merciful. I loved and admired him, perhaps to excess. The older I grew, the more I valued his genuine warmth as against my mother's sentimental affections, which I suspect concealed a chill centre to the heart. It was the more painful for me that in the end I found myself in the role of protector of my mother for the rest of her long life. My father I never saw again after I was twenty. The irony of this bit more and more deeply into my inner self as I grew older.

The pain of having had parents lasts from one's birth (and even before that) into old age. I feel I am not free of mine yet, not free from guilt, remorse, love, hate, unabsorbed elements in my blood.

There should be and indeed may be for some a kind of poetry that arises from one's parents, or one of them, a poetry that contains the essence of all the good that flowed from them, that reaches down through the guilt and remorse and gathers all the confusing and destructive elements into its healing embrace. This has not happened for me. I have attempted to see past myself to the man who was my father. This is far more difficult in the case of my mother.

Until recently I have not tried to come to terms with my relationship with her, or made a serious attempt to understand her complex nature. I do not clearly understand her now, and I am hampered by the fact that so much of the little I know of her earlier days has come to me filtered through the memories of others. My personal memory of her as a child is that I found her love for me oppressive and manipulative. She tried to draw me on her side, but I was too often hostile and defensive with her. Her women friends, with the exception of Nora, made me uneasy. Obscurely, I could see, long before my teens, that my father was being put in the wrong and belittled. I never enjoyed my mother's company as I did his, though I will admit that I came to enjoy it more easily when I was older and she was no longer living with me.

My mother had been beautiful when young, but the photographs I possess of her at the time of her engagement show a serious, rather withdrawn face, unsmiling and ungiving. What was she holding back? The same unsmiling face looks out from later photographs of her, taken with her three young sons around her, and later still with me. In fact, she had a great sense of humour. She was one of the best readers-aloud I have ever heard and the books she loved were those with plenty of humour in them, books like *Uncle Remus* and E. Nesbit's many children's books. In this field my parents had much in common, for my father, too, read aloud well, his contributions being mostly from Bret Harte's and Gilbert's verses, with Carroll's *The Hunting of the Snark* as his *pièce de résistance*. From these books were built up a fund of those sayings that many families adopt, that become common parlance among them – to the bewilderment of outsiders. 'How do yo' symptoms seem to segashuate?' was a favourite, and 'Miss Meadows an' de gals, dey set up a monstrous gigglement,' was another, both from *Uncle Remus*, now, alas, usually read from 'translated' texts that take out most of the characteristic, salty flavour. A rather more esoteric quotation came from an old rag book of my mother's, which on one page showed a little girl throwing her toys about in a nasty temper. Underneath was written: 'Little Miss Mince is *not* like Jesus.'

When my father went out of my life, our relationship was unfinished. My mother I knew until her death at the age of ninety-one. I see now that much of her life after we left Weymouth, and certainly after my father went, was a survival course, much as mine has been though for rather different reasons; nor has my version been performed with the courage and *élan* with which she conducted hers. She did not complain or moan about the break-up of her marriage. Once the initial shock was over, she set out to live a full independent life. When I started work in London after leaving the university, she shared the large flat where a college friend and I lived in North London and she went with us three years later when we moved to Denmark Hill. We were all three of us too poor to live separately. However, she realised that the position was unsatisfactory for herself as well as us, and she departed to a bed-sitting room in the semi-basement of a terrace house in Camberwell Grove not far from me, where her landlords were a printer and his wife who became very fond of her and cared for her devotedly during the Blitz. One night her windows and door were blown in by a bomb. She was a prisoner in her room, with masonry falling outside and plaster descending upon her head and the floor a mass of broken glass. They broke their way in and rescued her. She made a splendid comic story of her escape: how she was more or less frog-marched through the rubble-strewn garden in her nightdress, helped into the Anderson shelter and plied with brandy. She enjoyed it all hugely. She felt a part of her community, the true Londoner she had always been at heart ever since her Shadwell Dock nursing days.

Once independent of me, although she liked to see me frequently, of course, she set out to exploit interests which in some cases she must have had all her life. She was not, I think, a truly religious woman, but she loved a religious disputation, something her husband and family had never gratified and which the mild Anglican clergymen she had known had never provided. She joined the Roman Catholic Church but eventually her love of argument brought her into trouble. After a few years she was told politely but firmly that she could only remain within the Church if she refrained from arguing with priests about its tenets. She thought this over and then – I know it was with much pain despite her capacity to make an amusing tale of it – she left the Church. Her chief quarrel with it was the doctrine that her children would remain in Purgatory until the Last Judgment (or is it for ever?), because they had not embraced the true faith. Or indeed any faith. She became a wanderer from church to church, which saddened me, for I could understand the loneliness that drove her into this restless pursuit and I believe that her old age would have been far happier if she had remained a Catholic. The Roman Church looks after its own.

She had a great gift for friendship before deafness and finally blindness overtook her. Even in her seventies she could still inspire the somewhat sentimental adoration of one or two young women, but she also won the regard of two eminent men in Nonconformist churches in London. She never went to their services, but she corresponded with them, and went to see them and talk with them from time to time. No doubt she enjoyed discussing theological points with men who had no authority over her. She was equally at home with the Salvation Army, particularly with one officer who lived in her neighbourhood and became a close friend, an interesting character who had worked in Russia at the time of the 1917 Revolution.

My mother was charitable in an old-fashioned but unpatronising way. It was not a matter of giving away money to causes – she had little to give – but of interesting herself in individual 'hard cases', like that of the girl who lived upstairs and whose baby was found to be a 'mongol'. Mother befriended her with unstinted time and kindness when, unable to face the truth, she let the baby be taken into a home and subsequently went through a long period of suffering over the irrevocability of her decision. My mother was unjudgmental over moral issues and simply offered what warmth and practical support she could. Sentimental in some circumstances, perhaps her nursing experience had taught her to give help without a trace of patronage, and the difficulties and problems of the less fortunate seemed to have touched her heart more than her husband's love or her children's emotional needs. At Weymouth, she had conceived and carried out a piece of social work original for its time. Every summer, swarms of 'trippers' descended upon the town. In those days they spent their brief holidays in boarding houses, where it was the custom to turn them out after breakfast and not admit them again until the evening. Young couples dragged their small children along the esplanade and across the sands, often in sweltering heat or sometimes in pouring rain. My mother set up a day nursery on the beach, where families could leave their babies and toddlers all day for a trifling sum. There she and her helpers fed them and cared for them while their parents were set free to enjoy themselves.

Such natures as my mother's seek fulfilment of themselves in giving, but generosity can become burdensome. She could be intrusive where members of the family were concerned, especially her grandchildren. She did not understand them or try to. She regarded them as a new generation upon whom she could bestow her gifts in a situation where she was deprived of a family circle which might have mopped up her generosity. She loaded the grandchildren with food they didn't want and often didn't like and with objects they had no use for. And they shied away instead of returning to her the love she so badly needed. As she went into her seventies she became increasingly deaf, and was further cut off from communication.

After the war she moved to a North London flat provided by Tom, not far from where I was living. I saw her as often as I could. She increasingly needed help, for she began to go blind. I could not give it. There was no place where I could have had her to live in the house where I was confined virtually to a bed-sitting room, most of the premises being part of the school of which I was joint headmistress. I had very little money to spare, nor had my brothers with their growing families, at least in the case of Roger and Bob. Tom was unmarried but was never well paid. At least he provided her with the flat and could ill afford to pay the rent of it. Later I found her a room in one or two private households, but people found her difficult and demanding, and as she became more helpless she needed care. She had to be put – and what a terrible phrase that is – into a small inexpensive nursing home. I do not think she was treated with real kindness there, just kept clean and fed. Communication with her was now impossible. What went on behind that shrunken, unhappy face, with its often frustrated, ill-tempered expression? It is painful to me to remember her.

Why should anybody be condemned to end this way? Have we not a right to kill ourselves if we choose or to be helped out of life when it becomes a hopeless burden? I believe this profoundly. Death was once more indiscriminate, and many died young and before they had fulfilled themselves. Was this more terrible than the living death to which modern science condemns us by prolonging our lives into senility and incontinence? Why is society not shamed by the lack of adequate hospital and home nursing facilities? By the overcrowded, often understaffed geriatric wards to which the old are banished to endure a death without dignity? I feel a deep anger at the callous degradation which converts a stable if feeble old man or woman into a drivelling, incontinent idiot. My mother was for a short time in a hospital ward with a damaged knee. She was not blind or deaf at this time. She was perfectly rational but physically incapacitated and willing to spend a few days being looked after. But she was shunted from bed to bed, hardly helped even to wash, and she became increasingly 'difficult'. I must stress that this was thirty years ago and I cite it only as an example of ignorant rather than callous treatment. My brother Bob and I saw one of the doctors. She was senile, he informed us, and would have to be put into the ward for certified patients. We removed her at once and by taxi because no hospital car was offered. Indeed, no wheelchair was even given us to get her from her bed to the lift. We had to carry her. Once home, she quickly became calm and *compos mentis*.

I am unwilling to make general statements on this subject, which is an aspect of society that weighs upon my mind very heavily. It is more cogent to quote a case all too typical of what is going on despite the efforts of devoted doctors and nurses in many geriatric hospitals. They cannot do their work adequately as long as an uncaring society prefers to spend its money on arms.

Mary Handford (I have changed the name) was hospitalised because she was in pain and physically disabled. Her daughter visited her frequently until she was forced to go away for two or three weeks. She returned to find her mother not in an orthopaedic ward but a geriatric one, where she was confused and unhappy. Her daughter at once brought her home but as time went on lack of daily help made it impossible for her to nurse her mother and Mary Handford went into hospital again, this time into 'an overcrowded, dismal ward with thirty-four old women lying two feet from each other in low beds or crushed together in a tangle of chairs and walking frames in the makeshift dayroom'. Bells did not work. If the patients needed a bedpan they had to shout for the nurse. The daughter was convinced that her mother's incontinence was entirely due to these conditions. Another indignity was that she lost her own clothes. 'I went in and saw her sitting in an old dressing gown made out of what looked like a grey blanket. There were buttons missing, exposing an old vest that was not her own and a pair of paper panties.' Her own clothes had allegedly been lost in the hospital laundry. Further distressing incidents followed which I will not enumerate. Mary Handford stayed in that geriatric ward for three and a half months. She was then moved to a long-stay geriatric hospital. 'The move terrified her. She became even more confused, noisy, began taking off her clothes. She had to be sedated. In less than a fortnight she was dead.' This account is taken from an 'In Focus' report in the *Sunday Times*, 15 November 1981. It is not a criticism of hospital treatment as such but a comment upon a society which will not press for proper caring treatment of the growing population of old people.*

Such things occurring in a prison would cause an outcry and probably give rise to a public enquiry. An old woman kept in a relative's house in such Dickensian conditions would be reported to the social services or the police. Low-funded and minimally staffed geriatric hospitals are not to be blamed for a situation which society, that is you and I, tacitly condones or utterly ignores. As I write this in September 1984, hundreds of the public are gathered outside a magistrates' court where a multiple rapist is being charged. No doubt they exclaim against him in indignant and angry voices. They do not analyse the feelings which really inspire their prurient curiosity or ask themselves why they remain silent when they read of the conditions of old people. They must read them. Most newspapers report them. But, of course, they rarely have any sexual connotation.

And where, you may ask, has my own *saeva indignatio* over the plight of the aged brought me? For what crusade do I carry a banner? Am I active in any of the societies like Age Concern even if I support them with money, which I in fact do? I have no answer to this. I allow others to do the work for me. I salve my conscience by giving money and hoping it will do some good, and I pray to that God in whom I do not believe that he will give me the strength and the means to kill myself before my mind gives way, or I am paralysed and unable to act for myself.

I condemn my own pusillanimity that prevented me, fearful of a criminal charge if I was found out, from putting a merciful end to my mother's life when it had gone into the darkness within which she lived out her last ten years. *Mea culpa. Mea culpa.*

Recently I read much of the poetry of the American poet, Denise Levertov. From one of her volumes I take this perfect evocation of a dying mother.

---

* A work of imagination is often more powerful than a newspaper report. I urge everyone to read May Sarton's novel about an old woman put into a home by her relatives: *As We Are Now* (The Women's Press, 1984).

On your hospital bed you lay
in love, the hatreds
that had followed you, a
comet's tail, burned out

as your disasters bred of love
burned out,
while pain and drugs
quarreled like sisters in you –

lay afloat on a sea
of love and pain – how you
loved that cadence, 'Underneath
are the everlasting arms' –

all history
burned out, down
to the sick bone, save for

that kind candle.

In a strange way, though this mother died in such different circumstances from my own, I have found this poem – part of a sequence of poems about Levertov's mother which I have read many times – comforting and reassuring. It has purged me to some extent of the terrible feelings and thoughts that have burdened me for so long. The total burden of guilt will never fall from me.

10
We'll to the Elephant!

When I went to the university in 1930 I had no idea as to how I was going to earn my living except for a strong resolve never to go into teaching. I still wanted to be a writer, as I had determined to be in my teens, and I intended to be famous by the time I was thirty. I was not, however, so unrealistic as to think that I could exist by writing, at least for some years to come, nor had I any clear idea in what field my creative talent lay. I never doubted that I had it. One of the poems I wrote in my early twenties began:

> I will not live on the low levels,
> On the plains.
> I will rise like a meteor . . .

I no longer remember the next lines, but I know that it ended with an image of myself 'burning in flames across the sky'. Alas, it was not at all like that. I devoted far less time to writing in my twenties than I had when I was at school, and what little I wrote dissatisfied me. I hardly attempted to get it published, with the exception of a gloomy sonnet on suicide which was printed in the *New Statesman*. Probably I should have got down to writing if I had been more certain what I wanted to write, but my aspirations were very vague. Besides, London provided so many distractions. However, I have gone ahead a little and it is, I suppose, necessary to say something of my university years at Royal Holloway College in Surrey.

R H C was probably the worst choice that could have been made. It was hardly a choice, for no alternatives were suggested. My Latin teacher at Bampfield had emerged from it only two or three years before she taught me. She was a fair scholar and probably found favour with the elderly Head of the Classics Department and her colleagues. To me, R H C was simply another boarding school like Bampfield but without Bampfield's endearing eccentricities, and certainly without its inspiration and encouragement to me as a writer and lover of poetry. I had expected a great deal: intellectual freedom and stimulus, new worlds to discover. But I found myself in a narrow, half-dead institution, subject to stupid, illogical rules and manufactured traditions that I despised. I was there at a bad time in its history, perhaps, when the excitement and expansion of its early days were long over. The Principal was a most disagreeable woman who lacked any sense of humour, and was without the charisma that inspires or the humanity that breathes warmth into the chill corridors of such an institution, cut off as it was from the university proper. She was in appearance a squat, ugly toad, in contrast to her boon companion, one of the administrative staff, a peacock of a woman, tall, plump, with a shock of strikingly red hair.

R H C had at that time only a small number of students studying arts subjects. The majority were working in Maths and Science. Many of these were first-generation undergraduates from schools in the North Country, excited and happy and hard-working, their social lives a round of evening cocoa parties before the serious business of studying into the small hours. My own Classics school consisted of only four students, two of whom were scholars. These two were also ardent members of the London Inter-faculty Christian Union, a small body of militant evangelists, given to knocking on one's study door and asking if one was saved, or leaving little tracts with titles like 'God in the Slums'. I could not endure them and spent all my time with members of the English school.

I could have forgiven Holloway much if my course in Classics had been stimulating. I had arrived there with a passion for Latin and considerable aptitude for it, but unfortunately my knowledge of Greek was rudimentary. My Latin tutor read his notes from dog-eared typescripts, yet despite this uninspiring method he succeeded in giving me a liking for Silver Latin, for Tacitus and Juvenal in particular, and nothing could destroy my passion for the Latin language as such. The Head of the Classics school was the professor who had taught Ivy Compton Burnett thirty years before. No doubt she was then young and enthusiastic but she was now crabbed and pedantic. She had no time to spare for me when she had a couple of scholars like the two evangelists to teach, and their religious enthusiasm commended them to her, for she had a hobby-horse: women in the Church. I remember her simply as the woman who made me hate Greek and I do not feel forgiving. 'No, Miss Manning, you must not read Herodotus at present. His vocabulary will not help you with your Greek proses.' Many Greek lyric poets were denied me for the same reason.

I adopted 'agin the government' attitudes, refused to take any part in college life except for the music and, as I had done at school, I threw my weight about, behaved arrogantly, enjoyed playing the clown. I sought easy admiration to shore up the weak defences of my uncertain identity. Thus I played the fool in chapel although I was passionately fond of singing in the choir, which I did for two out of the three years I was at R H C. This meant compulsory attendance every morning (and evening? I can't remember) and two services on Sunday. As a convinced atheist, I regarded the words I sang as devoid of any religious significance but allowed myself to enjoy their poetry, if any. A psalm was sung every day of the week and sung antiphonally. Psalms were set to some of the most beautiful and interesting chants I have ever heard, and all chants and hymn tunes were arranged in three parts for women's voices to give more richness to the singing, especially for the unaccompanied service every Friday.

My poetic and musical passions did not prevent my clownish side from too often dictating somewhat childish behaviour. I sometimes went into chapel with stockings drawn up over my pyjama legs and my gown enveloping my night attire, the whole rig-out crowned by a mortarboard which, I expect in common with other renegades, I had deliberately bent up at all four corners. As a protest against Christianity and compulsory chapel, despite those lovely psalms, I always wound my watch ostentatiously as soon as the Principal started to read the boring prayers in her painfully unmusical voice. As I sat immediately in front of her in the choir stalls, this did not escape her notice. She summoned me to her study and requested me, with a cold and fishy stare, to stop the practice.

Despite hating much of my three years there, I have never regretted studying Classics, and the music I took part in gave me a solid foundation for future partsinging in madrigals and motets. I could have benefited even more in the musical field had my professors not interfered. The Director of Music, Dr Sybil Barker, began to teach me the viola and I became proficient enough to play in the college orchestra. I was soon hauled before the Head of the Classics Department and told that learning the viola would do no good to my Greek proses. A modern undergraduate would say, 'Fuck off!' (at least under her breath), but we did not talk like that in the thirties. Cowed, and all too aware that my presence in the college was now, in my second year, dependent on a college loan for my fees, I gave up the viola – to my lasting regret. That I did not take it up again after I left is one of the major stupidities and misdirections of my life. All in all, I look back on my university experience with repugnance, not least because it was undoubtedly partly my own fault that I did not enjoy it more, as others appeared to do. I emerged in 1933 with a degree – a second class, to my surprise and I've no doubt to the surprise of my professors as well – a passion for music, several good friends, and a backlog of hang-ups and personal problems which I had no idea how to deal with. I do not know why my friends put up with me but they did, so there must have been some redeeming features in me which I fail to see when I look into the mirror at the rather unlikeable person that I was at college.

I had then the extraordinary but not uncommon notion that graduates were eagerly desired by most employers such as publishers, advertising firms, newspaper and magazine editors. Quickly disabused of this myth, I was thankful to get a job as a shop assistant at thirty shillings a week in Bourne and Hollingsworth, a large Oxford Street department store, no longer in existence. The wage of thirty shillings was a reward for my degree and quite undeserved. Those girls whose education had ended at fifteen received only a pound a week but they were far more competent than any graduate. Indeed, I think that we were probably a liability, and most firms who set up these 'graduate schemes' only did so to give themselves kudos in the eyes of their customers. They must soon have regretted it. So did most of us who went into shops and restaurants, but there was little alternative.

I endured selling – or not selling – dresses in B and H for about two years. It was a strange interlude in my life. As I pause in front of this mirror, I see almost nothing of myself, of my appearance, my clothes (how on earth *was* I dressed? In a cheap black dress, I imagine), my actions. I am turned away, talking earnestly to another assistant, a short, fat young woman. A rack of dresses almost hides us from view. Far more in evidence is the figure of the 'shopwalker', as she was known in those days, a bony, angular lady with rather bulging eyes, clad in a severe black sheath of satin (of good quality). In the dull, spotted mirror that holds this episode, her figure blurs uncannily into that of Miss Christian Lucas, one of the most powerful members of staff in *The Chinese Garden*. She was the P T mistress at Bampfield, a woman with prominent china-blue eyes and stringy muscles, forming the outward carapace of a bullying sadist. No doubt the 'shopwalker' was bearing down upon the two of us, but she was not, as far as I recollect, a sadist like Miss Lucas, but a competent and strict monitor of the girls in her department. Her mouth is moving, I see. No doubt she is calling (as they did in those far-off days): 'Forward! Forward, girls!'

My companion behind the dress racks was not a graduate, but probably should have been. She told me that she was the sister of a poet whose name was well known in the thirties, Michael Roberts. I had no means of verifying this so I give her the benefit of the doubt, for she was certainly the only girl I met in B and H who, like me, knew that a book meant a book and not a magazine – a woman's magazine, of course. We talked together as often as we could behind those racks of dresses with their peculiar smell of printed materials, a dry, pungent odour dominated by the dyes used, I suppose. Yet I cannot even remember her Christian name.

I was thankful for the company of this poetical spirit, for to me she represented the inner reality, the true values I was struggling to reach. To me, selling dresses was anathema and for several reasons. Primarily, it was because I was no good at it, and I was so bent on being good at something, having spent my youth trying to emulate my older brothers, and very unsuccessfully, it seemed to me. But I think there was an element of snobbery, too. What was I, a Classics graduate, doing *selling clothes*? Though my family would never overtly have expressed derision about this form of work, the term 'shopgirl' was not one to be proud of at that time. It's an unpleasant truth to arrive at now, but perhaps something in my face in this mirror, as I answer the call of 'Forward!', tells me that I considered my job demeaning. This may seem strange to young people today, who for the last two decades have been accustomed to spend some time, often years, doing all kinds of jobs, before they settle down to the career they may at last decide upon.

There were two bonuses at B and H: the firm gave their staff an excellent lunch every day and one was forbidden to opt out of this. It was a slap-up meal and enabled one to make do with a small breakfast and a light supper, which was just as well for 'girls of slender means'. What must have been the *chef d'oeuvre* remains in my mind to this day: a succulent hot-pot (as we called casseroles) of pieces of pork with prunes, in a rich gravy. Most nourishing. No onions, of course, for fear we breathed a coarse culinary aroma in 'moddom's' face.

The other bonus was that Bourne's gave all employees a week's holiday in winter as well as two weeks in summer, which was very generous for the thirties. My first experience of the Cotswolds derived from a week's walking with my college friend Diana on those bleak uplands in January. We covered the length of the Colne Valley, and then fought our way in icy winds along the exposed Fosse Way to Bourton-on-the-Water, then an utterly unspoilt village. Frozen but happy, I recognised in the golden limestone of the Cotswold houses and the drystone walls in the windswept fields a country very like the Dorset I had lost when I was ten years old, uprooted from Weymouth to live among the conifers and sandpits of Surrey.

After my long day at Bourne's I studied shorthand and typing and, after two years which I am certain had never justified my hot dinners or my princely wage, I left to become the secretary of a young brick salesman. F.D. O'Halloran was a strikingly handsome fellow with an Ulster accent to charm the birds off the trees. I was not really much better at shorthand-typing than I was at selling dresses, but I was reasonably competent in running the office and I enjoyed the work, at least at first, for bricks, especially the handmade variety, are interesting things and craftsmanship goes to their making. I had always been interested in architecture and I was soon to be involved in some high-powered building schemes.

I was not at all attracted to the handsome Irishman but I did like the men in the building trade whom I met or certainly talked to, for much of my work was done on the telephone. Almost every swearword I know dates back to those exhilarating arguments with builders' foremen about the non-delivery, poor quality, wrong size, wrong quantity, etc., of the bricks we had or had not delivered. It was not that we were really inefficient. Builders' foremen are perfectionists and brickmaking is capricious. These are facts of life. There were visits to Yorkshire, for that is where in the early days most of our bricks came from. I remember my deep pleasure in the dark-red and purplish handmade bricks from Askern, the kindness and courtesy the Yorkshiremen expressed towards this strange young woman who tramped round their works in unsuitable clothes, speaking in an outlandish southern accent. It give me a lifelong love of brickwork and a fair knowledge of the variety of bricks that used to be made. When I built my Dorset house twenty years ago, my brother Roger and I jointly decided to build it of red, handmade, sand-faced bricks, of two-inch size instead of the usual two-and-five-eighths. My walls here in Dorset give me lasting pleasure, and it was the right decision for a village which is predominantly brick, not stone as in much of Dorset.

I have remained fascinated by brickwork, not merely by the bricks themselves but by the use of them, from Saxon and Norman herring-bone courses to modern design in this medium. I notice bricks as I am walking past buildings, and say to myself or to a companion: 'They're Kentish stocks, hard burnt, red and purplish, with a variegated face produced by the very imperfections in the clay and firing. But those over there – they are boring machine-made reds, with no variety, no quality. Touch them and they all feel the same. As for those on that spec. builders' estate, they're "flettons", a cheap Bedfordshire brick intended only for inside use. That firm'll use them for the outside walls and slam cement over them or pebbledash them.' All this I learned and more.

My honeymoon period with office work gave me more than a tech-nical knowledge of bricks and swear-words. It opened my eyes to the working of the capitalist system at first hand. F.D. O'Halloran was a smart alec, with no intention of remaining a brick salesman for long. Mrs Thatcher and Norman Tebbit would have loved him. He formed a consortium of suppliers of building materials: timber, aluminium windows, tiles, etc., and added to the group the chairman of a big building contractors' firm and a substantial London property dealer. With the weight of these established companies behind him, he persuaded the property dealer to provide the cash for buying a prime site in a London square, with a first option on the purchase of the building as soon as it was erected at, of course, a very favourable figure. Up went a block of luxury flats which the property firm then sold off at a large profit. They had been built with materials from the various firms in the consortium, which was a registered company with F.D. O'Halloran as Managing Director. A brass plate of this new property development company appeared beneath that of the brick company's, whose London salesman was the same F.D. O'Halloran. In return for the substantial brick order for the luxury flats, he was permitted to make use of the brick company's offices, my services and the company car. He also had an additional salary now as managing director of his property firm. While I was with him, he built three more blocks of flats in the same manner. Three more brass plates with company names upon them appeared below the first one, three more chairman's salaries flowed into his pocket, and the office and the car (for which he claimed expenses in each consortium that he chaired) cost him nothing. Fair perks, you may say, seeing the amount of business he put into the way of a fairly small brick manufacturer. This business also expanded quickly, acquiring a range of brickworks in the home counties.

The manner in which F.D. O'Halloran got his hands upon these first-class central London sites was often fraught with problems, and even legal pitfalls, about which we had to obtain Counsel's Opinion. I became familiar with Lincoln's Inn and the Temple. 'Ask him how near the wind we can sail,' F.D. O'Halloran instructed me on one occasion, and I framed a suitable paraphrase of this for the barrister to whom I was delivering the dossier about the site we wanted to buy. In due course we received his learned opinion on just how near the wind we could go without falling foul of the law. It was most instructive.

F.D. O'Halloran became a tycoon. There were cigars to buy for him and his friends now, an office supply of alcohol to maintain and a set of glasses of high quality purchased from the Army and Navy Stores, telephone calls to Portrush hotels to provide him and his cronies with comfortable and expensive accommodation for their long golfing weekends. He became a Freemason, and his apron and other outlandish equipment was kept in an office drawer. He bought his suits in Savile Row. A young man called Buster was imported into the office to take over the work of brick salesman, which F.D. O'Halloran was now too busy to undertake. Buster and I watched his progress, fascinated. He then became engaged, but as he rose to new heights of affluence – still with the same office – he decided that he had made a mistake and could do better. He broke off the engagement and became involved in a breach of promise case which Buster and I enjoyed hugely. We were rather regretful when it was settled tamely out of court.

All this hectic life in the office was interesting and educative, but there was a more important world outside the office. First Mussolini and then Hitler rose to power. Hunger Marchers were seen in Trafalgar Square and Whitehall, just outside the office which now housed an ex-salesman with four chairman's salaries and a soaring bank balance. I had discovered Collett's Bookshop in Charing Cross Road and was devouring left-wing literature. The Spanish Civil War was starting. The Left Book Club was founded by Victor Gollancz and I joined it immediately. It is easy to criticise the shortcomings of some of its authors but it opened the eyes of many of us to events we knew little about except through heavily-biased newspapers and Pathé-Gazette news films – events in Africa, for instance, and above all in Hitler's Europe. By chance I reread recently that cogent study of what was going on as country after country on the Continent fell to the Nazis, Geddye's *Fallen Bastions*, an L B C book published in 1939. His warnings were heeded no more in book form than they were when he attempted to get them published in full in the *Daily Telegraph*.

The Left Book Club produced historical studies on such diverse subjects as the English Civil War, colonialism in Africa and the trade union movement in Britain. It did a great deal to re-educate us and correct the mostly inaccurate, Tory-biased history we had been taught at school and some of us at university. Victor Gollancz was quick to publish accounts of contemporary events such as the Spanish Civil War and the march of Hitler's armies in central Europe described with such terrifying clarity by Geddye. There is no equivalent of the L B C today, although there is, it is true, a plethora of publications about the nuclear threat, about environmental issues, and such events as the sinking of the *Belgrano* in the Falklands War, but such books are almost too numerous. They vary in quality and depth of research and are so geared to commercial sales that, inevitably, subjects unlikely to have selling power because they are far away and relatively obscure do not find a publisher or perhaps even a writer. I could instance events in the Philippines (except when they briefly make news) and in Indonesia. Being assured of sales, the Left Book Club could and did publish studies about events and regimes not often in the news. It had coherence and consistency of political angle, and employed some of the finest writers of the day.

Yet it is true, I need hardly say, that Victor Gollancz's red-bound books were read almost entirely by middle-class readers. The same readers were inspired by some of the polemical poetry of Auden and his circle, notably Stephen Spender, but these poets were hardly 'popular'. The theatre should have offered a platform for a wider audience, for in many ages the theatre has been iconoclastic. The theatre of the thirties provided a number of interesting plays, but they were rarely polemical. There was nothing comparable to today's numerous fringe events, so many of them fiercely critical of the establishment. There was the famous *Insect Play*. There was Clifford Odets, and there was the small Unity Theatre tucked away somewhere behind St Pancras, putting on any left-wing play it could find. Even the Spanish Civil War threw up no popular literature, as far as I can remember, nor, closer to home, did the Jarrow Hunger Marchers. And what of Sir Oswald Mosley's Blackshirts stepping out like soldiers through the mainly Jewish East End of London? Mosley's terrorising tactics were well protected by the police.

It is worth while comparing those events in the East End with another exhibition of violence in our history only just over a hundred years before, the Peterloo Massacre of 1819, when troops were used against a peaceful assembly in the fields on the outskirts of Manchester. I believe that those of us who are articulate, the writers and artists, have a duty to criticise and castigate if need be the society we live in. The Peterloo Massacre brought a massive protest from the liberal press at the time. Men went to prison and incurred huge fines for their outspokenness. More than that, Peterloo brought a vigorous attack on Lord Liverpool and Lord Castlereagh from the young poets and writers of the time, notably Shelley.

It is unfortunate that Shelley is best known to most readers as the lyric poet of 'To a Skylark' and 'When the Lamp is Shattered' and other short poems, beautiful in themselves but not rated very highly by the poet himself. He should be more widely known for his ferocious ballad, 'The Mask of Anarchy', deliberately written in simple, forceful language, for it was Shelley's intention that it should be read by working-class men and women. In fact it was never published, gagged by the sedition laws.

Thinking back to the thirties, I realise how much Shelley still influenced my thinking then. It was my good fortune that I had studied the Romantics for my university entrance, but studied them with a difference. Bampfield had on the staff an eccentric old woman who did little class teaching, for she was almost stone deaf. With her I had one-to-one seminars and was taken through Shelley's political poems and prose and, most influential of all, his verse play, *Prometheus Unbound*, a kind of dramatic communist manifesto, or so Miss Taylor made it seem to me. She introduced me to 'The Mask of Anarchy', of course, and I can still hear this tiny old woman, her primitive hearing aid crackling and spitting ineffectively on her knee, while she intoned in a conspiratorial and bloodcurdling half-whisper:

> I met Murder on the way,
> He had a mask like Castlereagh,
> Very smooth he looked and grim,
> Seven bloodhounds followed him.

It is worth pausing over 'The Mask of Anarchy' for a moment, for the sake of the original thinking that went into it. Shelley was hard-headed and more clear-thinking than some left-wing intellectuals today or in the thirties. His attack on Lord Liverpool's ministers at the outset of the ballad is followed by the entry of a more sinister figure, Anarchy himself, seated on a white horse, like 'Death in the Apocalypse', and leading the establishment figures. Surprisingly, it seems at first, he is 'adored' by the multitude: Anarchy 'bowed and grinned' to everyone and led the crowd on to attack the Palace, the Bank and the Tower. The tight reasoning behind this is very relevant today. Anarchy is shown by Shelley as virtually a *member* of the establishment, because governments secretly desire his help. As in South Africa today, a government will provoke anarchy by harsh laws and then seize the excuse to put down 'mob rule' savagely in the name of public order and 'true liberty'. Shelley, however, does not allow the crowd to proceed too far on their way. They are halted by the figure of a woman lying under the very hoofs of the soldiers' horses. It was an image that haunted the poet for years. He never forgot that the opening incident of the Peterloo Massacre was the trampling down of a woman by a trooper, and the death of her child under the horse's hoofs. In 'The Mask of Anarchy' a maid called Hope walks serenely through the blood to address the crowd, while Anarchy falls dead and his horse flees, 'and his hoofs did grind/ To dust the murderers thronged behind'. She speaks of false freedom and true freedom, the freedom that means 'clothes and fire and food/ For the trampled multitude'.

Parts of this long ballad appear in anthologies, though seldom all of it. Hope's call to the oppressed is well known: 'Rise like lions after slumber . . . Ye are many, they are few.' What is perhaps not so celebrated is Shelley's advocacy of passive resistance, of a solid demonstration of the workers, 'calm and resolute', awaiting the attack of their tyrants, and relying upon the ancient wisdom of the laws of England, made by 'children of a wiser day'. This must seem naïve today, but is the use of passive resistance altogether naïve? I leave this an open question for it is too large a subject to pursue here. I do, however, find Shelley's clear warning on the provocation of anarchy by government worth serious thought in the context of the increasing use of force and harassment by the police in England.

I make no apology for this long diversion on Shelley. I read several of his quasi-political works at an impressionable age and I have never forgotten them, though I have not reread them. With his play *Prometheus Unbound*, they did a great deal to turn my mind towards communism.

Most of our university circle of friends were armchair communists. Only one of them joined the party, married a party member and worked seriously for the cause. I do not now admire the intellectual socialism I espoused, and I cannot blame working militants for despising it. It is, however, a myth that virtue resides only in the working class and I will not subscribe to it. The English class system is utterly pernicious, but to divide people into castes and classes is pernicious anyway and appears to be inherent in the human condition. Communism, as practised in, say, Soviet Russia or Cuba or Yugoslavia, merely converts it to a different kind of class system. To destroy this divisive pattern we shall have to go far deeper and discover the common pattern which unifies us instead of separating us not only into classes but into racial and colour groups.

War was clearly coming, deliberately prepared for by concessions to and encouragement of Hitler and Mussolini, the most significant for the immediate future of Europe being the betrayal of Czechoslovakia, its industrial power ready to Hitler's hand to be turned against its betrayers. A logical and just retribution, one could say, but who wants the politics of retribution? When war broke out in 1939 it was made to appear that we, the Allies, were fighting in a noble cause. At last we were standing up to a regime more beastly and also more insane in its manifestations than Attila's. What happened thereafter in the war itself has always seemed to me just as terrible as what happened before it, and very similar, only more of it. It is true that you cannot measure up cruelties one against the other. You cannot quantify murder, terror, torture and destruction. But it is as well when remembering the Holocaust and Hiroshima to remember as well Russia's twenty million dead, also murdered as a sub-human race by the *Herrenvolk*, and such landmarks of shame as Dresden. In Shandean terms, it may be wonderful how men and women survive through their own inner resources. It is also devastatingly wasteful that, having but one life and one only, a man or woman lay it down *pro patria*. Gertrude Stein has a less Shandean view: 'Wars are never fatal, but they are always lost.' These few pages must act as my political apologia for the present.

There were pleasures, too, in the thirties. Living in London, however poor we were, was to make me for ever part of it and in love with it, feelings I had already had brief stirrings of when my father took me to the theatre, and my brother Roger had me, a very dowdy and provincial girl, to stay in his Chelsea digs, and took me to revues and musical comedies.

I was acutely aware of clothes. It had mattered less at college, where a gown covered one's deficiencies, but I hated appearing in London among my brother's friends looking the most pitiful country cousin. We were never in the thirties as clothes-conscious as the young people of the fifties and sixties, it is true. Our clothes reflected the general conformity of behaviour of the times. One had to be brave to be eccentric, but both conformity and eccentricity cost money. Clothes were far more expensive then, and most of us were poor. I was burdened with reach-me-downs from my cousin Alison, a little older than myself, and living in the very provincial town of Malvern: inevitable suits – coats and skirts of good quality tweed or serge in abominable colours, totally boring and lacking in personal individuality. I felt embarrassed and miserable in them. Trousers for women were almost unknown, and the few lesbians who adopted a masculine style, like Radcliffe Hall and her circle, were well-off people who could afford to flout convention. I knew little of them, and it was not to emulate them, therefore, that I longed. But I did want to cut a dashing, a striking and strongly individual figure, and never achieved it. There was nothing for me between expensive eccentricity and cheap, usually second-hand dowdyism. Even if I had had a little more money, I believe that I should have been too sexually confused and unsure to experiment with clothes.

When I left college in 1933, I lived with a university friend, Diana, in a flat in Holloway. The North London Holloway Road must derive from an ancient track, perhaps a real 'hollow' way (that is, a lane between high banks), leading up to what is now Archway and Highgate. It was developed in the nineteenth century when the old estates like Tufnell Park were built over. Camden Town and Kentish Town were working class, though gentrified now, but Holloway was more genteel, with villas for the Mr Pooters of the later nineteenth century. When Diana and I came to the Holloway area, it was a warren of run-down, seedy Victorian houses with decaying brickwork and peeling stucco. The owners let out rooms and flats in houses that once held large families. We took a large first-floor flat in Tufnell Park Road, large enough to give my mother a bed-sitting room as well. It cost ten shillings a week and smelt of linoleum and gas.

After our two years at Bourne and Hollingsworth, where Diana had worked in the coats department, we rose in the world a little. I went to my brick salesman's office in Westminster, and Diana obtained a secretarial job on Denmark Hill in South London. A few months later we moved from Tufnell Park to a flat right on the top of Denmark Hill. In the thirties this district must have been much as Ruskin knew it. Large stucco-fronted family houses, standing back from the road behind spacious front gardens, lined the hill rising from Camberwell Green, with its small shops, Camberwell Palace of Varieties, and numerous Victorian pubs. The road divided near Ruskin Park. On the right it went on to Herne Hill, past a pub then called The Fox Under the Hill. On the left it turned sharply between the Salvation Army College on one side and the railway station on the left, then turned right again and went up to the top of Denmark Hill among stately houses with mulberry trees in the gardens. It then went down to Dulwich. At this exact topmost point, on the right, was a private, gravel road with a wooden barrier across its entrance. This led into Champion Hill, a lane with large, comfortable houses built on what was once the de Crespigny estate. In one of these was our spacious top-floor flat with its wide views over the Vale of Dulwich. The garden, which lay on the slope of the hill below us, must have covered at least an acre. The three flats into which the house was divided had each a substantial piece of land in this once beautifully landscaped garden. Our flat, where again my mother had a bed-sitting room, cost us thirty shillings a week, which shows how we had come up in the world. It had a very large, irregularly shaped sitting room of unforgettable charm. Until I built my house in Dorset nearly thirty years later, that Champion Hill flat remained the most unusual and beautiful place I have ever lived in. The Champion Hill houses have all been demolished, their sites and gardens built over, most of the trees gone. Unrecognisable now, the crown of the hill has been transformed by modern development. I have never had the heart to return and walk along what was once that gravel lane, and see if the narrow leafy track that led down to Dulwich is still there. It seems impossible.

Change and replacement must always go on. The eighteenth-century houses which we so much admire today often replaced Elizabethan hovels equally admired now by owners of second homes and retired middle-class couples. I am not complaining that Champion Hill as I knew it has gone, that even the name of The Fox Under the Hill has been reduced to the commonplace Fox. I simply make the point that there is no reason why this unusually beautiful site and setting should not have been 'developed' (hideous word) in an inspired way, worthy of it. This has not happened. It is a totally undistinguished 'development' and the blocks of flats that run along the edge of Denmark Hill, where it abuts upon Herne Hill, must be some of the crudest and most abysmally ugly that have ever been erected in London.

I came to love South London with a passion that I have never felt for Hampstead, where I have lived far longer. Diana and I both went to work along the Walworth Road, leading from Camberwell Green to the old Elephant and Castle crossing. We rocked our way to London Bridge and Westminster respectively on trams and we felt a part of the Elephant-Walworth-Camberwell community. Strictly speaking, of course, we were *not* a part of it, for we were middle class. But neither did we feel excluded. We bought cheap food in the Walworth Road, for we were still very badly off. In the 35 tram I looked down on a host of little neighbourly shops, one of which remains for ever in my memory – a tiny fish-shop across the window of which would sometimes appear the legend: EYEBALLS TONIGHT!!! We never got so far as sampling eyeballs, but we did eat eels and very delicious is the flesh of an eel, not unlike the white meat of a chicken. One could get one's shoes mended and clothes patched up at little shops whose owners had probably been there since the nineteenth century. Music Hall still flourished at the Camberwell Palace and at the Elephant, and I greatly regret that my overwhelmingly intellectual interest in the theatre made me overlook the entertainment on my own doorstep. I am not romanticising the rundown backstreet housing, the poverty behind the little Walworth Road shops and pubs. The arguments for improvement are well known enough, and so are the mistakes that were made. The mistakes were hideous, here and elsewhere. The old Victorian streets were bulldozed and replaced by Council flats of uninspired and dreary design. The old Elephant and Castle has become a desolation in which it is impossible to believe that any of the old sense of community has grown up again.

London today . . . it provides the theatres, films and art exhibitions which I love. Above all, it holds most of my inner circle of friends and has also brought me new friends in the last few years. Without these human contacts, old and new, I know that I cannot live. They mitigate my isolation. But it is more than these things that holds me to London, where I have spent so much of my working life. I criticise it often enough nowadays: the dirty streets, the noise, the fumes, the crowds, the incivility of those who work in shops and

buses and undergrounds, and yet . . . and yet . . . To walk through
Bloomsbury squares, through St James's; to stroll across Regent's
Park, Hampstead Heath, or over the hump of Primrose Hill . . . I
experience in the streets and parks both the intimacy of London, its
wide panorama of roofs and spires, and the green oases that make it
the most countrified of cities.

Recently I walked through Mayfair in streaming rain, to meet
friends in Nash House in The Mall, beside St James's Park. Afterwards, under still glowering skies and a steady downpour I walked
through Trafalgar Square, up the Haymarket, to the top of Regent
Street. Leaves were falling and glowing on the Mall footpaths, Trafalgar Square was like an underwater city, the Haymarket drowning
but waving to me a handful of memories of the St James's and Haymarket theatres, and suddenly a much older memory of something
long forgotten: a small left-wing club I belonged to in my twenties
that met in a room in Panton Street near Piccadilly. It produced a
revolutionary magazine with a blood-red cover. Everywhere I walked
among people whose faces streamed with rain, people who trod the
slippery pavements with who knows what in their watery heads. London was alive and I was part of it, my thoughts and memories washing
into my mind like rain. The crowd around me made up the beat of
London's heart. I know that to leave London permanently would
diminish my life.

When I was young, my chief love was the theatre. As I've said, it was
rarely political. It was really the players rather than the plays that made
it so exciting: the young Michael Redgrave, Laurence Olivier and Peggy
Ashcroft, John Gielgud in *Musical Chairs* with a thin pencilled moustache like Adolphe Menjou's. The Westminster Theatre was the venue
for Anmer Hall's wonderful seasons of modern classics like Ibsen and
Eugene O'Neill. There were a few off-beat plays, too: *Children in Uniform* and Hellman's *The Children's Hour*, the latter for members only
because of its lesbian theme. The vast suburban theatres then had starry
productions. I saw the Gielgud/Olivier *Romeo and Juliet* at the Streat-
ham Theatre and at the Golders Green Hippodrome, the never-to-be-
forgotten *Importance of Being Earnest*, with Gielgud, Edith Evans,
Peggy Ashcroft, Margaret Rutherford, and Gwen Ffrancon-Davies.

And there was the country at weekends, first on bicycles, and then
in an old Wolseley car with a dickie that we bought for ten pounds. I
look back on this London period of my life as happy in spite of the
many problems which beset me. I had not then learned, as I was to do

later, that my inner demons would only be kept at a distance by my creative talent.

I was increasingly unhappy in my job, as my socialist views formed and crystallised. The tension this produced was an intellectual one and could have been resolved. Far deeper went the tensions caused by my immaturity, my inability to direct my own life, and above all my sexual ambivalence. With a kind of last-ditch desperation, I imagined myself in love with a young man I had known for some time. It got me nowhere, indeed it disturbed me rather more for I was humiliated by his friendly indifference to me. My mother's presence in our flat was a perpetual reminder of the loss of my father, whom I had not seen since I was nineteen or twenty. Of my brothers, two of them married, I saw little or nothing.

The sexual ambivalence, or more truly sexual immaturity, was, I think, fundamental, though I rarely thought consciously about it. I had been driven into an emotional cul-de-sac and did not know how to get out. I had developed a wariness of human relationships while longing for their warmth and reassurance. This I certainly received from Diana, with whom I shared the flat, but she was soon to meet the man she would marry. I was increasingly closed in upon myself within a hollow chamber peopled by these cloudily perceived problems. Eventually, I gave way. I had a 'nervous breakdown' which took the form of acute agoraphobia.

For a short time I went to a psychiatrist at the Maudsley Hospital nearby. Before starting with him, I was interviewed by a man who was, I suppose the senior consultant. He was one of those bullying psychiatrists whom I met again much later in my life and who, in my opinion, should be removed from positions where they can get rid of their aggression upon patients. He shouted at me. Maybe that is an exaggeration but it is how I remember it. He framed in accusatory tones the suggestion that I was a lesbian – a sexual deviant, I think he called it – and that this was the root of my problem. It had causes which could, if I cooperated, be brought to light and uprooted. Like nasty weeds. I should then be 'normal'. I was allocated to a mousy little man who asked me to lie on a couch and tell him whatever came into my head. But I was wary. Even then I realised that my life was my material and that I would be foolish to give it away. This knowledge was little more than an intuition at the time. No doubt a stronger reason for my silence was fear. The fear of being found out, an aspect of the deep-seated shame of being different that dogged most so-called 'deviants' in the first half of this century.

It was my misfortune, perhaps, that I went to a man who I would assume was a Freudian. It damaged me, for it closed my mind not only to Freud, who, whatever you may think of some of his theories, was a genius and a seminal thinker for our times, but it closed my mind to psychoanalysis generally. My experience of it has certainly been unfortunate. When, years later, my doctor sent me to a well-known Middle European analyst after my attempted suicide, I found him not only unhelpful but bullying in manner, like the Maudsley consultant. He did not appear to see me as a distressed human being who needed help in exploring her inner self and making sense of it, but as someone entirely wrong-headed, whose tentative statements he usually met with brisk contradictions. I was *mistaken*, was his constant cry. It was quite otherwise. I found this exasperating and rather frightening. Whose mind was it? Whose life?

I have often suspected that I should find C.G. Jung a far more sympathetic figure but I never explored his writing or attempted to find out what he said or how he differed from Freud. Now at last in my seventies I have read books about him and a volume of selections from his own writing, and there is much in his attitude to his patients, especially, that makes me realise that I could probably have been helped much earlier in my life if I had found the right analyst or psychotherapist. For a start – and this greatly appeals to me – Jung always sat opposite his patients and they talked together face to face. None of that objectionable impersonality of lying on a couch with the analyst *behind* you that filled me with distrust in my twenties. Perhaps the trouble was that of the three men I have encountered, one was ineffectual and the other two were plain unpleasant types. Hostile is the word that springs to my mind. It was almost as if they wanted to *frighten* me into health, for of course from their point of view I was 'sick', whereas I myself, whatever symptoms of illness I experienced, was obsessed with the inner impasse I had reached. I wanted to make sense of it, to accept myself. For all I know, they may have had the skills to help me, but no surgeon or physician faced with, say, a patient suffering from cancer, would attempt to frighten her out of her condition or gain anything before an operation or treatment by behaving like a concentration camp commandant. I exaggerate, of course, but am unrepentant, for those two men had a damaging effect upon me.

Jung's *respect* for his patients strikes me as remarkable and something far too seldom met with in medical men. He insisted, for instance, that the story or dream that the patient told him was the patient's most precious possession and must be returned to her. Of understanding, that overvalued and often intrusive activity, Jung said: 'All understanding, in general, which is a conformity with general points of view, has the diabolical element in it that kills. It is a wrenching of another life out of its course, forcing it into a strange one in which it cannot live.' A unique view.

My knowledge of Jung's work and ideas is so small that I cannot pretend to anything but a feeling that a Jungian analyst might possibly have done for me what Jung himself did over and over again: break the code of the patient's dreams and give into her own hands the means to heal herself. 'I give you the end of a golden string . . . ' The words might have been Jung's.

When I consider how strong a lifeline writing has been to me since my forties, I find it curious, indeed, reprehensible that I did not make any attempt to fulfil the writing ambitions of my teens when I arrived in London just before my twenty-second birthday. I was uncertain at the time where my talents lay for I had been drawn away from writing towards music. Within a few years I had bought a baby-grand Broadwood piano. This was the more extraordinary as I was not at all a good player, and rather disliked most piano music. In my mind was growing the desire to be a composer and I needed a piano for that. I was moving into a world of music, not writing. I joined a small choir, meeting one evening a week in the old LCC building on the South Bank. It was directed by a quiet, unassertive little man called A.W. Cox, who introduced us to a range of madrigals and motets of extraordinary interest. Among them were many that even my later, highly expert singing friends did not know, and I have never ceased to be grateful to him for all he taught me, and for the wonderful Elizabethan music I learned to explore under his direction. English amateur musicians have reason to be grateful to people like A.W. Cox, truly dedicated musicians who want to share their expertise and knowledge with others. They are largely responsible for the network of amateur choirs of high standard all over England, derided by Kingsley Amis in that much overrated book, *Lucky Jim*.

I have two photographs of myself taken by Diana in our Denmark Hill flat in about 1935, when I was in my mid-twenties, and both, I would imagine, taken with tongue in cheek. They do, however, show that the dichotomy between music and writing was entirely unresolved at this time. One shows me sitting at the Broadwood piano, writing on music paper set up on the stand in front of me. It is labelled facetiously: 'The Composer at Work'. The other shows me seated at my father's oak bureau, writing, and is inscribed, I hope more seriously, 'The Writer at Work'. I see those photographs hanging on the walls of the Denmark Hill flat, as it appears in the mirror, this beautiful L-shaped room, with the baby-grand in the corner, and the windows looking down over leafy gardens, one of which was ours, to Dulwich Vale and the heights of Sydenham, crowned with the Crystal Palace. Yet it is remote, this room in which the division in my nature between music and writing is not as clear as the room itself, so that I have the sense of being someone looking into another person's room. No reconciliation, no resolution of the division within me took place in this flat, or indeed was to take place for many years.

To return briefly to my sessions at the Maudsley Hospital in my twenties. The mild little man to whom I had been assigned, far from bullying me, bleated rather ineffectually at me, begging me to tell him anything that came into my head.

Not only did I lie silent upon the couch, gazing with pleasure at the sky, something one usually has little time to observe. I eventually found myself the recipient of my psychiatrist's confidences about his unhappy relations with his wife. It dawned upon me that he should have been paying *me* fees, not the other way round. I brought the interviews to an end after about three months. I had had to leave my job and my friend Diana had supported me. Now I wondered how I was to earn my living for I was still suffering from agoraphobia which made it hard for me to go about anywhere. I suffered equally from claustrophobia in places like buses and undergrounds.

At this juncture, Chief came up to London from Bampfield on business and, hearing that I had been ill, made a point of coming to see me. I talked fairly freely to her. She said at once: 'What you need is a complete change of scene and to be among people who know nothing of your problems. Come down to Bampfield. I'll give you a job in the gardens and perhaps a little teaching.' I accepted. But it was a flight, a retreat from reality. I let myself be acted upon, instead of making my own decisions. I was sucked back into Bampfield with its memories, and desperately I turned in a new direction, the very direction I had always sworn I would never take: teaching.

I let myself be acted upon . . . most of my friends see me as a successful woman, with the positive manner that betokens one who has directed her life with assurance and success. I do not see myself like this at all. I see myself driven by circumstances because I was not mature or stable enough within myself to seek out and pursue my own direction – nor did I even know for certain what it was. There in the mirror stands an uncertain, wavering figure. No later rationalisation about my political motive for choosing to go into education can disguise the truth that I used it as an escape in order to evade my total failure to resolve my inner conflicts and to get down to writing. This had virtually disappeared underground, despite my determination to be a writer as I had so often declared in my teens. There were other fields of work in London which I could have explored. I shut my eyes to them. I was overwhelmed by the vast ocean of the metropolis – you have to realise that it took me years to get over that breakdown – and far from welcoming it as an immersion into experience which would enrich me as a writer, I saw it only as a frightening shoreless expanse where I might drown.

Many of the subsequent misdirections of my life spring from that desperate retreat into teaching, in spite of the happiness of the first five years I spent in it. I was like a tree with three main branches, each growing malformed, each blown from its true growing course by the ill-rooted condition of its parent trunk. These branches were love, creativity and music. In the end it is only the second which I have succeeded in pruning and redirecting into some semblance of an upward-thrusting, vigorous, productive branch, and this took all my years until I was forty, when I wrote my first novel.

Items of self-disgust rise to the surface of this book and it is difficult not to leave them on display in the name of honesty. But in fact my most devastating self-criticisms are hidden from the public eye. They are visible to myself, and perhaps to some who know me well, in aspects of many of the characters in my novels where I have broken down my personality and used different facets of it in imagined men and women. If this has been an attempt to exorcise aspects of myself, I have to say at once that it has not worked very successfully. It has been at least an attempt repeated all the years I have been writing to pull them out and examine them – or have I come to love them?

I found the following words in a diary of 1961 when I was finishing a novel called *Look, Stranger*, published by Jonathan Cape in 1962: 'It is impossible to write a book of judgment on the human race. Judge not that ye be not judged. But judgment on myself, yes. And upon myself as part and parcel of the human race. This is what redeems *Look, Stranger*, that the unkindest cut of all is reserved for myself in the character of Mrs Birkett.' I have given myself away piecemeal in my novels, never more than in *Look, Stranger*. It has hardly helped me to live up to the words of Montaigne to which I have aspired all my adult life: 'The greatest thing in the world is to know how to belong to oneself.'

11
Like the Dyer's Hand

The one area of my life which I have never drawn upon in any novel is my teaching career. As this occupied over thirty years, it may seem a substantial and significant omission. It is, indeed. The reason for it in simple terms is that I regard those years of my life as forced labour. During them:

> My nature is subdued
> To what it works in, like the dyer's hand.

In devoting this chapter to it, I have chosen to be silent on many episodes that I cannot bear to examine privately, much less to reveal. I feel an enduring humiliation about them. They are travels down roads I should never have taken. Thomas the Rhymer made only one mistake and paid for it with seven years in thrall to the Queen of Elfin. I paid for my mistakes with thirty-five years' imprisonment. Yet they started well enough, those teaching years. My interest in left-wing politics had led me towards the 'progressive' movement in education. Teachers today may not realise the importance of those heady days in the thirties and forties when A.S. Neill's school, Summerhill, was in the forefront of the revolt against the educational establishment, and when the New Education Fellowship was a beacon to those of us who looked to education to save the world. How naïve it seems now. Education will never save society, and we are today learning how callously society views the status of teachers and the erosion of education's true aims by its elected government. It will need a political and social revolution to save and recreate education. Of course, the 'progressive' movement did bring about a revolution not in the structure of schools but in content and method of teaching and the best of its tenets have long ago been absorbed into the state system, especially in the primary schools.

If I were today a young woman entering the teaching profession I should not hesitate to go into a state school, but in 1937 or 1938, because my upbringing and schooling had been middle class, it was natural that I looked for work in a boarding school and one run on 'progressive' lines. I did in fact start by applying for a post teaching Classics in a provincial grammar school, but the job went to an old pupil of the school. I looked in the advertisements for 'progressive' school appointments and was fortunate in finding a very small school of this kind in Sussex where the Headmistresses took me on despite my inexperience. They paid me £70 a year with full board. No need to cry: 'Sweated labour.' I should have received little more in a state school and in any case I cared little about the money – a typical teacher's reaction which has kept the profession ill-paid to this day.

I was enchanted with the school. It hummed with ideas. My left-wing politics were not frowned upon. They were indeed welcomed except by a few parents who complained that my history lessons were biased. They meant, of course, biased to the left. They were accustomed to teaching and textbooks heavily weighted towards the right. My Left Book Club volumes were passed around freely, as were my *Labour Monthly* and *New Statesman*, and also the *Soviet Weekly*, which when the Germans invaded Russia corrected the laundered news of the Eastern Front emanating from our own newspapers and newsreels.

I loved the freedom, the liberal and lively atmosphere of this school, the ready acceptance and discussion of new and sometimes hare-brained ideas from children as well as staff. Nothing was arbitrarily dismissed but views and suggestions were given serious consideration and, if necessary, support. There were only about thirty girls, all boarders, aged from about twelve to seventeen or eighteen. Many were children with personal problems, girls from broken or in some way unsatisfactory homes. Fees were extremely low. The two Headmistresses, one of them a Quaker, were totally but not narrowly dedicated to their work. The atmosphere was one of relaxed and ordered freedom, for this school was not on the wilder shores of progressive education and would probably have been considered old-fashioned by someone like A.S. Neill. It gave me personally among many other things a strong sense of what I had never really had, a family. Although it took only girls it was far from being a nunnery. There was no lack of visitors, men and women, and the two Heads were insistent that staff and children should get out of the place and take part in events and societies in the town near by. They were always aware of the danger that the school might turn in upon itself and they frowned upon us teachers if we stayed hanging about the house on our free days or weekends.

I had already the makings of a maverick and they gave me my head. I spent a wonderful five years there and no teaching was ever the same to me again. It was here, in the neighbourhood of a town where music flourished to a high degree, that I matured as a musician. I had already taken part in a regular madrigal and motet group in London and in the activities of the Workers' Music Association, for whom I wrote a small book on modern choral music. Now I had composition lessons from Anthony Bernard, then a well-known conductor of a professional orchestra, and also Director of the local orchestra and choir, which were both of high amateur standard. I began to write songs. Nearly all my evenings and weekends were spent making music and my days, too, since I directed all the music at the school. I had no qualifications to do this, but the Heads didn't care a fig for paper qualifications.

I had not been at the place a year before I suggested that we should stage a performance of Purcell's *Dido and Aeneas*, originally written for a girls' school in Chelsea. It was a work I knew well and was passionately devoted to. The idea was greeted with cries of delight. But the opera is somewhat short, the Heads observed, in fact little more than an hour long. Let's write a half-hour prologue in which Mr Purcell argues its merits with the dancing master, Mr Priest, whose girls were going to perform it. This would employ several children as actors who would otherwise be debarred from the opera by lack of musical talent. In this prologue the young singers were brought in to be auditioned by Henry Purcell, and Mr Priest finally addressed the audience on the importance of music in a school and their good fortune in being present at the first performance of a remarkable opera. The work was sung in a two-part version, since we had no men, though in some choruses I rearranged it in three parts to give the music greater depth and warmer tone. I, who had never conducted in my life, found myself with a small adult string orchestra and a harpsichord, played by the school's visiting art mistress, an excellent amateur musician with whom I shortly fell in love and she with me.

During my first Christmas term I introduced a mediaeval nativity play. This was long before these 'mystery' plays became well known and frequently performed as they are today. I had discovered a book of them and had also taken part at college in a performance of Rutland

Boughton's cantata, *Bethlehem*, the words of which come from the Coventry cycle of nativity plays. I, however, spatchcocked my own play together from more than one cycle, using the Coventry one as a basis but adding in sections drawn from other cycles. There are several fragmentary cycles extant, like that of Newcastle, and these of course never get a performance yet sometimes contain characters and scenes well worth preserving. *The Shepherds' Play*, as I called it, was printed together with a version of *Noah and the Flood*, put together in the same way from several cycles. These plays became a regular feature at the school and I took them with me and used them at the two schools of which I subsequently became Head. They came out in a small paperback, I think in 1941, and this was still selling to schools, churches and clubs thirty years later.

I was not pretending to be a scholar. I wanted plays that worked well on the stage and were enjoyed by the young performers and their audience. I updated the spelling and in a few cases altered words, but in general I retained the earthy, vivid language, wholly free from religiosity, and the plays were a refreshing change from the type of Christmas play too often put on by schools and churches. I was very sorry when in the sixties it became fashionable to insist upon plays being made up by the children themselves and when learning by heart was scowled upon. Most of the younger staff were totally unenthusiastic about these 'mystery' plays simply on the grounds that they required lines to be learned and were subject to the discipline of a producer. I was all in favour of original plays by the children themselves, though I have always doubted the value of the young child's saying and writing 'her own thing' if this is carried to excess and to the virtual exclusion of reading and hearing what has been said better by Homer, Shakespeare and the authors of the King James Bible. Nor do I think that the opprobrium now attached to learning by heart is deserved. If it is, it must be because of boring, stereotyped teaching. As for playmaking, the two kinds, learnt and spontaneous, are entirely different and both have their merits and their place, but I am no longer in the business of arguing about this.

At this Sussex school I gained a deep sense of acceptance and flourished in ways other than teaching, though this was one of my chief enjoyments. Though I had not yet found my true *métier* as a writer, I was at last beginning to produce something both in music and poetry. I was also reading widely, especially the contemporary poets like T.S. Eliot and the Auden circle. After about eighteen months my life became centred upon Edith, who came to the school to teach art and took part in some of the music – she played the harpsichord for *Dido and Aeneas*. She was a woman of about my own age – that is, thirty. She lived in a nearby village. She also wrote both music and poetry, as I did. When we fell in love, we experienced a romantic and intense happiness, the foundations of which were more than a little shaky.

The limitations were due mainly to my inability and unwillingness to commit myself to anyone and to my intense shyness and deep-seated inhibitions. To undress with someone else in the room was anathema to me. When we went for the first time on holiday together, I – without Edith's knowledge – booked us separate rooms in the pub. It was not a good beginning. The affair suffered further from my perfectionism, my restless search for an ideal. Being so self-obsessed, I was incapable of giving someone else what they needed from me. How much Edith longed for my whole-hearted commitment to her I was not perspicacious enough to see.

I think that inhibitions and sexual ignorance could have been overcome, for certainly we loved with a burning intensity and romantic fervour which ought to have consumed them to ashes, but with hindsight I realise how much more deeply founded the difficulties were. I was in a state of arrested development and Edith, lacking in experience as much as I was, could not help me to grow out of it. I was still set in the pattern Georgie Murrill had imposed upon me at Bampfield. This was stumbling-block enough to our love affair, but there was also the inescapable fact that I had not reached any certainty about my lesbianism. I was still a victim of the 'marriage syndrome' in which I had grown up. Nor was Edith much more mature in this respect or surer of her sexual orientation, as I was later to learn, for not long after we separated she married and, as far as I know, had no deep relation with a woman again.

Yet we found a great deal of happiness in each other. We read each other's poetry. I thought hers better than mine (which it was). We played and sang each other's songs. I was convinced that mine were superior to hers. I was given to this stupid, judgmental, comparative way of thinking that is so destructive. I found her all the same stimulating and delightful as a companion. Long walks over downland and through the Sussex woodlands opened up a new world to me, a world of trees and flowers and birds, for Edith was very knowledgeable in country lore. And there was the delight of walking for miles in a beautiful countryside which had strong affinities with my native Dorset. I took Edith there more than once on holidays which brought to the surface my tortuous desire to withdraw from a situation almost as soon as I had entered into it. About this time, prompted by Edith who was mildly interested in astrology, I consulted by correspondence a professional astrologer. Her long, detailed horoscope of my birth – I am a Sagittarian – was extraordinarily accurate about my character and contained a warning note: 'You are someone who will not commit yourself but will withdraw from a situation even when you are finding happiness in it.' I thought this a very odd judgment, so little did I know myself.

The affair ended. I doubt if younger readers would credit how ignorant both of us were. In our youth and circles sex had never been discussed. Books on the subject were not readily available and I doubt anyway whether either of us would have read them. *The Well of Loneliness* was no more than a name – neither of us had read it – and aroused more than a hint of those words that haunted lesbians in those days: deviance and abnormality. The pragmatical girls of today's generation don't waste so much time getting to bed together, nor do many of them, I hope, agonise over it in their minds or suffer from devastating sexual confusion. Our affair was all very exhilarating intellectually. It was a union of souls, but it wasn't down to earth, and the anchors slipped in the romantic riverbed, especially when my own craft was pulling so hard on the ropes. I had a brief affair with a man and a less brief one with a bisexual woman who, at least, instructed me in the techniques of sexual love fairly thoroughly. Edith was not prepared to be either forgiving or patient. She left me. She left the town. She went out of my life.

After five years I felt that it was time I left the school. I had had a wonderful – but as it turned out very untypical – introduction to teaching. I had been given my head in an unusually encouraging way. I had made mistakes and been patiently corrected. I had even nearly killed my two Headmistresses and been forgiven for the lapse. It happened thus. When the war started, we were all set to digging for victory in the huge kitchen garden. Children and staff together, we brought as much land under cultivation as there was, and geese, ducks and hens were imported to add to the menu. While I was digging, I learned a great deal of French poetry by heart, I remember, propping up my Rimbaud or Baudelaire in the crutch of an old apple tree near where I was working.

One day, I asked if I might borrow a double-bore shotgun from a neighbour and pot at the rabbits and pigeons which were devouring our vegetables. Of course, of course! Splendid! I was instructed in its use and succeeded in killing quite a number of rabbits. The pigeons always eluded me. They were endowed with an uncanny power of mind-reading. Long before I caught one in my sights ('had drawn a bead on one' is the correct term, I believe), it had risen into the trees chortling with delight. On one occasion I had emptied one barrel and was about to watch for another victim when I was interrupted by the gardener and engaged in a lengthy conversation. Quite forgetting that I had not used the second cartridge, I strolled back to the house and up the study steps, dangling two or three dead rabbits for the pot. I opened the study door to find my two Headmistresses seated on either side of the fireplace, reading. 'Look!' I cried, waving the rabbits in triumph before them.

Exclamations of delight all round. 'Come and sit down,' they cried. 'You're just in time for a cup of tea. They'll be bringing it in and can take the rabbits back to the kitchen.'

Unthinking, I stood in the study doorway, the gun held nonchalantly under my arm. I moved suddenly. There was a deafening report. The tiny study was filled with smoke and a sizeable piece of the mantelpiece fell to the floor. The shot had passed immediately between them without harming either. In their relief, they fell back in their chairs, laughing hysterically for a few moments. They never held this against me.

However, I was getting restless. I left them to go to a boarding school near Ascot, a school of such tedium and downright miseducation that I was amazed that anyone should send their children to it. It was a regime for which five years in a progressive and freedom-loving school had not prepared me.

With me had gone a fellow-teacher, Andrea, and it was in fact at her interview with the Headmistress that she let fall that I was wanting a new post. I was offered the sixth form and accepted without much thought. We both found this school so frightful that we were soon determined to leave. I myself decided to get out of teaching altogether. I felt that I had had enough, that I needed other experience, and the itch to get down to writing was now beginning to make itself felt. I looked around me and considered the possibility of returning to work in an office in London, but I was not enthusiastic. My Sussex school had spoilt me for most jobs. I could think of nothing better than one of the forces, perhaps the W R N S . This would probably take me abroad, or so I hoped, and it had the merit of being totally different from anything else I had so far done. I was still disorientated and unhappy after losing Edith. I was in flight from the present as I had so often been in my life and was to be again. At the time, I was conscious of little but an overwhelming desire to escape from this snobbish, illiberal school, where I detested the narrow-minded, bitchy staff so cordially that I lost a stone in my first term by getting up and going after the first ten minutes of most meals, unable to bear their gossip and idiotic opinions any longer.

Why the W R N S? Still consumed with doubts about my own sexuality and to a certain extent still dogged by the old imperative of my upbringing – to get married – I suppose I saw the W R N S as a heaven-sent chance to meet men. I thought that Andrea would want to go into the forces too. She was engaged to a man in the Army and was as unhappy as I was in this miserable school. For some reason she was unwilling to go into one of the forces. Perhaps she felt that a school post gave her weekends and holidays, times when she could meet her man when he was on leave. The one thing we were united about was our desire to get away from the Ascot school. In the end, I applied to the W R N S only to discover that I was now in a reserved occupation. I could not get out of teaching. Andrea put pressure upon me to go into partnership with her and buy a small school, or even start one, and run it for the duration. I resisted at first. I had always sworn I would not be a teacher. The five years in Sussex were a strange oasis. I realised that such teaching work was unlikely to be repeated. At least I resolved not to run a boarding school. A day school offered a certain degree of freedom. I was still at that stage when we believe that we have seen little of 'life', which we think of as a sequence of outward events. We have not learned that the life within our hearts and minds is lived more intensely and with greater reward. But it seemed that I was in the prison of teaching, and 'life' was as out of reach as ever.

It was with inner and unexpressed despair that I agreed to go into partnership with Andrea. The day I signed the agreement for the purchase of a small day school in Hertfordshire, I knew that I was making a mistake and that my lack of decision had led once again to me being acted upon by another. I wrote to a friend and told her what I had done. At the end of the letter I drew a picture of myself in the claws of an eagle sailing through the air towards Hertfordshire (mapped out below) and across the bird's wings I printed the word: N E M E S I S. The insistence that I felt myself 'acted upon' has a spurious element, in that what one does must be accepted and indeed often willed by the inner self. I do not find this a comforting doctrine for it implies that this subconscious, if that is its name, is not prompting one in one's best interests. I prefer to think that quite consciously I went into teaching for wrong and highly dubious reasons. Moreover, I believe now that it would not have been difficult to leave the profession if I had been determined to do so. I have an idea that the fact that I was not teaching in the state system would have released me from the category of 'reserved occupation'.

So I remained, though the move to Hertfordshire was a change for the better in two respects. We bought a preparatory school so that I now taught children from nine to eleven, an age I found that I much preferred to the fifth and sixth forms I had previously been responsible for, and of course I was now co-Head of the school I was in. None the less I remained at heart angry and disappointed with myself for giving up the idea of a different job altogether.

Complex reasons lie behind my strong prejudice against teaching. My experience at boarding school may have been an element in my distaste, but I think the roots go much deeper. I possibly felt unconsciously that in becoming a teacher or certainly in remaining one and now committing myself to a partnership, I was betraying my early hopes, my youthful decision to be a writer. Looking at it pragmatically, teaching is not a bad occupation for a writer – as many authors have found. And I enjoyed the teaching itself, or most of it. I loathed the status bitterly, the fact that I was now labelled 'teacher', not 'writer'. It is fair to point out that when I was teaching, at least in the early years, teachers were not much respected, at least by the middle classes. If they were men, their image was that of an out-at-elbow, pipe-smoking Mr Chips, with dandruff in their hair and mildew in their minds. Of women teachers the picture was no more flattering. Grudgingly admired for their dedication, by which was meant that the poor things had missed out on marriage and been forced to pour out their maternal love upon the children of others, they were usually depicted either as the hearty, hockey-sticks type in gym tunic and black stockings, breathless and infantile (the image owes much to Joyce Grenfell and St Trinian's), or as dowdy, greasy-haired nonentities, timid, ineffectual, unimaginative, the inhabitants of a grey world of tiny flatlets or half-empty Victorian mansions, where they supported elderly impoverished parents or idiot siblings. The most praise they could hope for was to be called 'the salt of the earth'; to earn it they gave up their lives to teaching for a meagre salary and execrable conditions. This may seem a crude exaggeration today but it was generally true of the image forty or fifty years ago; nor was the image always so far from the reality. Of course there were exceptions to this dismal scene. Most of us can surely remember at least one outstanding teacher, woman or man, who taught us at some point in our schooldays and inspired in us a love of poetry, perhaps, or music or maths.

I still remember an occasion – it was much later, in the sixties – when I was asked to a party by a very old friend. I had now had some half-dozen books published. My host greeted me and, turning to a group near him, introduced me to them as the Headmistress of a London school. I was so incensed at not being introduced as a writer that, after swallowing a glass of sherry, I made my way to the cloakroom, put on my coat and left.

However, having embarked upon my chosen – ill-chosen, I would say – profession, I must give some account of it, however brief. The small Hertfordshire school which Andrea and I bought in 1943 quickly increased in numbers with young and energetic Heads and we moved to a larger house. I have no happy recollections whatever of our years there, though this house was beautiful, part Elizabethan, part Queen Anne in period, with outhouses and barns of timber and warm red brick, with quince trees, medlars and a walled garden supporting peaches and figs. None of this could compensate for the fact that the house stood on the edge of an unlovely dormitory town in the muddy, foggy fields of Hertfordshire, the most detestable county of England for me, against which I am unrepentantly prejudiced. We were forced out by the grasping intransigence of the landlord. We closed it down and moved to north London to take over an old-established girls' preparatory day school. This was in 1950.

12
Words and Music

It was a move for the better. It could hardly have been anything else after the Hertfordshire experience. For me it was a welcome return to London. The fifties are rich with memories of theatre and opera, especially another visit of the Vienna State Opera. I had already seen them in 1947 in *Salome* with the unforgettable Welitsch in the name part. Now they brought productions of *Don Giovanni* and *Rosenkavalier*, with a host of glorious singers then in their youthful prime: Elisabeth Schwarzkopf, Irmgard Seefried, Sena Jurinac, George London and Leopold Simoneau. And there were the young Kathleen Ferrier and Dietrich Fischer-Dieskau in the concert halls. A new world opened up for me.

I had been to opera at Sadlers Wells in the thirties, but in those days I was equally, perhaps more, attracted to ballet, a taste which totally left me by the fifties. The turning point for my operatic enthusiasm came in 1939, when I went to Glyndebourne for the first time with Edith. The opera was Mozart's *Don Giovanni*. I had never heard music played or sung like this. While the overture was being played, with Carl Ebert conducting, I sat on the edge of my seat, transported. It was a revelation. John Brownlee was the Don, Ina Souez Donna Anna, Hella Toros Donna Elvira, and that unforgettable pair, Roy Henderson and Audrey Mildmay, were the rustic lovers. It was a hot June night – midsummer – and we walked on the downs above Firle afterwards.

Once the war was over, I had come up to London from Hertfordshire to go to the opera whenever I could afford the time or money. I went to Glyndebourne again on several occasions, to Covent Garden, and to Sadlers Wells, now far more adventurous than it had once been with, among other things, Stravinsky's *Oedipus Rex*, and Bartók's *Bluebeard's Castle*. It might be tedious if I were to list too many memorable operatic experiences. I can only add that the period was rich in outstanding productions such as Zefferelli's *Lucia di Lammermoor* at Covent Garden, *Boris Godunov* with Boris Christoff in the name part, and the superb Visconti production of *Don Carlos*, put on to commemorate the first hundred years of Covent Garden, with Giulini conducting and a brilliant cast that included Gre Brouwenstijn, Jon Vickers, Tito Gobbi and Boris Christoff. Finally, after years of stupid ignorance and prejudice against Wagner, I arrived at my first Ring Cycle. It had its unexpected moments. I had taken two tickets for seats right on the edge of the orchestra, where we had a clear view of Rudolf Kempe and felt almost as if we were members of the orchestra beneath his baton. I had beside me an old friend, a singer and an extrovert character who shouted, 'Brava! Brava!' at the end, and thumped the upholstered barrier top in front of our seats. From it arose a cloud of dust that nearly choked us and those around us, dust that had settled there through years of Garden performances. That first Ring Cycle removed all my scepticism. I was hooked for ever on Wagner, Norns and all.

Somehow opera, that curious hybrid, suspends disbelief and can even survive the risible. One of the highlights of my operatic experience was a Garden performance of Bellini's *Norma*. In it Maria Callas, then at the height of her powers, sang Norma. Her niece in the plot, Adelgisa, was played by the then ageing Stignani. The production was mounted with sets that looked as if they had been brought out of store from a production of *Aladdin* or *Robinson Crusoe* painted in the twenties. The ancient Britons were dressed in skins reminiscent of Gracie Fields' 'Granny's little old skin rug'. Callas and Stignani were wearing grimy nightdresses and pigtails made of what appeared to be raffia. But the music and the singing survived all this and never more so than when the beautiful Callas and the stumpy Stignani, aged nearly seventy, I believe, if she was a day, began the first great duet with its ringing cascades of thirds and sixths. Out from Stignani's throat poured a stream of notes like a blackbird's, so sure, so unstrained, a living proof of the wonderful *bel canto* training of her youth which enabled her to continue singing well into old age.

I was thirsty for the London life from which, except for school holidays, I had been virtually exiled for over ten years. But what I looked forward to more than anything when I returned to London in 1950 was the acquisition of a circle of friends, an intellectual stimulus and a companionship of which I had felt miserably deprived when I lived in Ascot and then in Hertfordshire. But friends, if one is single, are usually acquired through one's work. I made hardly any in this field. As a headmistress, I found myself cold-shouldered by several school parents whom I longed to know better. Occasionally I made overtures but there was always the barrier that I was their child's headmistress and it seemed hard to get past this. The last thing I wanted to talk about was school. What had I to offer? I had as yet written nothing. I gave no evidence of being anything more than a fairly original and stimulating teacher.

From all the years of teaching in Hampstead – nearly twenty-five of them – I can claim only two close, long-lasting friendships, although since my retirement I have renewed what were only acquaintanceships with two other couples, and can now count them among my friends. I had, of course, many friends in the amateur music world but few have remained close. Most belonged simply to the world of music-making. With them I clowned and fooled about and was, I think, regarded as a provider of enjoyable parties and someone with a *penchant* for writing musical parodies, for this was all that my composing talent now produced, and that not often.

After two or three years in Hampstead I at last began to write seriously, coming over from the school study to my own bed-sitting room at the end of the day, and sitting down at my desk to continue writing where I had left off the night before, sometimes in the middle of a sentence. I wanted to distance myself from the school and protected my privacy fiercely. Even during the school day, my mind was often occupied by the novel I was writing. The school was an intrusion. I resented bitterly that as a headmistress I was necessarily interrupted by children and even more by staff, who would meet me in the passages or the garden and make trivial complaints about a tap leaking (I acted as a kind of clerk of works), a child not doing her homework, a parent making demands for coaching.

Why had Andrea and I stayed together for over ten years? The friendship had started with apparent compatibility and then with joining forces against the awfulness of the Ascot school. It had become a partnership in Hertfordshire, but there the resentments and differences began to build up seriously, though as a school partnership it still worked well. In that field we were complementary to each other, but our personal lives were under strain, compounded because we had to share a house on fairly close terms. We had only a bedroom each, mine acting as my study as well, a shared sitting room and kitchen/dining room. We were very poor.

It had always been our policy to keep the school fees low for we did not want to exclude children whose parents were less well off, and such parents were often part of the artistic community which then still existed in Hampstead. Today I hold such radically different views about private education that I find it hard to confess to this romantic notion about running an independent school on low fees. I now think that we should have been honest, unromantic moneygrubbers or else never have gone into the business at all. At the time I never faced the appalling inconsistency of owning a private and fee-paying school, while professing socialist views. It has always been true that Labour Party members do not practise what they preach. That is their own matter of conscience. But the Party itself has never been bold enough to grasp the thorny problem of our educational system with its mix of L E A and independent schools and the various hybrids that have existed between the two. When the comprehensives were set up, Labour lost the opportunity to make radical reforms in our divisive and class-ridden education. Today the country is reaping the whirlwind of the years of neglect that followed an ill-thought-out and hastily scrambled-together plan.

One positive step in the direction of persuading middle-class parents to move towards state education we did take as soon as we arrived in Hampstead. In 1950 the comprehensive idea was only in its beginnings and there were several large day schools in the area, ranging from direct grant to wholly maintained. We had some sympathy for parents who felt that the large classes in primary schools – and at that time not all primary schools were as excellent as they are now – were often detrimental to the slower and shyer child, but we were determined to persuade parents against boarding schools and against at least some of the private day schools when children reached eleven. We held parents' meetings and invited the Heads of some of the direct grant and maintained schools to talk to our parents about secondary education within the state system. I shall never forget the notable occasion when Miss Doris Burchall, Headmistress of Camden Girls' School, gave a talk about the kind of education offered at Camden, a maintained grammar school with no fee-paying places. At the end of the meeting one of the parents approached me and said: 'That was *such* an interesting talk, Miss Manning. You know, I never realised that the Headmistress of a grammar school would be a lady!' Doris Burchall was immensely tickled by this when I told her. Subsequently, twelve or fifteen of our eleven-year-olds went on to Camden every summer.

There were occasions when I wished I had gone into a state grammar school in the first place, but perhaps it was as well that I didn't, for I doubt if I should have been capable of teaching in the later comprehensive schools. In any case, I had chosen to teach in the independent sector and then to become the owner of an independent prep school for girls. Making the best of what I knew had been a wrong decision in the first place, I determined to make the Hampstead school we took over in 1950 a place where the arts, especially music, were given parity of importance on the timetable with ordinary academic subjects like arithmetic and English. It was an ego-trip in a way, I confess, but a successful one in that the school soon became well known for its high standards and wide range in music. Our aim was to offer the children musical experience in singing, playing, listening and creating. It was not to turn them into virtuosi. I think it worked, and many ex-pupils have testified to this when I have met them later on in their lives.

If the music became increasingly my province, Andrea's outstanding gift was in helping children with their difficulties, especially in mathematics. Neither of us believed in an entrance examination as so many private schools do, and inevitably this meant that there was a wide range of ability, but this was precisely what we wanted. I think we ran a happy and educationally rich school.

There were two buildings, the larger of which was entirely devoted to school use, while in the other there were a few rooms for Andrea and myself. Financially, this was an advantage for it meant that we lived virtually free. We drew very small salaries – well below most of the staff – so we could not afford to live away from the school, certainly not in separate establishments. This meant sharing our lives in many ways, in meals, for instance, and to a great extent in the entertainment of friends. It was a very claustrophobic situation.

It ended in a kind of armed neutrality, as the differences in our tastes and lifestyles became more pronounced. Andrea was extremely conventional. I had been accustomed in my earlier life in London and Sussex to a free, almost 'bohemian' life. In 1956 I began a five-year lesbian affair and this placed an even severer strain upon my relationship with Andrea. It could not survive it. Our lives diverged more and more sharply until we were hardly upon speaking terms.

In the late fifties I decided to escape from the school, but I had to find some other way of earning my living. I applied for a number of administrative jobs in universities and training colleges, but I had left it too late. I should have made my escape attempt before going to

Hampstead, but I had been reluctant for various reasons, some that I certainly did not recognise at the time. I had not begun seriously to write. I had not found love. I was in a kind of vacuum and to break out into reality demanded, I see with hindsight, a courage I did not possess. At the time, I argued in my mind that I was too interested in this new Hampstead venture and, as the years went by, I persuaded myself, I am sure mistakenly, that Andrea would have found it very difficult to run the school without me. I had a responsibility to her, I felt, another way of telling myself that I was indispensable. We had taken on this rundown school in 1950. I must stay with her and build it up. I was deceiving myself. Andrea was extremely competent – far more competent than I was – and would either have carried on alone or more probably have found another partner and one who suited her far better personally than myself. Except in the actual business of running the place, we had been at odds long before we ever came to London. I take the blame for the quarrels and resentments. Andrea was essentially a gentle, lovable personality, much valued by her own friends, although most of my circle found her diffident and shy. How fragile the basis of our relationship was began to show as soon as we went into partnership, and the rift grew with the years, despite attempts to salvage it by going on holidays together, sharing evenings at the theatre and at concerts and in entertaining.

Andrea died very suddenly in 1971 of a brain haemorrhage. I felt – I do not hesitate to say this – very little grief after the initial shock and strain of watching her in a coma for ten days. I felt remorse because I knew that I had not always treated her well and had often worked out upon her the frustrations I felt. She once told someone that I had ruined her life. I think that this was an exaggeration, but I had certainly become an increasingly difficult person to live with. What I felt overwhelmingly at her death was a sense of relief. I could at last be free of the school.

I have to pay a tribute to Andrea. She was a very likeable person, at her best amusing and, with people she felt at ease with, sociable and attractive in manner. In dealings with parents and children she was patient and understanding. Indeed I left most of the parental interviews to her. My abrasive manner often caused trouble. There have been times when Andrea removed the telephone from my hand and took over a conversation from me. She was a first-class teacher of young children, in many ways a brilliant one, especially in mathematics. Her personal life was overshadowed by the loss at Alamein of the man she was hoping to marry, a man she had known since she was a child. I think that it was because they had been accepted as lovers for so long that she and John had not bothered to get married. She later had a certain happiness in a short affair with a married man, but the difficulties proved too much and it sank beneath the strain when his work took him to Ireland. Andrea was a woman who should have married and had a family. Before I met her when she was in her late twenties, she had had no lack of young men pursuing her, but she was an only child with a morbidly possessive father. In the end he succeeded in driving off any potential husbands except John, in whom I don't think he seriously recognised a danger of marriage. Andrea deserved better than to live on uneasy and frequently hostile terms with someone like me and die as she did at only sixty-one, when we were doing better financially and she was looking forward to retirement in a flat she had bought. When she averred that I had ruined her life, I felt bitterly and unreasonably that I could have said the same of her influence over me. I never forgot that eagle with N E M E S I S printed across its wings. But in truth we ruin our own lives and I have no one but myself to blame.

On the credit side of our association must be placed the principles on which we ran the schools in Hertfordshire and north London, for despite my personally antagonistic attitude to teaching, Andrea and I shared certain convictions which we tried to put into practice. This did much to keep us together. As I have said, we both believed that music and the arts generally must be given a place on the timetable in parity with the ordinary school subjects like arithmetic. As the more experienced musician, I was certainly the prime mover in this, but Andrea supported me fully, and it was in music, which is so time-consuming if fully pursued, that we were most insistent on our principles. As regard arts and crafts, we built an art room and eventually were able to employ a fulltime teacher in the subject, as we did for games and gym, both unusual in a girls' junior school where such things were and still are in many cases taught by the class teachers. In music, it was an uphill battle at first. It was a subject that few parents gave much importance to beyond a desire that their offspring should learn the piano. Nor did many head teachers give it more than grudging attention, singing classes and instrument teaching (if any) being often carried out at wholly inappropriate times, squeezed into lunch hours and mid-morning breaks, and seldom enjoying a suitable and well-equipped room. We refused to countenance this. It took us three or four years to overcome opposition from staff as well as parents. By the end of ten years or so, there were some forty children learning the violin, and twenty learning the cello, out of a school roll of just under two hundred. Academic subjects did not suffer, as we knew they wouldn't. The school built up a first-rate choir, and a small orchestra. We even for a time ran a choir and orchestra made up of old pupils, parents and staff. A good deal of original composition was done. There was no element of élitism in all this. For those who did not learn an instrument like the cello or violin, there were recorders of different sizes, and recorder consorts. There was plenty of listening to music and singing in simple parts, the more advanced work being given to the choirs, of which there were usually two.

Since I was by all accounts a good teacher, it would be unfair to leave the subject without saying what I found positive and rewarding about being a member of a profession which since my youth I had sworn I would never enter. In the classroom itself, I was happy enough. The best teaching will always arise from the demonstration and sharing of one's interests and enthusiasms. I never hesitated to wear my heart on my sleeve and children appreciate the knowledge that you are giving them something you yourself enjoy and value, even if it is difficult. I remember that at Bampfield I was an absolute duffer at maths, but I did manage to learn sufficient of the subject to get my Matric, and I became almost enamoured of trigonometry. This was entirely due to the teaching of a woman called Miss Colman, whose eyes glowed, whose voice thrilled as she expounded the equations I tried so hard to understand. She was unfailingly patient and willing to go over and over a point. I was remarkably stupid in the subject but I really loved her for her enthusiasm and looked forward to her lessons. I sensed that even if I could never get very far, there was a pure poetry in mathematics which she was afire with and longing to impart. I may have unconsciously modelled myself upon her.

It does not in fact matter very much *what* our interests and enthusiasms may be, for the content is in the end less important than the stretching of a child's mental muscles, the training of eye and ear, the encouragement of sensitivity, observation, discovery. I am not talking about the formation of taste. Training the mind and the sensibilities will enable a person to make her or his own choices later. Music is a discipline, but I did not insist on high standards in order to produce mini-professionals. What I was trying to achieve – among other things I cannot expatiate on here – was the formation of a base on which a child could later build up a musical life, or a pleasure in music, with some standard of reference.

When teaching English (which I did to the older children of ten and eleven mostly), I based much of my work on the poetry of all periods and on writing poetry. But I also taught grammar, which I consider a necessary framework and especially useful when learning a foreign language. I defy any pupil I taught to come forward and say it was boring. No subject need be boring if the teacher knows how to teach it properly and that usually arises from a love of it. I genuinely loved grammar and syntax and philology, and often found that parents became involved and excited by the exercises in grammar that I invented – for who ever found an agreeable and interesting grammar book? I am not a scholar. I am a sharer and a populariser. Perhaps the happiest hours I ever had in teaching, apart from the school music and English, were in my sixties, when I gave lectures at evening classes and at residential colleges on subjects which had a glorious uselessness: heraldry, and another course which proved extremely popular: the meaning of the symbolism used by the mediaeval artists in stone and wood and stained glass. This work took me all over England, photographing tombs, misericords, benchends and the like in churches and cathedrals to make slides for my lectures. I loved teaching adults and perhaps this is what I should have done from the start. I do not greatly care for children though I am interested in them, especially in the misfits and mavericks.

Music teaching gave me the greatest reward in my school life of some thirty-five years. It still moves me to hear occasionally from old girls how much it meant to them, even if they have never gone on to do anything practical in the field. About twenty years after she had left, an old girl wrote to me: 'Today I switched on the radio and heard Mozart's *Ave Verum*. I remember so well singing it in the choir with you conducting and I almost wept. I just had to sit down and write to you straight away!'

None of this musical work could have been achieved without a really good music staff, with whom I worked closely, and in later years supported and encouraged when I had ceased to do much of the practical work myself. Two of the most able came to us at only twenty years of age, immature and uncertain of their considerable talents. To the first of them, Gill, the music of the school owed a particular debt, for she came to us when we were still in the early stages of implementing our ideas. She it was who introduced the string teaching in the school, and when she left she brought to us another twenty-year-old musician who was to prove an outstanding director of music and stayed with the school for many years. My relationship with the staff who taught music was always close, for though their technical training might be greater than mine, they were usually either very young and inexperienced, or had come to us from a school where the music was conventional and did not play an important part. I had had a fairly wide musical education of a very empirical kind, which enabled me to assess their ideas and encourage and support them and to have the Head behind you is, as I knew from my first teaching post, essential. I cooperated with them in practical ways, of which I will give one example. In a search for unusual folksong material, the second very young music director I have referred to above used to go with me to Cecil Sharp House near Regent's Park, and there we would listen to records of folksongs we did not know, and if we liked them and wanted to teach them to the children, I would scribble down the words, while Dinah wrote down the tune and later set an accompaniment to it.

As to the first music teacher, who introduced strings to the school, she was a near disaster, a failure at her piano teaching, often rocked off course by her love affairs, but I was certain she had great potential. I sent her to classes to learn the recorder, supported her in building up the string teaching and forming an orchestra, and she went on to work with adults and in music administration when she left us. She wrote me an account of what it had meant to her to work at the school. It is too long to quote here, but it ended with these words: 'St Christopher's was my training ground. Pupil or teacher? It's hard to say . . .'

It is a relief to me to have reached the end of this chapter. Teaching occupied thirty-five years of my life. There were aspects of it which I do regard with pleasure and even with pride, like the music, but as a whole I have nothing but regret for having entered the profession in the first place. I went into it for the wrong reasons and, however much I take the blame for my own immaturity and mistakes, I believe that teaching tends to hold back one's development in personality, in ideas and one's mental and psychological growth. Ideally (for we must have teachers) no one should enter the profession under thirty, and all should leave it by forty-five.

Throughout the years after we came to London when I was just forty, the school occupied only the surface of my life. I was driven by two inner compulsions that, like streams long underground, now coursed strongly through my personal landscape and soon refused to be denied. One was the search for love and the other my imaginative awakening and fulfilment in writing. These two subsumed the image of the successful teacher which others accredited to me and which I detested. The mirror hangs in a long corridor and if there are other mirrors near by which would show me in different facets of my teaching profession, I am going to hurry past them and take the reader with me to an area of my life which is of paramount importance to me. The corridor, you must imagine, now opens out into a circular room. Here is the true centre of my life. The mirrors that hang here are not arranged in an orderly fashion, nor are the reflections in them always crystal clear. In taking you with me and admitting you to this inner world, I can only wander with you and endeavour to interpret in words images that sometimes almost leap out of the glass at us, and at other times must be peered at closely, images refracted by indirect, perhaps deliberately oblique light upon the glassy surface.

The first mirror at which I pause shows a school building in the background. Schools from Bampfield onwards still occupy my dreams in my seventies. This one reflects as it were a double image, myself as lover and writer. The observer who stands beside me will find the picture beginning to clarify, and the two aspects of my persona will fall into their close and fruitful relationship as we move into the next chapter.

13
Died for Love

Not particularly brave in all circumstances, I think I have been a risk-taker where love is concerned; at least, this is true of me once I shook off the inhibitions and fears that to a great extent had wrecked my affair with Edith. It is only fair to say that others are usually involved in the risks one takes. The risks have brought me loss and pain, but love is still for me the perfect sum of all delight, and I would not change its note, however often my feelings have echoed those of the anonymous Elizabethan poet:

> Fain would I change that note
> To which fond love hath charmed me.

When we have lost what we loved we may well wish that we had never engaged our hearts so deeply, but *au fond* I regard this as a heresy.

My conscious search for love began in earnest when I returned to London in 1950. I was living my emotional life in a vacuum. My essentially loving nature was without an object. I began consciously to search for a woman with whom I could live a full life, sexually and in companionship. I formed a resolution that if I did not find her, I could not go on living this barren life, empty of all that was most important and satisfying to me, even if it was agreeable superficially, with its music-making and the many pleasures that London afforded. I had attempted suicide when I was seventeen. That form of escape was never far from my mind. Now I gave myself till I was fifty. I resolved not to live beyond that if I had not found the woman I sought and also won recognition as a writer.

I was still lamentably immature and my search for love inevitably led me up some blind alleys. I fell in love for a short time with a peculiarly unsuitable young woman, heterosexual, separated from her husband, a published writer (that is, of one book), and, above all, boringly sorry for herself. All my protective instincts, all my generosity (she had very little money: 'God, he's *so mean*!') came to the fore at once and B— was an experienced taker. A few years later I saw the funny side of my infatuation, turned her into a tiresome, fey young man and put her into a novel under this guise.

The pain of the affair passed quickly. The young woman disappeared into the depths of the country to commune with nature, eat sorrel and dandelions, and produce another rambling little book about dormice and dewy mornings and (alas, have I not done just this, as you will see?) owls at eventide. I hope it earned her enough to keep the wolf from the door. As for me, it was a relief when she went. I had taken my risk and recognised fairly early on that I was wasting my time. And after all, I gained something: she provided a minor character in a future novel. As my lover Jan said to me years later, with a touch of bitterness: 'You writers – all's grist to your mill, isn't it?' Yes, it is. And that includes myself, of course.

Shortly after this episode I was to take a far greater emotional risk and involve myself deeply but with very different consequences. This was after I met a woman I will call Elizabeth, in 1956. We met through a mutual friend soon after I had written my first children's book, *Green Smoke*. She was a junior editor in a publishing house and very interested in what I was writing. Through her, *Green Smoke* went to the editor of the newly established children's books department of Constable and Company. It was published by them in 1957.

Elizabeth was also to have a fruitful influence upon the final version of *The Chinese Garden*. I gave her the typescript of this novel about my schooldays at Bampfield and she wrote me several pages of thoughtful and penetrating criticism of it. One weekend I asked her to come round to my house and discuss it with me. We spent many hours going through her notes. By the end of it I knew, if she did not, that I had come to the end of my search. That search was not only for the person I longed to love. It was for the recognition of my own self through her love for me. Not long after the affair had ended, I wrote a novel called *Man on a Tower*. Into the mouth of George, the non-hero of the book and in fact a disguise for my own persona, I put the belief in this need for recognition:

The old philosophers who asked: 'Is a rose red if there is no one to see it?' knew what they were asking. I am not George if I am not known to be so by the one person who will recognise me. The desire

and pursuit of the whole is not the desire and pursuit of another
half, a complement. I am not and have never felt incomplete, a
man only half-fulfilled. I have spent my life fulfilling myself to the
top of my bent, but in the final account, I remain the rose without
redness if I am not recognised for what I am. The medium of recognition is love.

Happy though this affair with Elizabeth was, it remained too long on
the plane of romance. We never experienced living together. We met
in coffee-shops, in pubs; we went away for weekends and short holidays. It was our spare time that we spent together and this gave the
affair too much of a holiday flavour.

I was tied to the school, or at least thought myself to be so. Neither
of us had much money. We talked endlessly about living together. I
had a little capital saved from my royalties and wondered if it would
be enough to buy a small terraced house in Camden Town, not then
gentrified. I even looked at one or two, but there was a fierce determination in my heart to keep my freedom. Today I ask myself what
freedom I was thinking about. At the time, I have no doubt that a
shared life with Elizabeth implied to me the curtailment of my liberty
to write, and I could not bring myself to jeopardise this just when I
had struck such a rich vein of creativity. As I contrived to do quite a
bit of writing even when we were camping in a small tent, I was clearly
deceiving myself – and Elizabeth too. I set up for my own inner satisfaction the idea that I was preserving my privacy as a writer and my
personal independence. My independence was an illusion, for I was
very reliant both personally and financially upon Andrea's friendship, however shaky, and upon the school which I hated so much in
many ways. Looking back more searchingly, I see Andrea as the
friend and enemy upon whom I worked out many of my hatreds and
frustrations.

My love affairs with Elizabeth and later Kay went down very badly
with Andrea. I can see now that my continual absences from home
left her lonely, and the stress put upon me by my way of life – teaching, running the school, music, writing, the necessity for secrecy in
my relationship with my lover – all this must have made me intolerable to live with. Andrea had never liked my musical friends or the
few bookish and intellectual ones I had acquired. She herself had lost
during the war the man she had hoped to marry and this had made her
the more dependent on my friendship, but the friendship itself was

frayed at the edges, based as it was on not much more than old association and affection, and too easily subjected to irritation and anger.

My affair with Elizabeth, despite its central happiness and fulfilment, held within it stresses that built up from the very start. One strain,
perhaps the most fundamental, appears in my diaries again and again:
the conflict caused by the desire to retreat into solitude even at the height
of happiness. Other enemies to the successful enduring of our relationship have clarified for me only as I have grown older and reflected upon
our five-year affair. Socially, although we had several good friends in
common and although I maintained my active musical life and Elizabeth her own friendships, we were forced in general to keep our affair
under covers. Neither of us felt any desire to seek out and join the gay
scene and in any case it hardly existed in the late fifties. It was a con-
tinuation of the habit of secrecy that I had practised all my adult life
and it was eventually to affect my writing career seriously. Elizabeth
had an added problem in that she had to conceal what was happening
between us from her parents.

Clearly no two people who live under the predicament of being
social outsiders will react in the same way to it. Their response will
depend much upon their own awareness of their sexuality, upon their
maturity and any stability they may have gained from the support of
friends and of other gays, if they are fortunate enough to belong to
such a circle. But we, as I've said, knew no other lesbians and neither
of us spoke of our affair and its nature to other people, even those
close to us. This was strain enough for both of us, but there were
other cracks across the plate. A person who is by turns depressive and
ebullient as I am is not an easy person to be with. Elizabeth herself
once told me that she found me somewhat larger than life – which at
first I think I took as a compliment – but went on to say that at times
she felt swamped and overwhelmed. I am demanding, egocentric,
easily irritated and angered. My better qualities of geniality, humour,
generosity, tenderness are evidently not sufficient to mitigate the
darker side of myself, and since I suffer from this desperately enough
myself, how should it not affect the person I live with, however deep
the love?

After about four years, when I think I can say with truth that the
happiness we experienced outweighed the stresses, there emerged
something that I had never foreseen and which was to prove crucial:
Elizabeth wanted children. The early sixties were not a time when
women contemplated as readily as they do today the idea of sleeping

casually with a man in order to conceive a child. In many ways Elizabeth was conventional, and as well as wanting children she wanted a home. She was tired of living in bed-sitters. Tensions increased between us and mounted rapidly when she embarked on a relationship with the man she would later marry. As the end of our affair became painfully inevitable, I knew that I had no desire to live any longer. I had found what I sought and lost it. I was nearly fifty. There seemed to me no future without Elizabeth, whose marriage was now certain. In April 1962 I made a nearly successful attempt to commit suicide. Two months later *The Chinese Garden* came out to a spate of eulogistic reviews which did nothing to console me for having failed to kill myself.

I had made careful plans over several months, once it became absolutely clear to me that Elizabeth was going to go out of my life. I decided that, for the sake of those who loved me, I wanted to be found – but not too soon. I therefore wrote a letter saying where I should be and what I was intending to do. I posted this letter in a small country town where the last postal collection, I noted carefully, had been made two hours previously. This meant that the recipient could not possibly open my letter for at least thirty-six hours. As it would probably arrive on his doormat, I reckoned, *after* he had gone to work, I could reasonably count on about forty-eight hours. I had some seventy luminal tablets. I was confident that I should be dead when I was discovered locked into my car on a lonely part of the Wiltshire downs. I was not to know, firstly, that there was an unannounced late collection from that post office, presumably for the convenience of a local army camp, nor, secondly, that the person to whom I addressed the letter was taking a few days' leave from work. He opened the letter the following morning, something that would never happen with today's slothful postal services. Another factor: I think I must have the constitution of a horse.

Even so, the luminal nearly did the job. The policemen who found me, after being alerted by the recipient of the letter, were so alarmed at my condition that they did not dare to transfer me to their police car. They drove my vehicle at breakneck speed along the downland track, tearing off a tyre in the process. Undeterred, they entered the town and rushed me to a hospital, with the car jolting on three tyres, and an iron rim grating discordantly over the road surface. Thus was my life preserved by the combined forces of the Post Office, the Law and, I suppose, Fate. The circumstances were bizarre, but I should not be here writing this book were it not for that extraordinary set of coincidences.

When I recovered, I did not immediately take up the partly written novel that I had been working on before my suicide attempt, *Man on a Tower*. I wrote an autobiography which I called *A Time and a Time*. These words I found in John Cowper Powys' novel *Weymouth Sands*. They are part of a biblical quotation which reads in full: 'A time and a time and half a time.' This is what I gave myself when I recovered: a year and a year and half a year. Then, if my life was still as empty of love, I would make a second attempt.

A Time and a Time was not an autobiography in the sense of a full account of my life. It began with my suicide attempt and went on to describe my search for love which ended in finding Elizabeth. On that search I was not looking for perfection but for response, for acceptance, above all for a shared experience of loving and living as earthy as a pair of walking boots and as rapturous as the flight of a falcon. I tried to assess why the relationship had ended as it had.

As I wrote the last section of the book, life caught up with me. I found myself writing events almost as they happened. The last part gives an account of a short but ardent love affair with a young woman called Kay, an affair that was over before the book was ended.

One of the surest aids to survival is a love affair. I am deeply grateful to Kay for all she gave me during this bleak period. It was she who began the affair, pulling me into her orbit almost by brute force. I was starved of love, starved of sex. Kay taught me to revel in sensuality. I once heard a young gay argue convincingly in defence of 'cottaging' and 'cruising' on the grounds that for him the act of sex brought him close to his partner in more ways than the physical. He began to understand him as a person, to know more than his physical self, and to want to share far more with him than the sexual act. I can appreciate this but my affair with Kay is the only one in my life that followed this pattern. The enormous pleasure of my sexual encounters with Kay was soon converted by my romantic nature into a conviction that I was seriously in love with her. It was necessary for me to follow this fantasy because this is the kind of person I am. Alas, our intimacy did not bring fuller acceptance and understanding of her, only a growing knowledge that I could never hope to integrate her into my life.

Kay was belligerent and quarrelsome. She hated my bourgeois values and attacked them mercilessly. Violence was utterly antipathetic to me. On the other hand, she was warm and I was living out in the cold when I met her. Her abandoned pleasure in sex taught me a great deal and released my sexual self into a relaxed happiness without guilt. This was a new experience for me, for guilt had always provided a ground bass to my previous affairs. My reading during the fifties, especially of Llewelyn Powys' hedonistic essays, had opened a new world of sensual pleasures to me, but there were limitations to what was produced merely by reading. It created an overplus of 'sex in the head', as Kay bluntly told me. It was she who dislodged it from that area to its proper territory.

Kay was a Birmingham girl. Her father was a meat porter, her mother a loving, supportive person but withdrawn for periods and unstable, while her much-loved brother was seriously into drugs. And now I have to venture on to dangerous ground. We suck in class-consciousness with our mother's milk and this is fortified by the kind of education we have. There is, or certainly was in my young days, a sexist middle-class attitude that a liaison between a son of the family and a working-class girl (however unfortunate, of course, for family standing) can only *improve* the girl, whereas it is intolerable for a daughter to ally herself with a working-class man. If this is less true today, it must be one of the few areas where social attitudes have become a little less offensive than they were in the first half of this century and before that. One might hope that the feminist and peace movements would act as catalysts and perhaps they have done so, and the comprehensive school system must now be breaking down barriers of class to a certain extent, but these will be *outward* manifestations of it. These social divisions bred in the bone, however disagreeable some of us recognise them to be, shift over the centuries but only to take up new forms. Twentieth-century social and economic divisions are different but just as rigid as those of the Middle Ages, and a revolution may destroy current systems but will soon give rise to a different pattern of classes. I am not hopeful.

My own ineradicable middle-classness is like a deformity to me. I hated things about Kay that were a part of her and that I had no right to hate merely because they made me uncomfortable. I rather envied her her working-class origins, a kind of Orwellism on my part, but I detested the outward manifestations of them and more than anything her strong Brummagem accent. I loathed her taste in food which she tried to force upon me by acting as cook: her passion for steak and tinned peas, for instance. I am laying myself on the line as a middle-class boor. I was frightened of the unfamiliar, as scared of Kay's family as if they were standing round me, armed with cleavers.

Do women find it more difficult than men to break the class barrier on the personal level? I remember Edward Carpenter and George Merrill, his working-class lover who lived with him for thirty years. 'Dear love of comrades!' Why did this not work for Kay and myself? I was too prejudiced, too class-ridden, too reluctant to have my roots disturbed, possibly grubbed up altogether. I lost an opportunity for radical change in myself. But all this guilt and blame . . . let me try to tell it as it was, with this rider: that I have never learned and accepted (until I am too old to profit from it) that life is anarchic, that if love is the supreme element in it, it is given to cruelty, selfishness and violence as well as ecstasy and tenderness, and these things cannot be brought to order like a knot-garden. This is how it was.

Kay was small, dark and rather beautiful with that dark-eyed Jewish type of loveliness, voluptuous and sensual. She had a passion for small objects that pleased her: a red leaf lying on the road, a twisted branch, a bird's rain-washed skull, a single black ash tree bud. They were all brought back into the house after we had been out walking and were loved and cherished and wondered at.

She cast away what she didn't want in life and walked with a face always turned to the future. From the past she valued only her family, for which she felt a strong loyalty, and encounters with people who had she believed enriched her life. She could be predatory. She expected people to give, to support, to advance her. She was unashamed about taking what she could get as her right in a harsh world which in her youth had given her so little. She felt especially deprived of education, having left school at fifteen, and she loved books with a greedy passion, indiscriminately. What did discrimination matter? Indeed, what *does* it matter? She quickly found out what she liked and what she didn't and had none of my puritanical sense of duty that sometimes makes me persevere with a book I don't really enjoy. Modern books held little interest for her. It was the classics that she sought out to enrich her starved mind: Montaigne, Plato's *Republic*, Charles Lamb's *Essays* — she devoured them all. She picked them off my shelves without any promptings from me and ate them as if they were the eucharist in a holy feast that promised her eternity.

Kay taught me how liberating a fully sensual love can be, and she brought out in me the sexual and erotic potentialities suppressed for so many years. Physical love with Kay was immensely rewarding and it was fun. This was an aspect of sex rather new to me. With Elizabeth it had been full of delight and not without its fun element, but there was ignorance on both sides and there were inhibitions. Kay swiftly swept these away. She laughed at them mercilessly and involved me in love-making of an ardour and inventiveness I had never dreamed of. Yet as time went by, the rows we had became more than I could bear – slamming-the-door, locking-me-out-of-the-house rows. I knew I could not live with her.

I shared my Dorset house with her for some time, it is true, and we went to France for an unforgettably lovely holiday which took in Chartres, Cahors and Bourges, with much of the Dordogne and a few days in Paris. But I never shared my London home with Kay. She remained a passing visitor there and not always a welcome one. She did not fit in – a revealing bourgeois expression, as she would have said. And there was less room for her disruptive tactics. I was still teaching, of course, and had to square her presence with Andrea, which was not easy.

She had come into my life unexpectedly and given me a thorough shaking-up. Her youth (she was only about twenty-five when I met her, I about fifty-five), her eager grasping at every new sensation and experience, made her often a delightful companion and a stimulating one, but she could switch from joy to anger in a flash. Often I hated this, though I knew at the time that it was salutary for me to have my foundations so thoroughly probed and even undermined. Kay went out of my life completely after a final row, but in retrospect I am glad that she was once part of it. At the time I felt much regret and guilt for her going and a deep sense of failure. 'If only I loved Kay [I wrote in my diary]. If only I loved her. The absence of hope has driven me in on myself. I have nothing but my writing and my fantasies. I am completely in retreat.' After she had gone I found myself in the wilderness again. The two and a half years I had set myself – a time and a time and half a time – had gone by and I was still alive and still alone.

14
Whistling in the Dark

When I was a child of eleven or twelve at Sandhurst, my father sometimes used to ask me to post letters by the evening collection. The postbox was at the end of a long lane. On either side were high banks, topped by trees so tall and thick-branched that they arched overhead, almost shutting out the sky, and in late autumn and winter the road became a dark and frightening tunnel. And always a rustling and scuffling in the undergrowth on either side. I am sure that I was given a torch, but I was deeply afraid of that walk and inevitably too stoical to complain. I sang or whistled as I walked to the postbox.

The subject of this chapter – my life as a writer – has prompted this Sandhurst memory and provided a title for it. Round the central circular hall hang reflections of love and creativity. It is my teenage figure that I see in the first mirror, a figure almost indiscernible in the leafy darkness. But perhaps, in the faint light at the end of that tunnel of trees I have described, you can see, as I do, a building: the elegant Palladian façade of Bampfield wreathed in the mists that so often covered its low-lying park. And in the mirror I am reflected as a kind of double image: walking back from the postbox as a child, and on a far longer journey from the place where I spent six years of my youth, from Bampfield; for it was Bampfield, I am persuaded, that made me a writer, and writing has proved my lifeline, the equivalent of whistling in the dark, as I have made my way through life. Among the various sources upon which an author draws, there must be one or possibly more that can be traced far back into the past. In my case, the source lies at the heart of the place where I spent the years from eleven to nearly eighteen.

Teenage years are often a period of creativity, but few children grow up to be artists in any field. At most they use their talents as amateurs. I am, of course, leaving out the creative element in other activities, and indeed in the living of one's life. Music was only mediocre at Bampfield, art non-existent, but it was a literary school. I was not only encouraged to write. My work was read by Chief and *criticised*. It is rare for a girl of sixteen to be taken seriously. Too often, startled out of dull routine by some piece of mildly interesting work by a pupil, a teacher may exaggerate the worth of it. My essays and stories, for instance, were overpraised. They did not receive ruthless enough treatment from my English teachers and this was regrettable. I was permitted to indulge in an over-literary style and a too-ready use of quotation. I still find it difficult to shake off these old habits, allowed to go unchecked when I was a tyro.

It was my poetry which most interested Chief, but her encouragement need not, of course, have made me a writer. What was more important for my future was that I won her respect. She never allowed me to think that I was or should eventually be a second Shelley but she made me feel that I had a gift for words. This was the talent (Chief was very fond of the parable of the talents) that I must never bury, and she sharpened it with her careful and generous criticism. It was this gift that I called to my aid in later life.

Bampfield damaged me, but we are all in some degree damaged by our childhoods. Family, school, surroundings, social pressures, economic position – they are what ill weather is to a growing plant. Somehow most of us survive them despite the havoc they cause. By what is called 'strength of character'? Well, perhaps. By religious beliefs? Certainly not in my case. Dedication to marriage and children? To work? We grab for these and other lifelines as we struggle through the rough waters of growing up, confused, vulnerable and often battered in the process. For myself, my creative talent eventually proved the one rope strong enough to keep me on my feet. It is a pity that I did not realise this much earlier in my life, but – it seems extraordinary to me now – I virtually abandoned writing after I left school. I lost or buried out of sight the dedication I had declared openly in my teens. When I began teaching in my late twenties, I did at last begin to write again, but even then I only produced the kind of poetry I should have grown out of years before. I turned more readily to musical composition, for which I had only minimal technique and no more than a slight gift. It led to the composition of a handful of quite agreeable songs, but left me frustrated. It was not for another ten years or so that I took up writing seriously, and then it was only to make a false start.

I was loaned some *Cornhill Magazines* when I was laid up for a while with back trouble. As I read them, my boredom encouraged me to believe that I could write better short stories myself. I recovered and at once wrote a long story called 'The Fox' and sent it to *Horizon*, certainly the most prestigious of literary periodicals at the time. Cyril Connolly accepted it and it was published in 1949, the last number of the magazine to appear. I was thirty-eight. Soon I had a handful of stories on my desk. They appeared in the *Cornhill* and one or two other periodicals. Encouraged by this, I made up a small volume of them and sent it to Rupert Hart-Davis. At that time, David Garnett was a reader or perhaps an editor at Hart-Davis's. He called me into his office and praised the stories highly. He had a wall-eye which fascinated me almost as much as his heady references to Chekhov and Turgenev. But the volume came to nothing.

'It's hopeless for a new writer to begin publication with a volume of short stories,' he told me. 'Write a novel.'

It was almost a commission, I felt, so elevated was I by his encouragement. I sat down at once to write what was really only a novella, a blown-up short story. It was called *Remaining a Stranger*, and it had some good things in it but it was hardly typical of what I was to write later. David Garnett wrote to me from his Northamptonshire country house. He admired it. He was going to recommend that Hart-Davis published it. I had an undoubted talent. This novel was a splendid beginning to what he was certain was going to be a distinguished writing career. It is very heartening to be told these things about a first novel and I went back to my teaching – now mercifully in Hampstead, for it was 1952 – in a state of euphoria.

About three or four weeks after that, David Garnett wrote to me again on his country house letter-heading. He was sorry. He was more than sorry – he was devastated. Rupert Hart-Davis had now read my novel and didn't care for it and was returning the typescript to me. He, David, realised that he should never have encouraged me to hope that it would be published by his firm. He still believed in its merits and wished me the best of luck with it.

The blow could have been destructive and I certainly felt very bitter about the episode, but writers have some resilience and I had already embarked upon a full-length novel. David Garnett's 'masterpiece' did in fact find another publisher fairly quickly in Heinemann, who were then starting to produce a series of new authors in a cheap, well-printed format (price 7*s*. 6*d*.). My *Remaining a Stranger* had good reviews and sold rather well. I published it under the pseudonym Mary Voyle, not because it had anything scandalous or erotic in it – it was extremely pure – but I wanted to be free to write on any subject and in any manner I desired, and used a pseudonym to protect me from my official profession and from the parents whose money I was living on and whose prejudices, I feared, might constrict me later. *Remaining a Stranger* brought me one of the most valuable friendships of my life, as I shall describe in a later chapter, my friendship with Alyse Gregory.

I followed up this first novel with another, *A Change of Direction* (Heinemann, 1955), also under the name Mary Voyle, a book better forgotten. When I have looked back over my first ten years in Hampstead, from 1950 to 1960, I have always tended to ignore these two novels. The fifties were, I remembered vaguely, the years when I had a sudden upsurge of creativity and wrote the first two novels that I consider worth recording anything about, *Look, Stranger* and *The Chinese Garden*. These were published under my own name, for I had begun writing children's books by then and it would have been foolish to use a pseudonym for these, so I wrote at last as Rosemary Manning, and I need not have worried about the school parents, for they were only aware of me as a writer of children's books. I doubt if more than half a dozen ever read my adult novels.

I have said that Bampfield made me a writer. This may sound simplistic and of course I might have been one, though probably of a different kind, if I had never been to that boarding school. But for me that statement remains profoundly true. I have described how I discovered a Chinese garden in a huge shrubbery in the park, but in the chapter given its name, I was dealing with events which affected my adolescence and my subsequent difficulties in reaching maturity. Here I am seeing the garden as a symbol which sank deep into my mind to become the central and secret fount of my inspiration to write. It was a *hortus inclusus* which held an essence from which I could and did draw nourishment. But it was not until my forties that I dared to enter it. When I described its physical appearance and my first discovery of it, the words streamed from my pen as though it was a painter's brush, creating the scene visibly under my hand as it moved over the canvas.

The quiet pools, greened over with weed, never-disturbed, the dense overgrown shrubbery which hedged it from the world without, the incongruous oriental appearance of the pagoda and its bridges, created an indescribable air of secrecy and strangeness. She entered an exotic world where she breathed pure poetry. It had the symmetry of Blake's tiger. It was the green thought in a green shade.

She wandered slowly about, mapping it out in her mind. Its dereliction did not distress her. She was used to decay and ruin. The Chinese garden still offered, it its broken bridges and peeling cupola, the symbols of a precise pattern, a perfection greater than itself. Its complex image held within it a world of images, unfolding to the heart unending sequences of dream.

'a world of images', 'unending sequences of dream' . . . I cannot dissect these sentences but I think an artist in any field would recognise their significance for my future as a writer.

Why did it take me until my forties to find my feet as a novelist? For some ten years – my university and London working years – the stream of inspiration had run underground. Nor was it simply a matter of 'inspiration' or even of finding the right medium for my creative talents, or I should have written *The Chinese Garden* much earlier, probably instead of those two 'Mary Voyle' novels. It was essential for me first to come to terms with the events narrated in Chapter Nine: my affair (if it can be called that) with Georgie Murrill, my housemistress, and the betrayal of my trust in her which nearly destroyed me. It took me more than twenty-five years before I could transmute the experience of Bampfield into a novel. It was more than a matter of 'coming to terms' with past events. The Georgie Murrill episode was only an *incident*. I think that some or much of my later sexual ambivalence and inhibition could be traced to it, but for me as a writer it had a deeper relevance. It became a kind of yeast in the depths of my consciousness. There, moving like God in a mysterious way, it had worked upon my inner self. When the material was ready, when it demanded to see the light, it travelled through an intellectual, shaping passage to reach the threshold of my mind as the novel, *The Chinese Garden*. When I wrote it, I certainly thought of it simply as a novel, not as a piece of self-expression, or as an experience to be exorcised. The rites of exorcism had been performed by the priestesses who presided over their arcane rituals in my unconscious.

Recently, curious as to the exact date of the inception and writing of the novel, I turned to the diaries which I have kept since 1939. Workbooks would be a better description of them for, at least throughout the first ten or twelve years, they contained chiefly notes of my reading, and only in about 1950 did I begin to record ideas and material connected with my writing. Personal and introspective pages also increase at about this time. They emphasise that I was bitterly lonely; my lack of congenial friends; my growing dislike of my profession as headmistress; above all the restless and painful need for fulfilment in love. It was at this time that I read that distressing book of Hazlitt's, the *Liber Amoris*, which moved me greatly. In it I found some words he had written on the flyleaf of his copy of Keats' 'Endymion' and as I copied them, I must have felt that I might have written them myself: 'I want a hand to guide me, a heart to cheer me, a bosom to repose on.' When I read that sentence I felt bitterly how much it reflected my own needs. It still does, and surely it is what most of us need and should respond to and offer to others, whether we are women or men.*

Searching for the first reference to *The Chinese Garden*, I was surprised to find that I had to go much further back in time than I had expected. The novel was not published until 1962 but I thought I had written it in 1956 or 1957. I was wrong. This was the first reference to it: '*Aug. 21. 1951.* I have begun Bampfield. Title: *The Bampfield Papers.*' I was then just forty years old. I only wrote about ten chapters and abandoned it until, a year later, I started again with the rather odd intention of cutting the autobiographical element out of it altogether and calling the book *A Landscape with Figures*. It was to have no dialogue at all. This was clearly in the nature of a retreat from the past on my part.

But *Bampfield* was not the only serious writing I started and then abandoned temporarily in the 1950s. A long, satiric novel, eventually published in 1960 as *Look, Stranger*, appears in these diaries as *The Island*. This went through several transformations before reaching its final form nearly ten years after its inception. Something was holding back my attempts to write. Apart from producing the two 'Mary Voyle' novels, I was distracting myself by much theatre-going, and by social and musical pleasures that gave me a surface satisfaction, but when I reread the diaries of my forties, I see that I was, at least occasionally, quite aware of what I was doing. I wrote: 'I have done

---

* The sentiments are universal. Cf. Gershwin's song – one of his most beautiful – 'Someone to watch over me'.

irreparable damage to myself as a writer by closing my heart. The artist must suffer, has almost a duty to suffer.' In this statement, naïve though it sounds, I was trying to force myself to thrust away distractions and reach down into myself, whatever it cost me.

The sentence about the necessity of suffering is one that I do not entirely subscribe to now, but I *am* convinced that an artist, painter, writer, whatever, has far more to do than use her imagination and subject herself to the discipline of her craft. The artist is, in the last analysis, a guardian of the trove, of the image created in solitude of spirit. It is not so much suffering as aloneness that the creator must accept. The poet/painter David Jones states at the very outset of his extraordinary poem 'The Anathemata': 'The cult-man stands alone in Pellam's land.' By cult-man he means the artist, and I do not think that the artist's position has been more clearly and succinctly stated by anyone, even if the phrase needs a footnote, as do so many of David Jones' observations.

In the summer of 1953 I began to read the poet Rainer Maria Rilke, confining my explorations at first to his *Duino Elegies* and *Orpheus Sonnets*. Rilke's poetry was a revelation to me and released my imagination as no other writer's work has ever done in my whole life. He is a poet's poet, a writer's writer, perhaps, as Spenser was for the Elizabethans. My diaries are packed page after page with passages from Rilke. The key quotation was undoubtedly this:

> Work of sight is achieved.
> Now for some heart work
> On all those pictures, those prisoned
>   creatures within you.

Rilke acted as a benign catalyst, releasing a flood of creative work in me, making my forties and early fifties the most productive period of my life. Rereading my journals now, it is extraordinary to me to see how I contrived not only to write so much in ten years, but to write two or three books concurrently. No sooner had *The Bampfield Papers* been conceived than I had started the totally different work referred to for several years as 'the island novel'. This reached 70,000 words and was then ruthlessly destroyed *in toto*. I started it again with a new set of characters, and it absorbed me through most of 1954 and 1955. This version was also destroyed, but its satiric theme was not abandoned. Side by side with it, I seem to have taken up *The Chinese Garden* again, rewriting it in its present form as a novel with dialogue:

'*April 28. 1955*. A wet day. I have written a huge amount of the Chinese garden. Now it is a question of welding it together, revising it, letting it sink into the lees of my mind. I shall leave it for several months, and return to my other work, to that damned novel, The Island.'

In July 1955 I went to Cornwall, to Constantine Bay near Padstowe, with my old university friend, Diana, her husband, Peter, and their five-year-old daughter, Sue. I took the typescript of *The Chinese Garden* with me and wrote in my diary: 'I have just reread C.G. and have a glorious conviction that it is good.' That hot July I began my first children's book, *Green Smoke*. Always hopeless at telling a story, I had mugged up a few Cornish folktales to tell Sue and keep her amused (I hoped) on long car journeys or sitting on the beach. Somehow, within only a couple of days, I had bowed myself out as a storyteller in favour of a green dragon, whom Sue meets near Constantine Bay, in a solitary bay where he has lived in a cave for hundreds of years. Since the days of King Arthur in fact, when he lived at the royal court. It is R. Dragon who tells the stories. He became the central figure of four children's novels, the best in this field that I have written except for my single historical novel, *Arripay*.

During that wonderfully hot July and August – for we were there for several weeks – I read *Troilus and Cressida* three times, and learned many passages by heart as I lay on the beach or stretched out on the camp bed where I slept every night under the stars, on the lawn beside the cottage. I noted in my diary some words of Ulysses and followed the quotation with an account of an episode, part of which became a chapter in *Green Smoke*, though in that novel it was not to me in my camp bed that Sue found her way late that night, but to the dragon, lying on his back on the lawn, contemplating the shooting stars which fell dazzling bright so often through the blue-black Cornish sky that August.

July 30. 1955. Ulysses' words: 'I have a young conception in my brain; Be you my time to bring it to some shape.'

This might almost stand as a dedication to *The Chinese Garden*. But time, time. I need time, an extension of the present time, of my happiness and creative energy. If this Cornish holiday could be prolonged. Last night I woke up about one o'clock to a clear sky, after a rainy evening, a sky full of stars, with a brilliant, deep honey-coloured moon, just waning from full now and riding much higher in the heavens. The light around was golden, not a cold, white moonlight but warm. The tide, just at its lowest then, was roaring as it does during these neap tides. I lay awake on a tide of happiness, fathomless, drowned deep in it, conscious of all I longed for yet not filled with the misery of longing.

About half an hour later, I heard sounds in the house and saw a torch wavering to and fro in the scullery. I called out. Lights were switched on and off and the backdoor tried and rattled. I called again and Sue answered me. I unlocked the door and she came out in her nightie. 'I'm awake,' she said, 'so I've come out to see the stars.' She came out on to the grass and stood wondering. Then she came into my camp bed for a while and looked all round at the sky. She stayed for about ten minutes and then went back to bed. It was an experience to see her star-wondering eyes.

After she had gone, the clouds came up quickly and as quickly dissolved, and the rest of the night I lay in a half-sleep, waking and sleeping by turns, opening my eyes to see the stars lower and lower in the sky, Hesperus vanished, the moon sunk below the sea, but conscious always of my utter content and peace, that now, as I recall it in the light of day, I know to be an utter delusion. 'In sleep a king, but waking no such matter.'

But illusion or not, the experience of happiness, of astounding, transcendental happiness, remains a part of my experience. It has entered into me and only bitterness will destroy it. I would prefer to preserve it, even if it is a delusion.

That September of 1955, I finished, as I thought, the final draft of *The Chinese Garden*. It did not in fact come out for another seven years and I did yet more revision on it so that it was virtually ten years in the making. When it was at last published in 1962, *Green Smoke* and its sequel, *Dragon in Danger*, had already been published by Constable Young Books. The 'island novel', now called *Look, Stranger*, had been completed and appeared in 1960.

Look, Stranger describes the irrational fear and hatred felt by many people towards the 'outsider', the one who is different. I created a small inbred community on an island where, cut off from mainland influence, the pressures upon those who do not fit in with society's preconceived ideas could be highlighted upon a small stage. I chose for my 'outsider' an epileptic woman, for epilepsy even today causes unease in people, even positive fear, and it was the *irrational* hatred of the outsider that I wanted to satirise. In casting a slightly fantastic air over the whole story and giving it no specific date, yet implying that it takes place in the twentieth century, I was trying to make the point that although we boast today of our liberated attitudes to minorities, we are in fact primitive at heart in our distrust and fear of the one who is different.

Halfway through 1955, when I was deep in the writing of *Look, Stranger*, I wrote in my diary: 'How good it is when writing comes fluently . . . The book begins to take shape. I can see the end. I can see the book stretching out like a road in front of me even if I cannot see the end itself. It is not an easy book to write with its large cast of characters, like a team of horses, to be kept moving forwards at an even pace.' The novel had, indeed, more characters than I have ever used since, and I borrowed an idea from Dickens, whom I love this side idolatry, by putting a character list at the beginning.

I am sorry that this novel is no longer in print. Its theme was one I felt deeply and still do. Twenty-five years on, I see us moving rapidly in this country into the New Intolerance, when it is not merely social pressures that act against the nonconforming individual, but laws and government-sponsored police behaviour. Under an increasingly centralised and authoritarian government we have surveillance in all its disagreeable forms, the undermining of the right to protest and to demonstrate, the increase of police powers, the deliberate erosion of trade union rights. In 1960, when *Look, Stranger* was published, many old intolerances based upon outworn moral and social codes were being swept away by young people no longer hobbled by dependency upon their parents. And it was in the sixties that two of the most fruitful movements of this century were gaining strength: the anti-nuclear movement and feminism. The latter has achieved a far from negligible revolution in attitudes and is still gathering momentum. The anti-nuclear movement, however, being more political – or rather claimed to be so by the government – is more open to attack by authority. I do not think, however, that we have yet seen one half of the moral backlash against the tolerance in sexual matters achieved in the sixties, and it is reinforced by the neo-Moral Rearmament movement in the USA, so much admired by many Conservatives. We have our Mary Whitehouse and our Mrs Gillick, but it is only a matter of time and we shall have our Dr Criswells, too.

Anyone who doubts the hideous power of irrational bigotry might like to ponder on these words spoken by Dr W.A. Criswell, one of

Ronald Reagan's 'men of God', at a Republican Convention in 1984: 'In our lifetime we are scoffing at the word of God . . . and opening up society and culture to the lesbian and sodomite and homosexual . . . and now we have this disastrous judgment . . . the disease and sin of A I D S.' Similar sentiments of incredible bigotry are increasingly spoken and written in this country,* by judges, journalists and members of the public who contribute letters to the newspapers in righteous indignation, that handmaid of intolerance. I would like to write another *Look, Stranger*, but I doubt if my satirical pen would be sharp enough for today's Yahoos. They demand the invective of a second Jonathan Swift.

Look, Stranger was a novel with virtually nothing of my personal life in it. None the less, despite its somewhat mannered style – a piece of camouflage – it was powered by my moral anger. After it, my talent was to become increasingly in bond to my emotional life. In this attempt to assess my writing, I see myself turning away from the direction of satire, from *saeva indignatio*, into a narrower field where intellectual passion would give place to the immediate need to make sense of personal love, loss and self-destruction.

I look back on my forties with mixed feelings, for in spite of what I have just said in the previous paragraph, I find myself moved with envy at the self who lived those immensely creative years, fired by my extensive reading of Rilke, and fuelled eventually by the end of my long search for love, and by my first really happy love affair, which began in 1957 – the affair with Elizabeth.

---

* At the Labour Party Conference in October 1985, Mr William Evans, from Ogmore, South Wales, declared that homosexuality was a sickness, and that it was because of this 'unnatural act' that A I D S was spreading worldwide.

15
A Mysterious Incest

Nadine Gordimer, in a review of Patrick White's auto-biography, coins a striking phrase for this form of book: it is 'a reve-lation of the mysterious incest between life and art'. I have drawn upon myself to a greater or lesser extent in most of my novels. How-ever, there is a difference between using the *events* of one's life in a novelistic form, and trying through the medium of fiction to make sense of the directions one has taken. The publication of *Look, Stranger* and *The Chinese Garden* was separated from the next work I embarked upon by the attempt I made upon my life. What I wrote after that was dictated by my private need to examine myself and dis-cover those elements and forces within me which had brought me to such a pass, and I did this in two ways: in fictional form and in a straight autobiographical account of events which had only just hap-pened, with little attempt to search deeply into my past, my parents, my upbringing.

Even my children's books have a strong autobiographical element, which can be simply stated. In the first three the central character of R. Dragon was more than a vehicle through whom I could tell stories to keep Sue amused. He took over completely and although he is, of course, a fabulous creature, he assumed certain of my more amusing and agreeable qualities. He is sometimes abrasive (he does not suffer fools gladly, as Chief once wrote of me); he is greedy and selfish, but he is also loving, sometimes sentimental and, as a friend and mentor to Sue, he is reliable and caring.

In the late seventies, twenty years after the first three were written, I wrote a fourth dragon book: *Dragon in the Harbour*. At the time, I owned a small early-nineteenth-century terrace house of great charm, right on the quayside of Weymouth harbour. I had bought it at the time I was sharing my life with my lover, Jan. I began the fourth dragon book while I was still living with her. After she had gone, I took it up again and it helped me to come to terms with the emptiness of my Weymouth house. In this novel, the dragon comes from his Cornish cave to Weymouth, moors himself in the harbour and creates his usual mayhem. But this is not the theme that underpins the story. When I found myself suddenly alone again, I did not turn to suicide, though I contemplated it as I walked bitterly down the quay to the end of the stone pier and looked across the bay to Ringstead and White Nothe and Bat's Head. Instead, I turned outwards towards everything of value that I possessed: my writing talent and my friends above all.

Dragon in the Harbour is dedicated to my friends and is one of the most celebratory books I have written. It is a tribute to the Weymouth of my childhood, especially to the harbourside. If *Man on a Tower*, which I shall discuss in a moment, gave a harsh portrait of myself, this fourth dragon book takes a kindlier, more tolerant look at myself in the persona of R. Dragon. It is an attempt to express and preserve what little I like in my character. In terms of the corridor down which I walk, two mirrors hang close together. In one, I see myself in the likeness of the despicable George of *Man on a Tower*, and in the other, as the rotund, genial R. Dragon.*

Fairly early in this children's book, the dragon meets two old friends, Fred and William, owners of a furniture removal van which in a previous novel conveyed the dragon from Cornwall to Sue's home near London. To celebrate the reunion with these two, now operating from a warehouse in Weymouth, the dragon gives a party on the quay, pulling a piano out from a neighbouring pub and placing it firmly right across the railway line that runs from the station to the Channel boats. The trains are still preceded today, as they crawl along at the statutory five miles an hour, by a railway official on foot. At the party, the dragon gives the toast: 'May the garland of friendship ever be green!' and I meant this from my heart. It is what the book is really about. I don't care that children will read it simply for the dragon's adventures. At the end, the dragon sails away to Cornwall, the grey African parrot he has acquired perched upon his shoulder, while the Weymouth Silver Band plays his favourite tune, 'Tipperary', on the end of the pier. A farewell to Weymouth and its associations.

---

* George and the dragon – was there some unconscious link that made me choose the name George for myself as anti-hero?

I should have sold my Weymouth house then, or even earlier when Jan left me, but I did not have the strength of mind. She and I had found it together and it became part of our joint lives. Jan had childhood memories of Weymouth as I did and the house on the harbour encapsulated our unshared past with our shared present. The late evening walk down the quayside past the lifeboat house and the little dry dock, under the dark, tree-shadowed Nothe fortress, and then out into the wind along the stone pier, with its winking light at the end . . . the town stretching in an arc round the bay, and behind us the black, brooding shape of Portland . . . yes, I should have sold it as soon as she left me. It took me five years to do this and to sink in the harbour water certain small objects – talismans, if you like – that Jan and I had collected. I am glad that they and the house are gone for good. All that was valuable in the memory of Weymouth remains, built into me and I hope into Jan.

I have gone forward in time nearly twenty years and must return to 1962. In the two or three months before that April when I attempted suicide, I had been obsessed with the dichotomy between life and art. In my own case this was represented by the apparent impossibility of reconciling the demands of love with the ruthless pressures of my writing. I wrote about 45,000 words of a novel called *The Man with a Wound*, a kind of reworking of the legend of Philoctetes, whose wound stank so abominably that his Greek companions abandoned him on an island and sailed on for Troy. Thus did I see the artist. I identified with a male writer, having no confidence in presenting myself in my true light. To me the creative gift was a stinking wound making us all unfit for society. I also wrote during 1961 a serious children's historical novel called *Arripay*. Its theme was the making of a crucial choice. The inferences to be drawn from these two books are obvious. *The Man with a Wound* later became *Man on a Tower* (Jonathan Cape, 1965), and was an exploration into the springs of creativity as much as an expression of the split in an artist's personality, and the solipsism which so often brings his private life to grief. I was more than a little influenced by Thomas Mann's *Doctor Faustus* that year and saw the artist as compelled to make a pact with the devil in which the price paid was personal happiness.

I took this half-finished novel with me when I set out for the place I had chosen for my suicide attempt. The manuscript was in the car when I was found. On it I had scribbled with dramatic desperation: 'Destroy this. It's no good.' But when I recovered sufficiently, I took it up again and gave it a new beginning. I prefaced it with the words of Delacroix: 'Bitter reflections on the profession of artist . . . the isolation . . . the sacrifice of nearly all the feelings that inspire ordinary men.' It says it all so clearly, it seems almost superfluous of me to have written the novel.

The central character was a failed cartoonist, George. He had reached an impasse, as I had. Love and his creative talent had failed him at the same time. In fact, my writing was not really failing me but I evidently considered it lost for ever when I wrote 'Destroy this' on the manuscript. I did not feel free to write as a woman, and George was an unkind – a very unkind self-portrait. I pulled the book together and finished it, but it took me some months for rehabilitation was slow. Despite its gloomy theme, it is in fact a book full of humour and irony, and I am going to quote a passage from it. George has gone to East Anglia alone, and found a ruinous water-tower in which he intends to live. He needs a small sum for its purchase, and gets it from a pawnbroker.

I knew this pawnbroker very well. The firm is an old one. Faustus was acquainted with it and it had a flourishing branch at Loudoun. The senior partner was to me what their bank managers and doctors are to so many people, a friend and confidant, an adviser on personal as well as business matters. He knew my needs almost before I stated them. I had parted with a good deal, one way and another, over his smooth counter. My painting equipment had recently been handed in there, and something else, something which I had come to regard as of supreme importance to me, had in the last few weeks been exchanged for a pawn ticket. This was no less than my own identity, an identity acquired and treasured. Why then had I put it in pawn? Because it had no further relevance. It was one of those objects which men dispose of in a pawnbroker's shop without much hope of ever redeeming them. The friendly senior partner of the firm was delighted with it, wrote out its ticket personally, and made a detailed entry about it in the ledger. I could just read, upside down, the last few words of his entry: 'for an indefinite period'.

'An artist,' he said, leaning confidentially across the counter, 'an artist has no identity. In the last seven years, I thought you came dangerously near to acquiring one, George, and I'm glad to find that you have decided to abandon it. I shall hope to see you painting again soon. The stuff's all here, you know, when you are ready to claim it. I wouldn't dispose of it.'

A little later, George visits the pawnbroker again, after losing his job as a newspaper cartoonist.

'So you've lost your job as well?' sighed the senior partner. 'I can't draw cartoons any longer,' I said. 'I don't want to be a satirist. I've no illusions left, no values, no aspirations, no standards. Truth, love, self-knowledge – the things I've pursued all my life, all are empty.' (One can always talk in this vein to the senior partner.) 'The pursuit was in vain. I am merely existing.'

'There's plenty of good fish in the sea,' carolled the senior partner.

'Liar!' I shouted. 'You know damn well you've taken into pawn with everything else the one and only thing that would enable me to subscribe to your trite opinion – hope.'

'Such a circumscribed hope, it wasn't worth having,' said the pawnbroker. 'As it is, I've given you a sum far beyond its value. You know well enough what I mean by fish in the sea. Find a nice girl to sleep with and cook your meals, while you get on with your painting.'

'I prefer what I've had for the last seven years.'

'If I had sat about in a lake of mental pitch, pining for what I'd had for several aeons, I'd never be where I am now,' said the pawnbroker, complacently. 'If you were able to buy back from me this identity that was so unbecoming to you, you think that your illusions about truth, love and self-knowledge would return to you, I suppose?'

'I suppose they would.'

'And how would you earn your living, may one ask? Could you get another job as a cartoonist – now, at your age?'

'I could teach art to little girls,' I said, darkly.

'A very dangerous occupation for one of your propensities, bearing in mind your past record,' observed the senior partner.

'I shan't have any propensities left soon,' I rejoined angrily.

The full account of my suicide attempt and my setting out upon a survival course afterwards is contained in the book I wrote concurrently with *Man on a Tower*, the autobiography *A Time and a Time*, of which I have already said something. In the forefront of my mind was a conviction that I must make another attempt, and that my survival course was only of a temporary nature, a crawl along a road, counting the telegraph poles as I went, like poor Fanny Robin in *Far from the Madding Crowd*. I gave myself two and a half years: 'a time and a time and half a time.'

But I did not make the second attempt. My life took a new direction when I met Kay, as recounted in the last section of *A Time and a Time*. This book has been praised for its honesty but it was not all that honest. Much was omitted from it. Details were altered or obfuscated. I am not perturbed, still less ashamed about this. I was creating a semi-fictional autobiography and a selective one. It was honest as a work of art. As for the omissions, they were absolutely justified, for to have included more than I did would have detracted from the main themes: suicide, how and why I had attempted it; an account of the love affair that led up to it; the long haul back to life.

Kay and I parted soon after I had finished the manuscript of *A Time and a Time*. As I typed the final version I knew that I could never allow it to be published under my own name, because of my position of headmistress. When I sent it to Tom Maschler at Jonathan Cape, I told him that the subject matter, lesbianism and suicide, made this impossible. Tom liked the book and offered to publish it, but only if I used my own name. He had brought out *Man on a Tower* in 1965. It was now a year later. He gave me the alternative of publishing the autobiography as Rosemary Manning or rewriting it as a novel if I still felt the former impossible. But I could not accept either alternative and he reluctantly handed it back to me.

It should be clear that with three novels now published one after the other by a publishing house of the quality of Jonathan Cape, and all three receiving good notices, this autobiography should have been the next book to come out, probably in 1967 or 1968. Continuity is important for an author. But I was still a headmistress. To be a lesbian and a teacher is a near fatal combination even today. In the end, in 1971, Marion Boyars published *A Time and a Time* under the pseudonym, Sarah Davys.

The failure to persuade Tom Maschler to publish the book under a pseudonym put me under great pressure to publish and be damned but here I faced implacable opposition from my partner Andrea. She even threatened to take out an injunction against my using my own name. I don't know whether in fact this would have been possible but I bowed to the threat. Life at home was almost intolerable, and had been so since my suicide attempt. Andrea felt shocked by this, naturally, but she also, I think, felt revulsion. I took a long time to recover and she was unwilling to do anything for me. When I started work again it was in an atmosphere of hostility, aggravated by my affair with Kay.

A Time and a Time appeared in the year of Andrea's death, 1971. It was the only adult book of mine published between 1965 and 1983. In the latter year, Cape published a new novel, *Open the Door*, but I was bitterly conscious that my first three books were out of print and that as far as the public and the reviewers were concerned, I had been silent for just on twenty years. It was true that I had written more children's books but this was a different field altogether, and many of those who know me by these, even today, are surprised to learn that I write adult fiction.

It was shortly after *A Time and a Time* was published under the pseudonym Sarah Davys that I came to know rather better one of the school parents. I will call her Liz Halford and we were brought together through a strange and somewhat unnerving episode. She was standing in the hall before lunch, waiting for her younger daughter, then in the kindergarten. I came down from my room and said, 'Good morning.'

Without even drawing me aside, she said quietly but clearly: 'I must tell you, Miss Manning, that I've greatly enjoyed and admired your recent book.'

There was a moment's silence. Other mothers were too busy to notice what she was saying, but I must have looked stunned. My recent book? My last novel had been published in 1965. At last I said: 'What book do you mean?'

'Your autobiographical one,' she replied calmly. '*A Time and a Time*.'

I drew a deep breath. 'I think you'd better come up to my room and have a sherry,' I said. She did and it was the start of our friendship.

She refused to tell me how she knew that I was the author, but I suspect that the other parents whom I referred to as friends had told her, for they were friends of hers, and the wife was a writer and probably heard who Sarah Davys was on the publishing grapevine.

You may well ask what stopped me from going on to write another novel in the sixties. Am I making an undue fuss about having to use a pseudonym? But things are not as simple as this. In the first place, I had thought that as long as Cape was willing to publish *A Time and a Time* under the pseudonym, it could be revealed unofficially that the book was by Rosemary Manning. This was ridiculously naïve of me.

Its comparative failure when it eventually did appear in 1971 was a severe blow to me for it seemed to me an original and unusual book. The few notices it received were good, but there were too few to put the book on the map. There was not that element of scandal that there might have been had I been already well known as a writer. And there were other problems.

The necessity to keep silent in public about being gay put a strain on me that young gays today have no conception of. And I was older. The strains were beginning to tell. They had been going on too long. I was finding that I wrote far more slowly. I did in fact write one fiercely concentrated book, a novella called *The Patriot*, but Tom Maschler was unwilling to publish it, for it was so short. This prejudice against novellas (unless written by a well-known writer) is something that I find difficult to accept. The book is still unpublished though it must be one of the best things I have ever written.

I worked my way through this period by turning again to work. Though *The Patriot* was written with an intensity that kept thoughts at bay for the most part, Elizabeth still intruded on my mind and heart, and I made the disastrous mistake of seeing her on two or three occasions. And I looked back and remembered that, only a year before, Kay and I were getting ourselves ready to go to France and how good much of that month abroad had been. I respected her for never trying to get in contact with me again, but I could not respect myself for the painful and still romantic longings for Elizabeth that broke into my thoughts.

Other troubles crowded upon me. In 1971 my partner Andrea suddenly fell seriously ill and died after ten days in hospital; I have written in an earlier chapter about my feelings when this happened. Here I will only say that I grasped the opportunity to get out of teaching, but this again was no simple matter. Andrea and I had owned the school jointly. It consisted of two buildings, standing in nearly an acre of land. Just before she died, we had bought the freeholds and I therefore entered into negotiations with the *ad hoc* parents' committee, to sell them the school. I ran into tedious and exhausting business problems over this, time-consuming and mentally harassing. They went on moreover for at least two years. During this period I continued to write with a kind of desperation and produced two novels, but neither were really satisfactory. There was no return to the marvellous creativity of the fifties, until I put these two manuscripts behind me and at last embarked on two new books. These were the novel *Open the*

Door, written 1980–82, and the fourth dragon book, written a little earlier than this and published in 1980.

Many a time I have sat alone here at my refectory table in my Dorset home and asked myself: Why the hell do I write? I do not need the money now. Why do I not live altogether in London and exploit the social round? Why do I not travel? Collect *objets d'art*? Join a movement? Take up golf? Make myself an expert on wine, or first editions or Gothic carvings? I don't know why I list those particular alternatives for really I care for none of them, though I do know something of Gothic and Romanesque art. But I am not an expert nor do I wish to be. Not now. I used to wish this, and indeed longed to be fanatically dedicated to some interest. But I prefer to be a jack of all trades. As far as the mediaeval carvings go, I gave lectures on the subject, as I have said, but I was a pure populariser. I have not the dedication nor the technical ability of a scholar. It must be very absorbing, but where does one kennel the imagination while one is delving into learned volumes at the London Library?

The itch to share my enthusiasms comes out in my writing, but it takes a far lower place than the imaginative faculty that creates a novel or the desire to discover myself and lay out the results on paper as though I were a mapmaker, perpetually correcting and checking measurements and alignments as I go on. There are others who write like this and I am not claiming to be unique. There are, however, far more in my belief who write in quite other ways. I quarry myself partly because I am not, alas, a storyteller in the great old tradition as many admirable authors are. I only wish I were. I have had to use the gift I have. I sometimes think that it is a misfortune that my gift has been for words rather than paint or music.

Words are awkward customers. Intractable creatures. A word is a word is a word, Gertrude Stein might have said, and perhaps did. 'What I have written I have written,' declared Pilate and look what that has led to. Dictators are naturally addicted to words and use far too many of them. A kind of verbal diarrhoea. They love them for their double meanings and their capacity to convey specious lies. Can Bach's music lie? Or Picasso's pencil line? Or Turner's brush? But I know that I have used words to conceal or obfuscate and it would be pretentious and dishonest of me to deny it. And this despite my intention to tell my own truth clearly, for I regard this as the commission laid upon every artist. Although I recognise that it is possible to be sentimental, meretricious and even downright dishonest in painting or in music – do I have to spell this out? – I still maintain that it is the writer who falls into these traps more easily, more willingly, I fear, than any other kind of artist. I am trying to make a statement and not finding it easy because I so fear pretentiousness. Or really, what I fear is to be *accused* of pretentiousness.

There are painters and musicians who feel the urge to expatiate on their work, to explain themselves, harassed no doubt by the misinterpretations and superficial judgments of their critics. At the 1985 exhibition of Marc Chagall's painting, quotations from his written works appeared among the pictures. One ran something like this: 'To love all the world, that is the important thing.' Literary critics would have sneered and dubbed it naïve and simplistic. 'Simplistic' is used pejoratively, but truth is often simple. None the less it is difficult to write with that pure simplicity that makes Blake one of the greatest poets in the world. Instead of making my own statement of belief, I wrap it up in an obscure reference to 'Pellam's land' and grasp David Jones' hand while I make it. I have painted myself into a corner and now, to get out of it, I'll write my convictions on the wall: the artist is the guardian of creaturely love, of the freedom of spirit, and if he does indeed stand alone in Pellam's land, it is against cruelty, intolerance and the destruction of civilisation that he or she stands like a post in the waste of waters. As I have learned from the feminists, the personal is the political.

Despite my occasional wish that I had been a painter, I accept that for better or worse words are my medium. And just because words are common coin, I know that the writer must strive the more to make her words give out that individual bell-like tone whereby is conveyed the image or idea within her mind. And I know that I love words. I accept their intractability, their erosion by overuse. That is my problem and the writer's problem generally. I have no doubt that were I a painter or composer I should find myself facing the same challenge.

Do I love writing? I am sometimes asked. Do I even enjoy it? The words are irrelevant. Writing is my lifeline and it is a support and encouragement to me to discover that in this if nothing else I can claim kinship with many other writers, with Kafka and Virginia Woolf in particular. Of Kafka Erich Heller wrote, referring to writing being used as a survival course: 'This is a disposition akin to madness, separated only from it by a writing table, an imagination capable of holding together what appears to have an irresistible tendency to fall apart, and an intelligence of supreme integrity.' He might equally well be writing of Virginia Woolf, who said in a letter to Vita Sackville-West – and there are many similar statements throughout her diaries: 'What one imagines, in a novel, is a world. Then, when one has imagined this world, suddenly people come in – but I don't know why one does it, or why it should alleviate the misery of life, and yet not make one exactly happy; for the strain is too great. Oh, to have done it, and be free.' (3 February 1926)

I think the children's books gave me more pleasure in the writing than my books for adults. But then I pause to think for a moment and I know that I have experienced pure ecstasy as I am working on a novel. The words flow from my pen – I always write by hand – and it brings a joy like nothing else in life. But the argument that I threaded into *Man on a Tower* still seems to me valid. The artist in any field pays a price.

Perhaps I shall pay a price for writing as openly as I have about my work in these last chapters. Some may think that it takes courage to claim oneself a lesbian and to describe one's attitudes to sexuality and love. This depends on time and circumstances. In the 1950s, feeling myself like a lone patrol in no man's land, creeping across a mine-strewn battlefield, I did not have the courage to stand up under the searchlights. Today, I make a simple assumption: that those who meet me or read my work think no more of my sexual predilection than they would if I were heterosexual. Those who find it distasteful, or immoral, or more likely are made uncomfortable, even frightened by it, can leave me and my books alone, can they not? And deprive themselves thereby of an opportunity to widen their obviously narrow horizons.

I need far more courage to 'come out' as a writer who honours inspiration and whose literary tastes may be what some will consider élitist. Why do I share these private things with you, the reader? Partly because communication is my trade, but more importantly, because they are the essence of me. I do not go about thinking of my sexual orientation. I *do* conduct my life and work with constant reference to the books I read and that I allow gladly to influence and inspire me, provoke and stimulate my mind.

I was once talking to some London primary school children about my 'dragon' books. I never make a long speech, but after talking for six or seven minutes I invite the children to ask me questions. Many are what you might expect – 'How long does it take you to write a book?' and 'How much d'you get paid for it?' Every now and again I get asked something out of the ordinary, as when an East End boy of about ten grilled me about my upbringing, education, interests, children (if any), political attitudes. That boy must be working in Fleet Street by now. But the question I want to quote here came from a nine- or ten-year-old girl, and it was unusual and percipient, I thought.

'I say, miss, d'you ever get your ideas from other people's books?'

'Yes, I do,' I answered. 'Do *you* like writing stories?'

'Oh, yes, miss.'

'Well, then,' I said, 'go ahead and write and don't be afraid to get ideas from stories or magazines, or maybe from the telly.'

I fear and hate the indifference I sometimes meet to what matters so deeply to me in books and music, far more than any scorn, derision or avoidance of me because I am a lesbian.

I must include in this chapter my belief that form and style develop out of the content of a book, at least of the books that I myself write. The pressure of the subject matter, however subtle and unperceived, is insistent for me, and brings about the shaping of the material and the definition within which the story has its life. This is why my four novels are so different from each other. A friend once advised me to write in a more uniform style if I wanted popular success. 'Your readers like to know what to expect,' he said, sagely. 'They are disconcerted by the unexpected differences in Manning novels.' I don't really believe this and in any case it is alien to me. Arising from this subject is a statement that I feel compelled to make: I regard my novels almost as extended poems, or meditations upon their themes.

This brings me to one of the most important ingredients in the material I use: memory. Writing for me involves a continual transmutation of what is observed and felt and thought. Those processes existed in the past and therefore may require a double transmutation. First, the material is spun through the web of memory, and later, craftsmanship, the conscious working upon it, brings it upon the page. The material may be something I have read that, sinking into my mind, sets in motion the waiting imagination. As an example of this, I shall describe at the end of this chapter how a single paragraph inspired my last novel, *Open the Door*, a paragraph that had rested in a corner of my mind for over twenty years.

If one had total recall, one would produce something more like a series of photographs than pictures, and this is what some readers expect and like when they read memoirs, a kind of verbal album of coloured prints. It is not what I am trying to create. My materials are often inadequate, maddeningly so at times: scraps of conversations, old humiliations, half-remembered joys, tiny ineradicable wounds, unresolved disappointments, unaccepted losses, brilliant flashes of pleasure, even of ecstasy. From these shards lying about on the floor of memory a construction can be made, a meaning deduced, sometimes household gods recovered and replaced on the shelf above one's head to inspire and give protection. The use of memory implies a risk, but artists must be risk-takers and, with a mixture of arrogance and humility, will open the door for you upon what they have found or recovered.

A question about my writing which I have often been asked is this: Did the habit of secrecy about your lesbianism affect your writing? Was it a strain for you that you were forced to depict characters who were really gay as heterosexuals? No, it was not. The questions are based on a misconception about the power of imagination. It is not necessary to write about gays because you are gay yourself, any more than you would feel compelled to write about hunchbacks because you were so deformed. I am quite simply interested in people and their motives, and the circumstances that make them what they are; I feel passionately about certain moral issues; I am on a perpetual voyage of discovery about myself – I think that these three themes cannot be put in any order of priority. They coexist.

Whatever my feelings about patriarchy, I do not envisage a world without men, and feminist writers of more extreme opinions resort to fantasy, I notice, or thrust any male characters in their novels well out on the sidelines. I admire some feminist imaginative writing, but I don't feel that this is what I either am able or want to write. Men are not all the same. Of the three male characters in my 1983 novel, *Open the Door*, I loved the elderly alcoholic, Ralph, and tried to analyse with tenderness why he was as he was. The young climber, Alan, was odious and was obviously going to grow more odious with time. The central figure, Hubert, was a realistic study, I hope, of a man with thoroughly patriarchal attitudes. When I created the characters of the two women, Gwyneth and Meg, part of the *raison d'être* of the novel was to show how they reacted to the men and their attitudes.

Why should it be impossible for a writer to make the imaginative leap, and write of someone of the opposite sex from the inside? Many writers have done so. John Cowper Powys' women are extraordinarily true *as women* and he is on record as saying that he at times felt himself a woman as he was writing of them. A modern American novelist whom I would place in the top rank is May Sarton, whose novels are at last becoming better known in England. One of her finest is *Crucial Conversations*, a study of a marriage breaking down. There are really only three characters: the husband and wife, and the bachelor friend who has in a way battened on the marriage, lived vicariously upon it. He is a most convincing, subtly realised character. Here is a woman and an avowed lesbian writing with total success about two men and a woman and their relationships.

A more interesting question is this: Should we have been better writers, we who wrote twenty-five or more years ago when we were forced into secrecy – should we really have written *better* if we could have come out in the open and written our books from a lesbian angle? I don't think that this is necessarily so, though my own experience over *A Time and a Time* shows clearly enough the damage that an enforced secrecy can do to a writer and her/his career. Economic necessity and the grinding exigencies of motherhood, wifehood, eating up time and energy, have silenced more women, I believe, than their sexual predilections. And there are gay writers who are not explicit about these matters but who are none the less major writers. I will cite one example: the American writer, Willa Cather, who as far as I know never wrote overtly about or from the standpoint of a lesbian.

Willa Cather has inspired a long and fine poem from the feminist-lesbian poet, Adrienne Rich. In a collection called *A Wild Impatience Has Carried Me This Far*, she writes a letter-poem to a friend, Julia, in Nebraska. At the outset she quotes some words set up on a marker board by the Historical Landmark Council near Red Cloud, Nebraska: THIS IS OFTEN CALLED CATHER COUNTRY.

On this beautiful, ever-changing land –
    The historical marker says –
Man fought to establish a home
    (fought whom? the marker is mute)
They named this Catherland, for Willa Cather,
lesbian – the marker is mute,
the marker white men set on a soil
of broken treaties, Indian blood,
women wiped out in childbirths, massacres –
for Willa Cather, lesbian,
whose letters were burnt in shame.

Dear Julia, Willa knew at her death
that the very air was changing
that her Archbishop's skies
would hardly survive his life
she knew as well that history
is neither your script nor mine
it is the pictograph
from which the young must learn
like Tom Outland, from people
discredited or dead . . .

And Willa who could not tell
her own story as it was
left us her stern and delicate
respect for the lives she loved –
how are we going to do better?

This seems to me a cardinal point: are we going to do better, now that we are free to say what we like in sexual matters, and this goes for heterosexuals as well as gays? The answer cannot be other than: No.

I do not believe that my last novel, *Open the Door*, is in any way better than my first three, written when I was a 'closet' lesbian and therefore did not have the freedom I had when I came to write *Open the Door* twenty years later. If the sexual material has to be seriously distorted because of prejudice and false social *mores*, then it must be the readers who lose out if anyone does. They lose the chance to have their perspectives and experience widened. But I am not eager to be dogmatic even about this.

In *Open the Door* I used a cast of five characters. One of these is a lesbian, but she is only one of five characters. The conception of this novel goes back to 1951. I was then rereading the Welsh tales collected together by Charlotte Guest under the title *The Mabinogion*. Again I was fascinated by the tale of the Blessed Bran and its ending. Bran was killed in Ireland on a war expedition, and commanded his followers to cut off his head and carry it back to London and bury it under the White Tower. He told them that throughout their long journey, the head would converse with them as merrily as it had done in life. They were only warned that they must never open the door that looked out upon Aber Henfelen. Once they did, they would have no further cheer, but would be conscious of every loss they had ever sustained, every kinsman they had missed, and every ill that had befallen them.

After copying this last paragraph of the tale into my diary, I wrote after it: 'What a title for a novel: Open the Door.' The idea remained in my mind for nearly thirty years, for not until 1979 did I begin to write this novel. The paragraph had surfaced several times but I had not found the theme I wanted. When Jan left me it crystallised at last. It is a book about the different losses suffered by a group of five people working on an archaeological site in Wales. I tried to explore the ways in which these men and women had coped with the losses they had experienced in their lives. If I put my own pain into the character of the lesbian Gwyneth, she is not a self-portrait, and the circumstances of her loss are invented. This is, with my first novel, *Look, Stranger*, the least autobiographical of my books. In both, my imagination worked strongly for me and I distanced myself from the tale I was telling. Both books also engaged me in problems of craftsmanship, which I enjoy.

In *Open the Door*, pain became for me 'profitable loss', or so I hoped. And that phrase takes me back to the poet Rilke. I used to think he wrote those words himself, but in fact he did not. He was influenced by some sonnets he read, telling of the love of a woman, Stampa, for her false lover, Collatino. One of the sonnets contains these words: 'Why, prompt in my own losses, do I beg love to disburden me from such profitable loss?' The comment I made in my diary was this: 'A theme for a novel.' That was in 1953, when the two happiest love affairs of my life were still to come. I used the words to good purpose eventually in both *Man on a Tower* and *A Time and a Time*, both of them books in which I attempted to turn loss to gain.

When I came to write *Open the Door* I did not need to use them, for I was attempting, with fair success, to deal with my loss in other ways. None the less, I think Rilke's obsession with them, and my own, is justified. The words inspired the Ninth Duino Elegy, which has been so major an influence upon me ever since I first read it in my forties that it seems fitting that lines from it should end these two chapters on my writing life. These lines are very close to David Jones' statement that the artist stands alone in Pellam's land, guarding the *signa*.

> *Here* is the time for the Tellable, *here* is its home.
> Speak and proclaim. More than ever
> things we can live with are falling away, for that
> which is oustingly taking their place is an imageless act . . .

Praise this world to the Angel, not the untellable: you
can't impress him with the splendour you've felt; in the
cosmos
where he more feelingly feels you're only a novice. So
                                                show him
some simple thing, refashioned by age after age,
till it lives in our hands and eyes as a part of ourselves.
Tell him *things*. He'll stand more astonished: as you did
beside the roper in Rome or the potter in Egypt . . .

                            These things that live on departure
understand when you praise them: fleeting, they look for
rescue through something in us, the most fleeting of all.
Want us to change them entirely, within our invisible
                                                hearts,
into – oh, endlessly – into ourselves! Whosoever we are.

16
Fain Would I Change That Note

This circular room in which I stand holds more than the reflections of my writing life. What I have written has always been to a greater or lesser degree autobiographical, for that is the type of writer I am. I quarry myself, as the last chapter will have made clear. The pursuit of love which led me to Elizabeth was inextricably bound up with the creativity of my forties and early fifties, as was my affair with Kay, for this occurred when I was just finishing *A Time and a Time*.

Life does not offer the same experience twice and I did not set out on a deliberate search for love again when I parted from Elizabeth. It came to me unexpectedly just as my affair with Kay was ending, during a winter when I spent many evenings with Jan, an artist who was illustrating a book for me. We fell deeply in love with each other as the winter wore on, though we did not acknowledge it for many months. Thomas Hardy wrote that love was lame at fifty years, but for me this flowering came when I was nearly sixty. After a few years Jan came to live with me. This was in 1971, soon after my partner Andrea had died. Jan shared the flat we created for five years.

So far I have only mentioned her briefly. I must say more here, though I find myself unable to give a full account of our love affair, which lasted for nearly ten years. I can only say that much of what I shall write subsequently on the subject of love, sex and sensuality springs from the experience of loving Jan, the only lover with whom I have shared a home and with whom I have explored the widest spectrum of love I have ever known. Close friends said to me when they first met her: 'Jan is the best thing that's ever happened to you.' This remains true and its opposite is also true: that the loss of her was the worst thing that ever happened to me.

Jan was many years younger than myself. I was her first lover. But if I awakened her and released her into sexual love, she on her part enriched it for me by her own marvellous warmth, her lovable sensuality. On her side, she told me more than once that I was a fire at which she warmed her hands. It is a statement that I cannot forget easily.

By the time that I met her I was, in some ways at least, far more mature than I had been when my affair with Elizabeth began. But I was more of a depressive than I had been earlier. As well as the failure of my affair with Kay, I was no longer successful in getting my books published. When *A Time and a Time* eventually appeared in 1971, it was not under my own name. It made little impact, which disappointed me bitterly. My writing was now an engagement with a long novel which went through revision after revision and was never really completed. This central failure, which was comparable to a writer's block, made me unhappy and too often reduced me to a depressed state which must have been extremely hard for Jan to live with. It is something that only the depressive can deal with herself and, in common with some other things like jealousy and ill-health, it is all too easy to use depression as a weapon and no doubt I did this. Like an unlovely squid, it sends out such a poisonous cloud that the depressive loses any ability to see clearly either herself or her behaviour.

I had not recovered, moreover, from my attempted suicide nor from the bitter experience of losing Elizabeth. Since I have written of this in depth in *A Time and a Time*, and many people will not have read this, I make no apology for quoting a short passage from the book. It sums up a deep fault in me that affected my relationship with Jan. It did not destroy it, though it came perilously near it and must have contributed to her final decision to leave me. Yet I have to say that despite my depressions and hang-ups over my past, we survived for many years. Our love for each other was not shallowly rooted.

Writing of my suicide attempt at the very beginning of the book, I said: 'I see it as a massive blow of waves upon a headland. Half the cliff face has fallen into the sea. Old strata are revealed. I see myself and my past far more clearly than I did before. I see the mounting wave, the moment of impact when circumstances suddenly rose up like a wall of water, engulfed me and tore away a major part of my life.' The indulgence in metaphor disguised something more than my near-death. It dramatically obscured the fact that a cliff, whether ravaged in this picturesque manner or not, is *static*. I should have been nearer the truth if I had used a metaphor for paralysis. Jan – I do not blame her – found it difficult, sometimes impossible to cope with my inability to free myself from my past. I can say little by way of excuse. Happy though I was with her, I was still clinging to the wreckage. I had failed to heal myself and I demanded too much of Jan in asking her – even if unconsciously at the time – to help me to rebuild my fractured life.

Despite this, and despite tensions for both of us due to outside circumstances and the difficulties inherent in two rather disparate characters sharing a home, the years with Jan were good years and they remain for me, at least, more meaningful and rewarding than any other years of my life. Love was renewed each day in the common commitment to building a life together, made up of those small essentials: eating and drinking together, the quick phone call often to say no more than: 'I love you – I miss you', the return from work, a visit to a pub, perhaps, reading, talking, listening to music, the shared night. So fluent when I talked to her, when I wrote letters to her, I now find myself unable to put on paper all I felt for Jan. Sometimes I meet with words coined by some other writer and immediately recognise in them a reflection of my own experience. The American poet, Marge Piercy, puts into verse feelings of my own that I have not been able to express:

> Love is our minds stretching out webs
> of thought and wonder and argument slung
> across the flesh or the wires of distance,
> Love is the name I call you.

(from *Stone, Paper, Knife*)

That says it all.

I leave my relationship with Jan to reflect more generally upon my attitude to sexual love. As I've already said, these thoughts are closely linked up with the experience of loving her but their roots go far back into my childhood, as all people's must.

Bed is the ultimate intimacy. The private and exclusive world. This particular locale of love returns us in a sense to those long nights of childhood spent beneath the blankets in a warm darkness, sometimes mysterious, occasionally terror-ridden, but essentially consoling and protective. Those hours also gave us the privacy we are so seldom allowed when we are young. Bed was a place for secrets, for the fiercely guarded notebook or diary, for the forbidden book or the cherished but outgrown toy. It is not surprising that there often grows up between some lovers a childlike, funny, even esoteric 'little language', intimate jokes, disguises, masks, a kind of raree show between the sheets. It is only embarrassing or even, to some, shameful when it is brought to light. Swift's baby-language to Stella: alas, that it could not have been confined to a blessed warmth beneath blankets, but there was no such privacy for Swift and it's exposed for all to see on harsh sheets of franked notepaper.

Within everyday living there exists for lovers the central, sexual core, private to them yet common to all in its manifestations. Sexual love runs the gamut from childish play to erotic fantasy. Rather as we are said to travel in the womb through the history of the race from amoeba to sentient, intelligent human being, so in bed lovers move through the years of growth from childhood to maturity, or we can do so if we want more than a blind coupling.

I have found it difficult to accept some young lesbians' unwillingness to share a house or even a bed with a lover, though I understand their revulsion from the patterns of heterosexual marriage. Sexual patterns have indeed changed since the feminists came upon the scene. And thank heaven for them and for Women's Liberation, giving women the freedom to infuse sex with erotic pleasure. Being 'in love' is, however, a phrase that some lesbians reject wholly. I want it as a preliminary to erotic pleasure. I need sex to be part of a total emotional involvement. It is my personal view and may seem old-fashioned or mistaken to some women. For me, it diminishes the sexual act to isolate it from the delicate, pleasurable and sometimes indelicate and orgiastic preliminaries that within a shared bed pervade the experience of sleeping together in the practical sense.

Again, Marge Piercy captures exactly this aspect of love, an aspect which I missed far more than sex when Jan left me and still miss today.

> but love cherishes the back pockets,
> the pencil ends of childhood fears,
> the nose-picking and throbbing sweet tooth,
> the silly hardworking toes that curl
> now blamelessly as dwarf cats
> in the warm covers of the sweet
> tousled nest of mutual morning bed.

(from *Stone, Paper, Knife*)

The enjoyment of a lover's body, the celebration of it, lies at the heart of physical love-making. The exploration of it can be repeated endlessly (one of the rare things in life that does bear repetition) and is for ever an America, a new-found land. It is a tactile joy that moves outwards from private pleasure to public, to walking hand in hand, an arm round a shoulder, sharing a wine glass, a plate of food.

All this we had, yet Jan left me. In my third novel, *Man on a Tower*, I had portrayed myself in the anti-hero, George, a man who had reached an impasse, who had given his whole commitment neither to love nor art. In another major character in the book, Mrs Bogue, I delineated a woman whose love for George contains an unexpressed question: What have *you* got to give? That question I did not ask myself and George never answered Mrs Bogue. Though the novel was written before I ever met Jan, there was in it an element of the prophetic: flawed as I was, I never gave Jan the commitment that she sought and needed. It cost me dear.

There is an element of love which I am unwilling to omit, yet it involves a minor writer like myself in a dilemma, one in which I know I have placed myself more than once in this book. Now I have decided to take it by the horns. The dilemma is this: the little-known artist who arrogates to herself ideas, feelings, interpretations and so forth that are readily accepted if they emanate from someone established and famous, can all too easily arouse derision, even condemnation for venturing into this field, no matter how seriously she regards her work. I have decided to risk that danger and to end this chapter on love by illustrating the part played by a passion for a specific person, not as the subject matter of a book, but as inspiration.

It is difficult to deal with this aspect of love, for 'inspiration' is itself derided by many writers and critics. It is also intensely personal, so personal indeed that it would be almost impossible, I think, to analyse it at the time of writing. Indeed, one is almost always unaware of it. One can only look back and say, without even any certainty: But for the love I felt for A or B I should not have written that book. And it is undeniable that A or B need be in no way remarkable, beautiful, or even worthy of one's passion.

This aspect of love is rarely charted except in diaries and letters. The work inspired need bear no specific allusions to the beloved, not even a dedication. This is where I envy the painter and the composer, for words can become clumsy about what inspires them, except in poetry, perhaps. Music and painting can both pay tribute to the muse and at the same time leave her elevated to an airy distance where she can hover unrealised in flesh and blood. One can hardly interrupt a novel with footnotes about the personal source from which a particular paragraph or chapter has arisen. The whole matter of 'inspiration' has a fascination for me. I would like to illustrate it. Few works of art pay tribute to their muse so openly as Janáček's second quartet, entitled 'Intimate Letters'. As he was composing it, he gave the woman he loved an almost daily account of his devotion, his frustration, pent-up anger, desire, his bursts of happiness when he knew with absolute certainty that some phrase expressed all that he felt in his heart, his misery when he recognised that his passion was not reciprocated and was certainly doomed to unfulfilment. Yet this beauty, Kamila, could hardly understand a word of music, was married with children, and forty years younger than Janáček. Though she answered his letters, she was not disposed to break up her marriage for this lover whose torrent of words almost matched his spate of notes. Did it matter to his music that she never became his lover, though his wife was as jealous as though she had been? I suspect that she was far more valuable to him as the inspiration of some of his greatest works than she might have been if his longing for her had found fulfilment in an affair. As Bernard Shaw cruelly remarked in *Man and Superman*: 'Marry Ann; and at the end of a week you'll find no more inspiration in her than in a plate of muffins.'

However bitterly Janáček suffered in his passion for Kamila, he had the fulfilment of eleven years of wonderful creativity that included *Katya Kabanova* and his two quartets. Janáček died suddenly a month before the Moravia Quartet was to give the first performance of 'Intimate Letters' in the presence of its 'onlie begetter'. On the whole, I think, he was fortunate.

I offer these reflections, set off by hearing an intensely passionate performance of this Janáček quartet. And I feel, after it, inspired to expose my own heart and make explicit the personal inspiration behind this autobiography. It has been written under a stress far greater than any other book I have written. *A Time and a Time* was produced rapidly as a personal therapy, I recognise now, to lift me back to life. This book is not so immediate. I have waited long enough for it to be reflective. I have not described in explicit terms my love affair with Jan nor the nature of its end. I can, however, say that this love and its loss inspired this autobiography, inspired even the self-searching and retrospective analysis of my childhood and youth. Janáček's second quartet, has persuaded me to make this statement.

This autobiography, now drawing towards its end, has been written over more than three years, during which my life has been subject to change in an accelerated form, change which began ten years ago when Jan left me. Some of this has been fortuitous, but much has been due to a deliberate shaping of my life, a move outwards towards new ideas, new friends, new relationships, accompanied by a deeper exploration of old loves, old interests, old values. I have quoted the story of Janáček's inspiration because it touched me profoundly. This book has been to a great extent inspired by the loss of Jan, the coming to terms with that loss, and the formation of a new and redemptive relationship with her. The writing has often been done under stress, yet it has also been driven by a strong creative impulse. The book itself is only a part of the result of that impulse, a creativity that has pervaded my life in a far wider sense than the immense productiveness of the ten to twelve years that followed my fortieth birthday.

Jan left me in 1976. Her loss has not been metamorphosed into a novel. I have deliberately used it, instead, as inspiration. Apparently so creative since my childhood, I have neglected to create myself. After Jan left me, I was forced to do just this. The break was complete. No seeing each other. No letters. After the initial shock, I decided that I must live somehow. It was very different from 1962 when Elizabeth had gone out of my life. Then I was isolated. Now I had the warm support of friends. I turned my face in a new direction. Creativity, I believed, had been too confined to the written page. I looked back over much of my life with utter dismay. I realised how much of it had been closed in by circumstances, allowed to run in a groove like a train in a deep cutting.

I saw, too, as I took stock of myself, that for most of my adult life I had sought happiness in another person. After Jan left, I have sought it where it can only be found: in myself. I have not made as good a job of it as I had hoped, but I have not lost faith in the direction. Indeed, it is the only direction. I have tried deliberately to harvest all the experiences, the pleasures in places and activities like theatre-going which can enrich me and that for so long I could only enjoy and value if I shared them. The process should be the other way round: one must accumulate some inner wealth before it can be shared, and then, if one ends up alone, the wealth is still there to draw upon. That, at least, is the blueprint I drew up. It has not always been easy to build from it.

These years have been a voyage of self-discovery, in some ways of *re*discovery, finding again the capacity to enjoy things long forgotten or neglected. And there have been rich and often entirely new deposits in books, people, places, music. Unhappiness – if it has any virtue at all – does open up one's heart to new impressions, new emotions and pleasurable experiences, leading one into realms one hardly knew to exist, providing a bank of perceptions and possibilities. All these I have needed to prevent myself being knocked off course by the loss of Jan, but I find myself at this point in the book unable to give any account of my love for her. And I resist the old temptation to dress it up in metaphor. I know my dangerous tendency to use words as a barrier or throw them into the air before me like a smokescreen. So I strip off the verbiage and write of my response to this loss, a response which rather to my own surprise, did not lead me to attempt my life as I had done when I was fifty.

I look about me at the resources upon which I have drawn, the resources that make up the income on which I have lived for seven years. Music has provided me with much of it. It has always played a large part in my life – in my twenties I thought I should be a composer – but now it took an unexpected turn in a new direction. I began to take part in chamber music.

Thwarted in my desire to learn the viola when I was at the university, I subsequently took up first the clarinet and then the oboe, but my main musical activity was singing, and I foolishly never went back to a stringed instrument until I took up the violin when I was just on sixty. After an unfortunate start, I found a superb teacher who brought my playing up to a standard where it was possible for me to take the second violin parts in quartets, which had been the sole object of learning the instrument. It gave me some of the deepest pleasure in music that I have ever experienced. I came to know 'from the inside' many of Haydn's and Mozart's quartets and some early Beethoven. I was even capable of taking part in that greatest of all chamber works, Schubert's C-major quintet. It was at this point, when my technical shortcomings were all too apparent to me, and when the Rasumovsky quartets and much of Schubert were making demands upon me that I could not meet, that I realised that I could only make further progress by dedicating myself to the violin almost exclusively, as did many of the amateur players I knew. But I was first and foremost a writer. Writing is a discipline. So is learning the violin. There was not room for two major disciplines in my life. I stopped playing and gave away my violin. I have never regretted it. I feel an immense gratitude to the Fates, who brought a remarkable teacher and friend into my life and allowed me to experience chamber music from within the circle, as a player.

The other major resource on which I have drawn is friendship, with the deepening of old friendships and the acquisition of new ones. As for the lifeline that writing throws out to me, that has had its own chapters.

Leaving these on one side, nothing has served me better throughout my life than that permanent inhabitant of my inner self, my sense of humour. For one thing, there is a fundamentally comic element in my character: I make so much effort to stay alive, while proclaiming at every opportunity that I am a pessimist and that death can come for me when he likes. I am not sure that pessimism is an accurate word for my cast of thought, though it certainly describes the attitude I am taking towards world affairs. Scepticism is a better term, implying a residual hope that all may not be lost, that one's worst fears may yet be overturned, and that cheerfulness against all expectations will break through. Humour surfaces in all my novels to a greater or lesser degree. It plays over the pages of *A Time and a Time*, despite the dark circumstances in which that autobiography was written, evidence not only to the reader but also to me that I cannot take myself altogether seriously.

I should not like this book to be glum, so at this point I will pin down a memory that has been hovering in my mind during the last page or so. Suddenly it floats free and robustly interrupts the tenor of my thoughts. Perhaps the paragraph on music set it all going, a reminder that music comprises more than Mozart and Haydn. My head rings with a medley of cheerful, banal tunes, starting with:

> Do – a deer –
>   A female deer,
> Re – a drop of golden sun . . .

And I am back with Jan in the Dominion cinema in Tottenham Court Road, when we went to *The Sound of Music*, the most cliché-ridden film I have ever seen – but here I must interrupt myself to say: *there's* the explanation of its popularity and the abiding popularity of its equivalent in paintings of cosy thatched cottages in gilt frames, and in pulp novels and soap operas. The cliché is not to be despised. It is safe. It engages only the surface of the mind. We don't have to let down the bucket to understand or appreciate it. It demands nothing of the listener, viewer or reader as it slides into their consciousness on oiled wheels. Banalities cushion us against the hard truth, against unpleasant realities, against the unfamiliar or disturbing.

We took with us to *The Sound of Music* a young friend of ours in her late twenties, who insisted on having this as her birthday treat. She wanted to be informed and everyone she knew seemed to have been to it. We rolled in our plush seats with laughter until the tears poured down our heated cheeks. The moment that caused our virtual collapse, unbelievers all of us, was when the Reverend Mother, or someone in a religious habit, stood by a window and sang a meaningful song, the burden of which was, as far as I can recollect, that when God shuts a door he opens a window.

It amuses me that memory, that joker in the pack, should first fill my mind with ennobling thoughts about my survival, about acquiring an 'income for life', etc., etc., and then suddenly thrust into the forefront of my mind the vision of Julie Andrews skipping across flowery meadows and, in another hilarious scene, instructing a row of fat, fair-haired Aryan boys and girls – real little *Herrenvolk* – dressed up in window-curtains, how to sing:

> Do – a deer –
> A female deer . . . *und so weiter.*

Why is the pun so excruciating? What constitutes its banality? And why are clichés so ubiquitous and seductive that even the best writers fall into them at times? *Au fond*, presumably because they require the minimum of thought, they are the reach-me-downs of writing that can be picked off the hook almost without a glance. In this same film there is another song relevant to this theme, so cliché-ridden as to end all clichés: 'Here are a few of my favourite things'. I need not quote it further.

But memory is running free now, and conjures before me one Wilhelmina Stitch, a poetess (I think she deserves that title) very popular in my youth with readers of, as far as I can remember, the *Daily Mirror*, in which she appeared weekly. I have on my shelves – for I collect such trivia – a little volume of hers called *A Triple Stitch*. This sounds like a ring of bells – grandsire triples? – but, alas, is nothing like as mellifluous or inspiring. She wrote quite a number of these slim volumes of poetry, I see from the inside cover of mine: *Joy's Loom*, *Mingled Yarn*, *Homespun*. She evidently ran out of titles inspired by her simple seamstress's surname, so there are others less pertinent to it. *Catching the Gleam*, for instance, and, simply, *Life*. You will readily see that Stitch's poetry is not far removed from the lyrics of *The Sound of Music*. That sunny, window-opening phrase I have quoted may well have been inspired by Wilhelmina, who had a strong odour of sanctity about her.

Here is a list of the poetess's favourite things:

> How many lovely things there be: the ever-changing
> restless sea; the gracious, friendly, shady tree; and
> children laughing in their glee.

Wilhelmina Stitch was very original in the layout of her verses. I would myself substitute 'a really fragrant cup of tea' for the children, etc., but that is a singular taste perhaps.

I am compelled to take a serious look at my own writing and its clichés. Continually in my diaries I write of the western sky in the evening, as I see it, when I sit at the long table across the west-facing window in my Dorset house. I know that I relapse into cliché in my diary at times, if not elsewhere. In a diary I am, of course, writing only for myself, but why do I need these reminders which in any case I rarely reread? I make the hardly original observation that the sky never repeats itself, the shadows of the clouds over the ringed hill a few miles away create an ever-changing pattern. Perhaps I hope that I shall somehow capture in words what I see, words as fresh, unworn and vivid as the sky and cloud patterns themselves. I now begin to doubt the value of this diary activity that has occupied me since 1939. Too readily the words take over. The clouds and sky become dead hieroglyphs on a page. Unrecorded, would they have been lost, these natural pleasures of vision? I do not believe so. But they require a poet's pen.

Ivor Gurney, supreme poet of English skies and a new discovery for me in my seventies, put what he saw into his poetry with the direct clarity and luminousness of a watercolour. The following short poem was written when madness was already pressing upon his brain, madness that was to confuse his words but never his perceptions, nor his love of men and of the Gloucestershire countryside:

> Dawn brings lovely playthings to the mind,
> But sunset flights and goes down in battle blind.
> The banners of dawn spread over in mystery,
> But nightfall ends a boast and a pageantry.

> After the halt of dawn comes the slow moving of
> Time, till the sun's sudden rush and the day is
> > admitted.
> Sunset dies out in a smother of something like love,
> With dew and the elm-hung stars and the owl
> > outcries half-witted

This silences my diary.

Years ago, more than twenty years and shortly after death had nearly claimed me, I built this house in Dorset where I am now writing. It stands above the sprawling village, the spire of the church rising through clusters of roofs and trees, the cottages dwarfed to toy proportions by the distant mass of a solid green hill, a neolithic hillfort, with dark woods lying along the folds of its flank. The shrubs I planted over twenty years ago are, many of them, in flower now, for it's late June. A strong-scented honeysuckle wreathed around an oak post, deep-pink escallonia, purple clematis. Along the terrace a tangle of wild roses. Hibiscus, sturdy and shapely in growth, but not in flower for many weeks yet. Its branches brush the wide window where I am writing. In a couple of months its purple flowers will be host to thousands of bees.

I only arrived here an hour ago and, before I unpacked, I reached for the secateurs and went out to the rosebed. I have battled with the unloving chalk for all these twenty years to grow roses for me, and last year I put in some new ones. How are they doing? I cut some of those that are out and have my first pleasure in them: heavy-scented, strong-stalked, dark-leaved Prima Ballerina, elegant and shapely – the hostess with the mostes'. Precious Platinum – what terrible names they give to some of these roses now, and it's deep-red anyway. It opens out into a huge bloom, dark and richly scented, not unlike that paragon of roses, Josephine Bruce.

Arriving here full of grief, I grasp at these consolations as I have done for so many years. They are my own. All the associations of days and nights spent here with a lover who has gone out of my life must be forced to give way to things that have permanence: the ringed fort, the twenty-year-old honeysuckle that was here before her, the roses. But these new ones will have to come up to scratch in shape, colour and smell. If they don't like the chalk, if they don't please me, I shall root them out. Ruthlessness is not a strong element in my

nature but I should do well to cultivate it. It is a defence against sentimentality. Perhaps even against sentiment.

And now, having unpacked at last, I can put on my shoes and take
my stick and walk for a couple of hours, and before I leave these
flowery consolations, I can laugh at myself and see how like Wilhelmina Stitch I am (and so possibly are you).

> Oh, soul! [she exclaims] garner more zealously each
> quiet joy, each ecstasy, each sound, each touch, each
> sight, whate'er has given delight. Then when the
> summer days of life draw to a close, from Memory's
> fair garden – we can pluck a rose.

Splendid stuff. I might have written it myself.

Two hours later, I sit imbibing gin and reflecting upon the
unexpected bonus that this walk gave me. Not God. Not Fate. Just
the walk and the decision to take it, prompted, I suspect, by my
unhappy, consolation-seeking heart. It wasn't deceived for once: it
gave me the sight of a barn owl flying low over a field close to my
path, circling in wide sweeps in the late afternoon light. And he was
no unfamiliar creature. It is now nearly July and I first saw him on a
sunny afternoon early in February last year, when I had taken a
rutted track through farmland, and observed across a wide field a
brick and flint farmhouse and barns, their red roofs glowing in the
slanted rays of the sun. The buildings stood on the edge of
Cranborne Chase, and my track took me towards them along the
border of some woods, mostly ancient oak trees. Suddenly a huge
bird swept up on wide wings almost from underneath my feet. It
alighted on a low branch near by and turned to look at me. It was a
white-faced barn owl. When I reached the farm I found that it was
derelict. The barns, however, were in use and there perhaps the owl
lives.

It was a new discovery, this walk, though comparatively near my
house. I have taken the same track or variants of it several times
since that February afternoon in 1982. I have seen the barn owl
standing motionless on a fence post and more than once flying low
over the fields near the farm, but last winter I lost sight of him.
Knowing some farmers' ready hand on the trigger and their stupid-
ity and ignorance about such birds as owls, I feared that the
creature had been brought down by a bullet. But this afternoon,

when I was tired with driving and might so easily not have gone for a walk, there he was, and circling so near me that I could look into his stern, impassive face with its searching black eyes. And on this walk there was a kestrel thrown in for good measure, and hares as common as briar roses, a nosegay of which I picked to bring home with me, though I have sweetbriar growing on my own terrace. Those along the path to the derelict farm, where I hope the owl will breed a family, seemed the sweeter for their association with this noble, wide-winged, field-circling bird — white breasted, this one, though some are dark — with heart-shaped face and long, white-stockinged legs.

17
Thoughts on Being a Middle-class Intellectual

Love and writing – there is no significance in the order – are central to my life, but if I pursue this metaphor of mirrors, I must allow some reflections, in the sense of mental comment, upon the moral and political world in which I have lived for over seventy years and which has occupied my mind seriously from the heady days of the thirties; through my radical history teaching at my first school; then throughout the fifties and sixties. The world has changed and so have I. I have found myself taking new and, to me, dramatic directions as I have grown older, and have also looked back upon my earlier ideas with a critical eye. I seem to be more open to new ideas in my seventies than I was in my thirties and forties. This is a relief to me.

I am not and have never been a writer on political matters, but I want to clarify my present view of socialism and say something about my belated acceptance of feminist principles. In the last two or three years the two have become interlocked and an important part of my thinking. Nevertheless, having said that, I must add that my imagination and creative faculty are the most important part of my life. I remain *au fond* a novelist. I think in fictional modes, in terms of characters, stories and themes. So in this chapter I shall for the most part eschew political argument in favour of reports of injustice, exploitation, and so forth. They are more eloquent than theories, and my convictions, as I have grown older, have been formed by them far more than by argument or polemic. Often they have started as gut reactions. I then back them up by studying books and reports on the particular subject that has aroused my anger and indignation. To give a concrete example: Hiroshima shook me profoundly, as it did many of us. The subsequent development of nuclear weaponry and the testing of it on territories belonging usually to people powerless to protest against it, appalled me, morally as well as politically, and put me firmly in the anti-nuclear camp.

At first content to be vaguely anti-nuclear, my woolly opinions were given a timely shove – and I use the word advisedly* – by the protest of the Greenham women. I studied several key books and articles by writers on nuclear weapons. I think I am now reasonably well informed. I am not moved by the British and American defence of the build-up of nuclear weaponry known as the deterrent argument. It sounds reasonable and is certainly very persuasive to millions of people, but reduced to Thomas Schelling's parable, the wicked absurdity of it becomes clear: 'He, thinking I was about to kill him in self-defence, was about to kill me in self-defence, so I had to kill him in self-defence.'

An important factor, glossed over by the deterrent-mongers, is the cost of making and stockpiling nuclear weapons, a constant drain on any country's resources, resources which could and should be used to improve the quality of life for tens of millions of people. This of course means little to the wasteful societies of the Western powers, but it means a great deal, I believe, to the Russian government, for whom I do not cherish the relentless hatred and distrust of some. There is another facet of this expenditure upon nuclear weaponry rather than on socially valuable products: the stockpiling of bombs and cruise missiles, etc., freezes money that governments would otherwise have to spend on, say welfare, and on creating jobs to improve the infrastructure of their countries. This would mean that there was no longer a docile, poverty-stricken citizenry. Western governments are frightened to use public money to do away with poverty, to improve housing and overstretched medical services. It is more convenient, to put it mildly, to soak it up in arms.

If the manufacture and stockpiling of nuclear weapons is the most dangerous game the soldier-boys have ever engaged upon, I also have serious doubts as to whether nuclear power should be developed for civil purposes until the problem of the waste and its disposal has been openly discussed and resolved, instead of being pushed under the carpet or, in some cases, deliberately obfuscated and suppressed.

---

* *With Enough Shovels,* Robert Scheer (Random House, 1983). The title is based upon the statement of T.K. Jones that 'if there are enough shovels to go around everybody's going to make it', i.e. we are all going to survive the fall-out following the explosion of a one-megaton bomb (eighty times the explosive power of the Hiroshima bomb) on, say, New York. Or of course on London or Berlin.

Despite the nucleus (a good word, I feel) of books on the subject of the bomb and civil nuclear power upon my shelves, I always find myself stirred more deeply by the words of poets and writers and by paintings, for artists possess that compassion and empathy through imagination which statistics and theory cannot provide. Politics inevitably produce legislation, and extreme political movements protect themselves behind a positive electric fence of laws and prohibitions. Artists in all fields lead the protest against the inhumanity of tyrannous governments and also succour those who suffer under those regimes. One need only think of modern samizdat literature.

It is not only authoritarian governments that are guilty in the wider sense of cruelty and wanton destruction of life. Few governments have clean hands when it comes to the exploitation of natural resources. The connection between cruelty, war, environmental destruction and patriarchy has been brought home to me during the last few years, as I have studied feminist writers, and by no one more than Susan Griffin. So it is that we live and have done since Hiroshima in a world which is increasingly threatening and frightening.

The effect of this upon the young is something that anyone in the teaching profession and of course many parents can testify to. This is a poem written by a seven-year-old boy. He had in secret constructed an extraordinarily powerful head, in clay or plaster, its features distorted and its mouth open in a scream, like one of Francis Bacon's figures. His parents found this poem he had written:

> Helping Words
>
> help me.
> and me.
> me too.
> don't forget me.
> help me too.
> the ship has sunk help me please.
> so has my ship sunk help me
> too not only them please me too.
>
> rescue me at once I demand you
> too or i will tell a pliceman.
> i'll do the same if you're not quick.
> hurry up i'm drowning,
> if you don't be quick i'll send you to court.

Replys.

yes i will.'
I am being as quick as I can.
all right I am coming.
you're not in all that of a hurry.

(Printed in *The Times Education
Supplement* [5 December 1969] with a
photograph of the head he had made)

The poem may not be specifically about the nuclear threat. What it *is*
about, taken in conjunction with the terrifying, Baconesque head, is
death by violence. The sinking ship is a symbol and a powerful one.
In 1969 this small boy could well have heard of Hiroshima, of course,
but I do not quote the lines for this reason, but because they point up
sharply the impact of our violent, death-threatening world upon the
mind of a child. Children can sometimes be more eloquent than their
elders.

My growing interest in C N D during the sixties coincided with a far
from easy period for me. I need not again go into how much this was
due to my unsatisfactory personal life. I took no active part in C N D,
nor did I join the women's liberation movement. I turned increasingly
inward upon my own problems. Not even the brief affair with Kay
effectually brought me out of my solipsistic condition. Only when I
met and fell in love with Jan at the end of the sixties did I come to life
again.

Looking back to this period of my life, I see a yawning gap in my
experience. I remained in the closet and made little effort to join any
women's movement, though I made a nervous attempt to find women
in my own situation by having a brief encounter with the Minorities
Rights Group. It came to nothing, though it was there that I met Kay,
and also made one lifelong friend, Di Chapman. But I too easily felt
myself almost as much an outsider as I did from the heterosexual
world, for I had still not come to terms with my lesbianism and, moreover, had created for myself a lifestyle among my musician friends
that was totally different from the one I encountered among the few
acquaintances I made through M R G. With the young people of the
fifties and early sixties I felt out of touch, already middle aged, and I
never recognised that they might have felt quite differently about me
and welcomed me, if I had opened my heart and mind to their iconoclastic ideas and ideals. I failed to understand that by going halfway

to meet the women in the movement, I could have found the friends I so badly needed, the warmth and support of my own sex which could have ended the claustrophic way of life I was so miserably enduring. I believe now that this period had a profound effect upon the direction of my writing, driving me into the straitjacket of autobiographical work instead of letting my imagination run free.

When I emerged from my isolation, now established with Jan and happier than I thought I could ever have been, I reconsidered my political allegiances. I was disillusioned with the Labour governments of the time. They seemed to be setting up a form of state capitalism, something that could easily be dismantled by a Tory government, or worse: seized and made use of by a fascist one. I was even more disillusioned by some of the Marxist governments abroad.

During my early flirtation with communism in the thirties, an important book was published that is now probably forgotten. It was written by Dora and Bertrand Russell after a visit they made to Soviet Russia and its very title influenced us: *Soviet Russia: A New Civilisation,* it proclaimed boldly. Yes, that is how it seemed to us then, and throughout the war we had contrived to forget the show trials and to ignore books like Arthur Koestler's *Darkness at Noon.* By the time that the details of Stalin's reign of terror were fully known, we were well on into the fifties and I was adding a question mark to the Russells' title. I am not sure that they did not add one themselves in a later edition. Now, in the seventies, I was increasingly disturbed by the spectacle of a world in which states were being taken over by military dictatorships, communist or otherwise. My admiration for Russia's achievements during the war remained undimmed, but I was dismayed by the stranglehold Stalin had gained and was tightening over the East European countries, most of them far more closely linked in culture with Western Europe than with Russia. The silencing of opposition, whether working class or intellectual, the attacks upon intellectuals and artists of all kinds followed a pattern that was leading, I felt, to a new barbarism. Imagination was being stifled, art shackled by ideology, personal lives put through a mill of conformity. I joined Amnesty International and a new fact of life as it is lived today filled me with despair: the growth of physical and psychological torture, often in countries whose revolutions I had welcomed and seen as full of hope for the future.

One of the chief aims of feminism is to expose and bring to an end the treatment of women as objects. But the evil extends beyond the abuse of women. Cruelty has always been with us, I recognise, and it is impossible to prove that it is worse now than in the days of Attila. It does seem to me, however, that cruelty was formerly blinder, more insensate than the well-reasoned and deliberate brutality of this century. The word 'objects' in this context chills my heart. It was as objects that the Nazis regarded not only the Jews but their Russian prisoners. Long after the war was over, we were given evidence that the most hideous experiments were carried out upon war prisoners by Japanese doctors and scientists, who anaesthetised their imaginations and therefore their sensibilities by referring to their victims as 'logs of wood'. Some of those who perpetrated these monstrosities hold high positions in Japan today.

Cruelty is not the monopoly of any nation. There is no outside compulsion, no special ordination from on high that directs any of us to seek power over others, to be hypocritical or to be greedy – all ubiquitous vices; but cruelty, surely, is a special case. It has been proclaimed the greatest vice under the sun by thinkers and writers as far apart as Montaigne and John Cowper Powys. It thrives where there is tyranny, where there is civil or religious conflict. Faulty though democracy may be, Montesquieu, and Kant after him saw that some form of democracy was desirable, and the former philosopher described it as 'the organisation of the state (which does lie in man's power), whereby the powers of each selfish inclination are so arranged in opposition that one moderates or destroys the ruinous effect of the other . . . and man is forced to be a good citizen even if not morally a good person'. A cynical view of human nature, some may think. I consider it a sane and reasonable assessment, for I cannot believe in the perfectability of men and women. Democracy – the term needs qualifying, of course – gives us some chance to exercise our more agreeable traits, whereas tyranny and strife evoke our worst. What came to the surface in the conditions of the 1939 war and later in Vietnam and Kampuchea, to mention only three recent fields of human misery, is a *wantonness* of cruelty, whose only positive achievement was the gratification of the perpetrators. This is to equate the power-mad men of the twentieth century, and rightly, with their power-mad predecessors in history, going back to those who made human sacrifices to Moloch. Men may have split the atom, but they have failed to heal the split in their psyches. I cannot pretend to be very conversant with the works of Jung, but the more I read him the more I find him a man for our times. There is a truth worth pursuing in his statement: 'In the collective unconscious, already all men and all races and colours are kin and enjoy one and the same parentage.'

There is a capacity for cruelty in all of us and whoever drew up the ten commandments evidently realised the uselessness of including any embargo upon it. One can see in oneself how close it is to fanaticism. I know that the more convinced I am that I'm right, the more likely it is that I shall give rein to the urge to ride roughshod over someone else. Then it is only a short step to mental cruelty, and how do I know the precise length of the step that would take me to the threshold of physical cruelty, or over that threshold? It is this deeply vibrating string that is played upon with such virtuosity by tyrants, and most of the world now lives under some sort of tyranny.

A closely reasoned account of modern cruelty forms the long first chapter of a book published in 1985: *Ordinary Vices* by Judith N. Shklar (The Bellknap Press of Harvard University). In a detailed critique of Nietzsche and his influence upon European politics, Professor Shklar pins down the physical and moral aspects of cruelty as they appear to her:

> Mankind in fact has only two possibilities: a cruel self-mutilating conscience ruling the empire of the weak [she is writing of Western puritanism], or ruthless egotism in which the strong cruelly dominate their inferiors. We are reduced to a choice between physical and moral cruelty. In such a vision [i.e. Nietzsche's vision] the world is turned upside down. The weak are powerful, thanks to their guile and numbers, while the genuinely strong individuals are really the victims. That is how Nietzsche managed to teach the socially powerful classes and the various megamaniacs of interwar Europe to fear the weak. Indeed, not only were poverty and physical weakness to be hated; the poor and the weak became justifiable targets of cruelty. Europe's most flourishing ideologies of those years were not violent attacks on socialism. Fascism really hated the weak. That may not have been Nietzsche's intent, but the cruel hatred of moral cruelty underwrote physical brutality.

As far as Europe and America are concerned, the eighteenth-century Age of Enlightenment, the age of Voltaire and Rousseau, did have a beneficial effect upon some areas of human behaviour, but it has to be said that the effect was limited in time as well as scope. It is uplifting to learn that the use of torture was actually abolished in Europe towards the end of the eighteenth century. A hundred years later, when humanitarian ideas appeared to be and indeed in some fields really were moderating the worst features of Western society, Victor Hugo proclaimed confidently – the date was 1874 – that torture had ceased to exist. In Europe, perhaps, it was at least less openly used, but it still flourished in countries dominated by Europeans, like India and Africa, and in the States, where Americans carried out the 'pacification' of the native American Indians and tore their lands from them with unspeakable and ruthless cruelty. Moreover, Hugo could not foresee that in another hundred years torture would have become more widespread than it had been for hundreds of years.*

The despot has enemies innumerable. He must find out from his prisoners as well as from his spies who his opponents are. Fear triggers cruelty and the world is now peopled with Herods: it is *de rigueur* to torture captives before you even know their political alignments. This is called 'softening up'. Unlike some other vices, cruelty is irreversible. You cannot withdraw as torturer or you will yourself be tortured. The political colour of the regime makes no difference. It has now become universal. An Argentinian torturer, questioned by a journalist about his motives and feelings about his appalling practices, gave among his answers: 'We all had to learn to give punishment to the subversives . . . Do not draw blood . . . You can watch the body arch and bounce under electricity, but never draw blood . . . Electricity is clean. The rest is for maniacs . . . Soon, perhaps, they will use the same methods in Europe. There is no other way to beat the Communists' (*Observer* report, 15 January 1984). He is right, though it is not always Communists who must be eliminated. Caroline Moorhead, who covered *The Times*' 'Prisoners of Conscience' column, found that in all, during 1984, she wrote of prisoners held in twenty-nine different countries, with Soviet Russia and Turkey heading the list.

When I write a letter under the Amnesty International scheme for prisoners of conscience, I find myself addressing the letter to the head of a state which usually calls itself something like a 'People's Democratic Republic'. I know with fair certainty that it is neither popular nor democratic and that its rulers will imprison those who do not agree that it is popular and democratic.

It may seem a more heinous sin to destroy a man by beating him to death than to cut down a tropical forest (though this usually involves

---

* A searching book on torture and its origins has recently appeared: *Torture* by Edward Peters (Blackwell, 1985).

the displacement and often the murder of its native inhabitants), but the cruelty and greed which prompt these acts, respectively, have a common root: love of power, which like 'an universal wolf, So doubly seconded with will and power, Must make perforce an universal prey And last eat up himself.' That we are 'eating up ourselves' must be plain to anyone with eyes to see. The Judaic god whom Christians have adopted gave men dominion over women and animals and all living things of the earth. He made him, the psalmist says, a little lower than the angels. I assume therefore that those heavenly beings must have the power to destroy worlds and star systems. They need to look to their laurels, for men are creeping up on them. An American flag now flies on the moon and that is only a beginning.

Though cruelty is to my mind the greatest vice in our world, greed comes a close second. It is greed that is turning good land into prairie, that grossly overproduces food that must be stockpiled while millions starve, and it is hypocrisy – the 'cant' that Byron inveighed against so cogently – that tries to justify the destruction of valuable habitat in the name of 'better land use' and even 'progress' and that describes over-fishing as 'sea-farming'. In December 1982 I watched a B B C 'Horizon' programme, reporting the U N Environment Conference which meets, I believe, every five years. Our own Michael Heseltine made an anodyne opening speech, a shaming speech, I thought, in which he suggested blandly that things were getting much better in the ecological field. This was contradicted by nearly a hundred world experts. Peter Scott warned of the loss of genetic resources caused by the extinction of so many species of animals and plants. Especially impressive and inspiring contributions came from some of the Third World speakers: the aged, ascetic Indian, Sunderlal Bahuguna, who started the Chipko movement to conserve the Himalayan forests; the black woman speaker from Kenya, Professor Wansari Maathai, who made the final speech, summing up the sorry evidence of destruction and waste with the words: 'We are on trial.' I felt that if world rulers were of the calibre, expertise and dedication of these men and women, we should not come to be regarded as the ultimate endangered species, a state which cannot be so far away.

My political views have changed. I have had to rethink my attitude towards certain countries which claim to have built a socialist system. I can no longer accept and excuse the atrocities of revolution in the way I used to. I am not going to quote horrendous accounts of torture, nor give examples of that unforgivable crime, the psychiatric manipulation and abuse of helpless prisoners. Nor should readers suspect me of anti-Soviet bias because I choose to write briefly of an episode in the life of a Russian poet. Totalitarian states of every political persuasion have always attacked artists, especially writers, and they always will. Language is the prerogative of human beings and proclaims our individuality. The juggernaut state has no use for individuals and fears their language, especially in the work of poets and novelists and journalists, who speak for those rendered inarticulate through fear and degradation. All who want to understand this fully should read Nadezhda Mandelstam's two books, *Hope Against Hope* and *Hope Abandoned*, which describe the life and death of her poet husband, Osip Mandelstam, and the persecution of their friends. One of Russia's dissident exiles, the poet Joseph Brodsky, says memorably of these books: 'In that light history winces, and an individual realises his choice.'

Anna Ahkmatova is one of Russia's greatest poets. Her reputation is worldwide. In 1946 she was denounced by the cultural commissar, Andrei Zhdanov, in the following 'criticism', if it merits the word (she was also expelled from the Union of Soviet writers):

Ahkmatova's subject matter is . . . miserably limited: it is the poetry of an overwrought upper-class lady who frantically races back and forth between boudoir and chapel . . . A nun or a whore – or rather, both a nun and a whore who combines harlotry with prayer . . . Ahkmatova's poetry is utterly remote from the people . . . What can there be in common between this poetry and the interests of our people and state?

(Quoted in a review of some new translations of Ahkmatova's work in the *New York Review of Books*, 19 January 1984.)

Certainly she was hardly showing sympathy towards the interests of the state when she wrote this:

No, not under the vault of another sky,
not under the shelter of other wings.
I was with my people then,
there where my people were doomed to be.

She was expressing, *pace* Mr Zhdanov, her oneness with all those who suffered not only in the last war but later for their political opinions. She refused to leave them, to remove herself from Russia of her own will. She was standing up as a comrade to the many who stood 'under the blind, red wall', waiting for news of their imprisoned, possibly murdered, relatives and friends. She had 'found out how faces droop,/ how terror looks out from under the eyelids'. The Kremlin would never forgive her for her knowledge and for giving voice to the woman

> who came out of the numbness which affected us all and whispered in my ear (we all spoke in whispers there): 'Can you describe this?'
> I said, 'I can!' Then something resembling a smile slipped over what had once been her face. 1 April 1957. Leningrad.
> (Words from the opening of Ahkmatova's long poem 'Requiem 1935–40')

Such eloquence is gall to totalitarian governments. Czechoslovakia banished or silenced many of its finest artists. Milan Kundera, now living in France, has retained that marvellous instrument of balance, a sense of humour. His vision is wider than national. He is a true European and as uncompromising and eloquent as Ahkmatova, in his different field of novel-writing. However, do not draw the conclusion that because I have mentioned two eminent writers I ignore the fact that imprisonment, loss of status, despair and suicide are also the lot of the humblest citizens in many totalitarian countries. 'Police files are our only claim to immortality,' writes Kundera. It may be objected that it is misleading to take evidence too readily from dissidents. This is a fair point, but it is surely more misleading to put much credibility in the pronouncements of those in power. If a balance is to be struck, I would bring it down in favour of dissidents. They often provide evidence in their own bodies.

I believe that the well-known words 'from each according to his capacity, to each according to his need' have little meaning in terms of politics. Perhaps they would be better regarded as a key moral precept, like 'love thy neighbour'. As a moral imperative the words would not of course change the world any more than the Christian commandment has, but they would do less damage in a moral context. Political ends, no matter how high-sounding, are usually achieved only at appalling cost, and too often the original precept is forgotten. Political ends justified the slaughter of the Russian kulaks. Morally, such an act could never be justified.

Some readers will by this time be dismissing me as appallingly simplistic in my views. I have explained that I am not writing a political treatise. I must state the truth as I see it and truth is often startling in its simplicity. To sum up, I can no longer forgive the cruelty of regimes proclaiming themselves socialist or communist, regimes which have had plenty of time, in some cases more than half a century, to adjust and moderate laws often absolutely necessary in the stringent days of early revolution; I cannot accept the disregard for the quality of life of their citizens, the blithe acquiescence in a class system which has replaced the old one with managerial and party echelons possessing privileges denied to the 'toiling masses' so frequently referred to. I cannot forgive such regimes for their almost total unreceptiveness to outside ideas, for their cynical signing of declarations of human rights. Indeed, I condemn them for writing into their constitutions high-sounding clauses on freedom for women and for racial, regional and religious minorities, clauses which in reality are contemptuously disregarded, though frequently mouthed. I am not excluding British governments from these strictures. I do not forgive the way we have treated Ireland in the past, producing now a hydra in the North which successive parliaments have attempted to control or kill by cutting off its heads, resulting in two growing where one grew before. Having said that, why should I gloss over or forgive the persecution of Anna Ahkmatova and other artists in the Soviet Union, or the jailing of homosexuals, Jehovah's Witnesses and other nonconformers in countries all over the world?

Condemnation of abuses in some communist countries cannot destroy my belief in the socialist system for which their revolutions were fought, nor do I deny that rigorous and even cruel laws will persist while a state is struggling to set up a new system of government based upon a socialist economic structure, and the more so when that country is subjected to powerful hostility and even military interference from its neighbours or from further afar.

It is however useless for us, the socialist intellectuals whom the left wing despises, to try to wash our hands of guilt and preach to the oppressed and deprived and starving: 'Take heart. At least in most developed capitalist countries laws are reasonably just, humanitarian ideas have influence.' This is the middle-left argument, the gradualist argument, which wants to moderate and control capitalism. Is this true of Latin-American capitalism? Turkish? South African? Northern Irish? Words like 'humane' and 'just' will sound hollow to a prisoner on the parrot-cage in a Turkish prison, to an abused and beaten-up black South African lying in his own urine on the concrete floor of his tiny cell, in a country stuffed with investment from Western capitalist institutions and governments.

Cruelty and violence, whether it takes the form of rape, child murder, or bombing a village or destroying a whole class, cannot be (as it often is) excused as 'men's natural and uncurbable lust' or the state's reasonable necessity to destroy its enemies without and within. Rarely do these acts spring from uncalculated urges. They are deliberately planned and undertaken.

This chapter has been leading inevitably towards feminism. I had known for years that feminism was a far larger issue than its critics made out. Belittlement is a prime weapon of hostility and hatred. Yet knowing this, I have to admit that at first I allowed myself to be seduced by facile criticism. I followed the women's liberation movement . . . from a safe distance. I read with admiration the unfolding story of Greenham Common and women's peace camps elsewhere. I collected a stack of cuttings about them. Somehow . . . sometime . . . I told myself. I had another huge pile of cuttings classified under the heading 'Rape of the Earth'. I did not make the connection.

I have never been a joiner, still less a marcher. I can never even bring myself to shout 'Brava!' (or 'Bravo!') at the end of an opera or a concert. Yet I have no timidity about speaking in public and I was not in the least disconcerted when I 'came out' on I T V in 1981, the event that really brought me to turn in the direction of feminism, for it was after this that I began seriously to read feminist literature and buy books on the subject. I acquired a long row of them. I did not understand or like all of what I read at first. But like them or not, they deposited a rich silt upon the ground of my understanding.

It was a single article that finally drew the threads together and compelled me to see that I could no longer remain indifferent to the women's movement. A friend in the U S A sent me a magazine called *Trivia* (Spring Number, 1983). The word 'trivia' is used here in the sense of 'threefold', the magazine being devoted to feminist theory, scholarship and book reviews. Andrea Dworkin, feminist writer, had an article in it called 'Anti-feminism'. This long, hard-hitting piece made an immediate impact upon me. It convinced me that my tepid indifference to the women's movement placed me in a position which Dworkin summed up brutally thus: 'Anti-feminism is the politics of contempt for women as a class.' I surely wasn't *anti*-feminist, was I? I wasn't contemptuous of women as a class? But yes, I began to see that unconsciously I might be so. I realised how deep-rooted were the masculine attitudes and values inculcated in me during my childhood and youth.

Dworkin described the whole spectrum of forces ranged in opposition to radical feminism. It is made up, she claims, not only of men but of some, indeed far too many, women. During her attack upon the anti-feminists, she makes a simple statement that had a strong appeal for me: that feminists must work to create an equal dignity for all people, regardless of race, creed, class or sex. This seems to me unassailable as a goal. I have not found myself reading Dworkin's books. Indeed, now that I call myself a feminist, I read very little theoretical writing on the subject. I quote her in this context because it was her article in *Trivia* that forced me to think out my position as a woman.

In my heart I still reject gradualism, I suppose, and think in terms of revolution, but it is clear to me now that as radical feminism is in itself a comparatively new concept, so it must create an entirely new form of revolution. How otherwise can we avoid the trap of violent confrontation which will mean that women, who have always done conspicuously badly in revolutions, will find themselves, willy nilly, the supporters of men who grab the leadership, make promises to women that will never be kept, and use the age-old revolutionary violence that we as women oppose? But 'a new form of revolution' implies that feminism has or should have a political structure which is not the case.

There are many different strands in the women's movement. There may be dangers in this looseness of structure but perhaps there are also virtues, provided there is some hope that the different elements can work together. I would like to quote more experienced political writers than myself upon this thorny subject: Anna Coote and Beatrix Campbell in *Sweet Freedom*,* a book that has not pleased everyone in the women's movement. Writing of the gulf that arose in the late 1970s between heterosexual and lesbian feminists, they say (under the significant subtitle 'Divide and Rule'): 'What remains to be done is to explore the experience that lesbians and heterosexuals *share* and to build on this common ground a political understanding of sexuality.' These two writers emphasise that while a variety of views and certainly the ability 'to learn and to change ourselves' is important, they were already concerned in the early eighties, when writing this book, about the divisions in the women's movement. Variety is one thing, rigidity and intolerance quite another. They wrote:

* Published by Pan Books, 1982, in association with Basil Blackwell Publishers Ltd.

> Women's liberation must reproduce the means of its political survival. We need an autonomous feminist movement no less now than we did in 1970. It is much larger than it was, although its identity is less distinct. It shows no sign of melting away, but there is a danger that it will if we don't actively encourage its growth and development. There is a case for stronger organisational links between women's groups and campaigns . . .

I agree with this and I believe that the writers might express this view more strongly today. Feminists seem to me to be more divided than ever, at a time when the backlash against them and against lesbians, gays and all 'nonconformers' is far fiercer than it was ten years ago, and when a senior Tory politician can be applauded for a speech declaring single parents to be 'evil'. See also the anti-gay words of a Labour politician quoted on page 154. What revolution could change such prejudices, based as they are on male hatred of any woman who does not conform to masculine needs and desires? I ask myself the question: Once – if ever – a broad feminist party could be formed and were to confront its enemies, is it conceivable that it could win even a bloodless revolution without women resorting to many of the psychological weapons used by men? That women can be motivated by masculine ruthlessness and a naked desire for power has always been evident.

   It is not a shift of power from men to women that is wanted. Power – how can one avoid quoting this cliché? – power tends to corrupt. As Susan Griffin says: 'Men, valuing power, produce nations, conflict and wars, and (that) women, valuing life, produce relationship, continuity and peace.' I am, however, left in despair that such a profound shift of values will ever be brought about. The generality of men preach loudly about the virtue of 'caring', 'forgiveness', 'truth', etc. They write the religious dogmas and the tomes of philosophy, but rarely practise their own precepts when they are against their own interests, which they usually are. Not that I am implying that women are paragons of virtue, but I do believe that whereas men pontificate on virtues as related to an abstract humanity, women not only know the truths of freedom, tenderness and peace at an intellectual level, but also experience them within their hearts and bodies and in their own relationships with each other.

   Abstract ideas and even accepted rules of conduct can always be set aside when convenient, or argued out of existence. For instance, a study of the Vietnam war shows that the U S government refused over and over again in the early stages of the conflict the opportunity to withdraw and allow the Vietnamese to work out their own destiny. U Thant, Secretary General of the United Nations, made strenuous efforts in the mid sixties to give the Americans a chance to 'withdraw gracefully'. These efforts were deliberately undermined by the American bombing campaign known as 'Rolling Thunder'. The opportunity to end a long and appallingly destructive war with a certain face-saving on each side never occurred again. Vietnam emerged and the Vietnamese people did indeed work out their own destiny.

I end this chapter with a story which is an indictment not of communism but of man's power-mad nature, a parable if you like of the way in which the values in which women believe, and to which many men subscribe verbally, can be and are ignored completely by men when it comes to the living, breathing creatures who compose that convenient abstract, 'the human race': the women, the men and the children.

I found the story of Madame Dinh and her family in a personal account of a visit made to Vietnam by Gavin Young, traveller and writer, printed in the *New York Review of Books* in July 1985. Young gives me some kind of hope for the male sex. The story he tells is not an indictment of communism as practised in Vietnam or anywhere else, but a warning that forgiveness, with many of the virtues and values that make us human, is unacceptable to totalitarian regimes. It is seen as one of those bourgeois forms of weakness which must be eradicated to produce a uniform society with no chinks in its rigid armour-plating through which a tender feeling can creep. This story finally destroyed the classic delusion I indulged in, and still minimally retained, when I believed in my twenties that education would change the world, by which I really meant that left-wing political systems would bring about the millennium. Only the education of the male heart, yes, and many women's hearts, will change the world, and I am nearly convinced that it is too late. There will be no world to change.

Gavin Young met the Dinh family when he was a war reporter in 1965. He became friends with them and returned to see them whenever he could during the subsequent eight years. A long and close friendship. After the communist liberation of the country he heard no more from them. At last, in 1985, Young revisited South Vietnam and set about trying to find the Dinh family, whom he had not seen or heard of for twelve years. He found Madame Dinh still living in the house in Hue which he had known so well in earlier years. He crossed the familiar bridge over the Perfume River and went up and through the open door.

> There Mme Dinh stood staring at me in an almost empty room. I was shocked. She seemed to have shrunk . . . Unsmiling, as if dazed, she led me to a bare table where we sat facing each other in silence as if it were visiting time in jail.
>
> After a while she whispered, 'This is too dangerous.' She kept glancing fearfully about her . . . 'The Communists . . . the terror,' she said into my ear. I felt I had stepped into a nightmare.

Her son Minh and his cousin Chinh had both been through seven years of 're-education', that process that sound so civilised compared with imprisonment or execution. In reality it was hard labour. Having served the sentence, this did not mean that the cousins were now free to lead normal lives, despite the promises contained in the government's booklet called *Whose Human Rights?* This explains that 're-education' spares the prisoner 'a stained police record which would follow him throughout his life and would even influence his children . . . a re-educated person could return to normal life.'

Chinh was now an agricultural labourer. In happier days he and Gavin Young had discussed books, and Chinh, then hopeful, would quote Camus' *Sisyphe*: 'Est-ce le globe terrestre est beau? Ah, oui, très beau.' Mr Young was not allowed to see Chinh.

He ran into Minh in the streets of Saigon, where he was peddling sweets for a meagre living. He was even permitted to give him dinner. He learned from his old friend that there would never be a better job for him, that his sons would not be allowed to go to the university. Mr Young gives the Communist regime credit for combating illiteracy (despite denying the university to Minh's sons) and drug abuse, but he ends his account with words that contain the tragedy of millions of the wretched all over the world, men, women and children trapped in situations they did not create and from which only death will set them free: 'Since the victory [of the Communists]', he writes, 'too many people have died, or have been in camps, or have left out of fear of the simple horror of living in a place ruled by privileged cadres, where there is no incentive, no chance to question authority, and above all no forgiveness.'

18
Give to Me the Life I Love

What is the life I love? What do I value most? What, more precisely, could I not live without? If I pare away the obvious inessentials and even much of what has in my younger days seemed indispensable, I am left as surely most people must be, with love. Do I mean the whole spectrum of love, from the fiery core of sexual passion to the companionship and stimulus of friends? I should have felt this to be true once but find it imprecise and soft at the edges now, like damp cardboard. It belonged to my youth and early middle age, though I didn't analyse it at the time, but was able to see its negative aspects only – not finding love or losing it when found.

The loss of Jan has made me define love more maturely. Since I cannot live with her again, I turn to friendship and make an art of it, not, I assure you, regarding it as second best. Friendship has its own validity, its own rites and, in my opinion, its duties, for I do not believe you can afford to be casual and take it for granted. Certainly there are some old friends whom you see seldom, and may rarely communicate with, yet you find on meeting them that you take up the threads with ease where they were dropped, perhaps years ago, and it may be true that this is really easier than it is with friends whom you see frequently. The invisible cords that bind such friendships are spun from the thread of your being. It is the relationships with people you see most that need a care and a consideration that will prevent any fraying of friendship at the edges, that will keep the pattern tight and preserve its colours and texture.

As I grow older, I place a more thoughtful and conscious value upon my friends. Perhaps this is partly because I now see myself as a more valuable person, though there are other reasons. To disparage yourself, as I did fairly consistently when I was younger, banishes you to an outer darkness of depreciation from which you gaze in, as upon a lighted room, and see the friends you long for chatting together, separated from you by the chill pane of glass.

I have always been able to put on an act in a party of strangers and often I have mistaken passing interest for reciprocal liking and respect – I mean on my own part. Then my puritanical conscience gives me the probably quite erroneous idea that I have a duty to keep up some sort of relationship with someone, even though it often becomes irksome. Better to end it. You are not as indispensable as you think and you can be as mistaken about other people's interest in you as you are about your own in them. I do not for a moment imply that you should break the legitimate ties of responsibility if you have incurred them, nor of course that you should ignore the ties of old-established friendship by unkind neglect. I am pleading for the right to be selective, especially as one grows older. In fact, my circle of close, permanent friends has become wider, but less and less do I want an outer circle of 'fringe friends', what Virginia Woolf picturesquely called 'ramshackle jerry-built houses run up here and there'. This reference to 'fringe friends' is not meant to be offensive, nor does it imply that I do not enjoy meeting new people; simply that unless we eventually warm to each other to the point where rapport can be taken for granted and differences relished, I am disinclined to add to those of whom one is obliged to say: I *must* see so-and-so. At the other end of the spectrum, I can do without sex. I mean precisely what I say. I have not become incapable of sexual love but I have met no one since I knew Jan with whom I could enjoy it. I only want it as part of a total love relationship and when, within my inner self, I am totally engaged. It would be a different matter if I had the kind of temperament that enjoys casual sexual encounters, but I have not. I can forgo them without regret.

I am now very rich in the companions I have always longed for. The last eight or nine years have been a success story in this field, adding to old friendships several new relationships that span a wide arch of love. Each bond differs more or less from others. It is an important truth for me that many close friendships have a trace, or perhaps a potentiality for the erotic, certainly the sensual. I need from friends something more than to be accepted, to be entertained, more even than to share a few similar tastes. I want to be entirely at ease with them. I like the warmth of physical contact and seek the intimacy that comes from sharing experiences; the pleasure of walking together, eating and drinking together, talking freely without inhibitions, exciting a response to my own enthusiasms and returning a welcome to theirs, disagreements also being included; I want the liberty to kiss them, to put my arm round them and find a reciprocal warmth, a feeling of no holds barred, although in fact I don't want to go to bed with them or they with me. All this applies to most women and men friends, heterosexual or gay. The erotic element in friendship, however tacit and unexpressed, is an exciting and enriching element, but if it is not there this does not necessarily impair the relationship. My old friend Alyse Gregory, the subject of the following chapter, opened her essay on 'Friendship and Solitude'* with words that I have never forgotten: 'It is not to be wondered that Epicurus placed friendship among the highest rewards to be enjoyed by human beings. It is a daring thing to give over our reticences into the keeping of another and to accept the responsibility of being custodian of theirs.' This element of daring has always attracted and intrigued me.

Once I had reached my thirties and embarked upon my teaching career, I found myself deprived of the warmth in friendship that I longed for, with the exception of my lifelong university friend, Diana. I think I have always needed to expend myself in loving almost more than to be loved. Anything of worth I can offer from my own personality I want to bestow and to share. Though I had found this reciprocal warmth in two or three friends as my life progressed, they remained a small circle. It is a kind of relaxed absorption in another that I have always looked for. Time passes imperceptibly and one feels at ease because the absorption is not so intense as to raise the temperature to a point of discomfort. I enjoy not only the responsiveness and quick awareness of my friends, but also an appreciation of their physical selves, even their idiosyncrasies, and I hope that this is reciprocal though I recognise that it is not always so. Such an appreciation certainly belongs to sexual love, but it can be found with friends of either sex where there is no timidity or inhibition, where there is a willingness to take the risks that any relationship entails. As always, Wordsworth fortifies my beliefs:

> Give all thou canst: high Heaven rejects the love
> Of nicely-calculated less or more.

It was not until eight or nine years ago that I formed new and rewarding relationships, and deliberately moved outwards towards

---

* from *Wheels on Gravel* (John Lane, The Bodley Head, 1938).

other people, setting myself upon a positive course for almost the first time in my life. I found myself drawing towards me a closer and more diverse group of friends and, as always happens among like-minded people, the circle shifts like a kaleidoscope as one shares some of one's friends with others, and oneself moves into new relationships, the whole process providing continually enriching and sustaining experiences. That most of my friends live with a partner causes me privately some pain, but not so far as to impair the friendships.

It is an aspect of the patriarchal system under which we have lived for so many centuries that women's friendships have been consistently played down or totally ignored until feminists began to discover and celebrate them. All women, feminists or not, should be grateful to the publishing houses that have rescued and reprinted such celebratory writing: poetry, novels and diaries by women of past ages who have had the education to record their life experiences. But alas, what of the millions who have not? I myself am one of a privileged few. I am white, middle class, and university educated. On the other hand these advantages have been weighed down and conditioned by that very privileged upbringing and education to accept for far too long patriarchal attitudes and values which intelligence and a different range of books on my shelves might have made me question.

During the last few years I have learned more consciously to appreciate qualities in women which, when I was younger, I took for granted or even felt guilty about valuing. More than that, the inhibitions of a lifetime in the closet induced in me a kind of defensiveness about men, an 'Ah, but . . . ', an 'Of course, my men friends . . . ', a delicate hint that perhaps it was not choice but chance that made me gravitate towards the pleasure of women's company, whereas, the older I grew, the more critical I became of male attitudes that for too long my upbringing had taught me to ignore, condone or even admire.

Places have always been so important to me that there have been moments when I wonder if I do not love places more than people. This sounds extravagant and absurd, but the very fact that I can write it down and leave it written implies that there is a grain of truth in it. Love of place rooted itself in me very early in my life. Above all, I love England itself. I have little of the travelling passion that lures so many of the British abroad. In what travelling I have done, all in Europe, I have come to realise that I love foreign cities, like Florence, Venice and Bologna. England has nothing to compare with these. Its best townscapes are in smaller places, like Richmond, Warwick and

Tewkesbury. I am only sorry that I do not know Paris well, but I am seriously inhibited by my lack of French. This makes me feel very uncivilised. In Germany or Italy I am prepared to plunge into speech as best I can. I never feel that I can bring myself to do this in France. But if I have loved some of the European cities I have visited, nowhere in the world can give me a countryside like the Dorset downs, the North Yorkshire Moors, the Penwith peninsula, with the sea on three sides of it. The list comes readily to my mind, for these very disparate places have something in common. Walking in them, I am always aware of wide space around me. This is something I need in my life and I find myself savouring it with conscious pleasure as I walk along a chalk track or over the heathery tracts of Yorkshire or the Cornish cliffs, with huge skies above and around me. It is space that I am immediately aware of when I walk through the front door of my Dorset home and out on to its terrace. I look down on the village, with the Blackmore Vale rolling into the distance and Hambeldon's hillfort with its tremendous walls and ditches two or three miles away. Beyond it stand ranged the central Dorset downs with their beautiful names: Bulbarrow, High Stoy and Dorsetshire Gap. Space unfolds before me in cloud and hill contours.

Not long ago, a walk in the downs gave me an experience of the purest sensual pleasure. I still discover lanes and tracks quite near me which are unfamiliar. They are a kind of handsel, a pledge of surprise and pleasure. One day I drove to a small village a few miles away, left the car and started to walk up a long straight track between high hedges and trees, leading towards the summit of White Sheet Hill on the skyline. I emerged from this 'hollow way' into fields. The track still climbed steeply. At last I found myself on the rim of a deep bowl in the downs. Below me was a precipitous drop and opposite, three clefts as if a three-fingered hand had plunged into the chalk just below the ridgeway track on White Sheet Hill that runs for some twenty miles to Salisbury.

I sat down, glad of the breeze, and watched a pair of kestrels, then three, four and finally five of them, gliding in the green bowl below me, or rising level with my eyes, borne on air currents, and from time to time beating a swift upward course that carried them almost out of sight into the clouds. As last I walked on to reach the track and, about half a mile along it, turned down past Norrington, a grey stone house with farm buildings among trees. Walking is a pleasure to me almost as deep as reading, though on a different plane. It satisfies something in me that otherwise is in danger of being starved, my sensuality. I get a physical joy out of the rhythm of it, a sense of well-being, a marshalling of the senses, for almost all are engaged, watching the kestrels, noticing scabious, harebells and restharrow, that tought little purple plant in the ruts of the track, catching the darting flight of butterflies, hearing a rush of bird-song from a hawthorn.

Making my way across the fields, I dismissed all thoughts to allow myself the pleasure of the sun's warmth and the sweat on my face and neck. A long briar caught my bare arm as I climbed over a gate. I watched the blood running slowly down my arm and drying in the heat and didn't trouble to wipe it off.

I shall never live permanently in my Dorset house, though this is what I intended when I built it. I need the company of friends and most of them are in London. After a day of work, whether it's writing or not, and it may include a long solitary walk, I feel isolated when evening comes. I can bear this for three or even four weeks. After that, the solitude becomes oppressive. I think I really yearn for the soap-opera of neighbours. I often find it odd that I've lived in a London road for thirty-five years and am on no more than nodding terms with two or three people in it. It emphasises the fragmentary and mobile nature of modern society. When I first came to this Hampstead street it was full of rooming houses, student hostels and cheap hotels. Now it has risen in the world and the houses have mostly been converted into expensive self-contained flats. These are equally impermanent in their clientele and barricaded against neighbourliness. I think my intermittent longings for this kind of street friendliness belong to those daydreams where one sees oneself living in a small street on cosy terms of borrowing a screw of tea, grumbling over the fence about the Council, popping into someone's house for a cup of coffee and a bit of gossip. There's an element of soap-opera in most of us.

Returning to the question which opened this chapter, what is essential to me? I should have found it hard to find an answer until a few years ago, for I never seriously addressed myself to it. While Jan was with me, I should have declared that my Weymouth harbour house was essential to my happiness, yet when I sold it in 1983 I felt only relief, and have never missed it at all. It was much the same with my violin. Music *is* an essential part of my life, but when I stopped playing and gave away my instrument, I knew that I had shed a burden, even while I retain pleasurable memories of the chamber music I took part in and gratitude to Fate that I have had at least a few years' experience of playing quartets. We mistake the object with what it stands for.

Writing of music reminds me of another major pleasure in my life: the discovery of new composers and writers. By 'new' I do not mean necessarily modern. In music, I have becomed devoted to jazz only in the last few years and this is possibly the most important addition to my musical pleasures. No discovery in any field, however, has equalled the shock of surprise and joy that led me through the maze of Rilke's poetry when I was in my forties. Since then there have been pleasures in books far too many to enumerate here. This is a real restraint on my part, as I could willingly share with the reader the delights of T.F. Powys' novels, and the richness of his brother John Cowper's writings of many kinds, and there is my love affair with Virginia Woolf's letters, diaries and novels. The latter I knew fairly well from much earlier on, but when the letters and diaries were at last published, I read them concurrently, and added a rereading of the novels as the writing of them appeared in her journals, a system I recommend as very rewarding.

Of the main themes of this chapter, love and friendship, music and books, the quasi-country life that I live in Dorset needs a little more said of it. To be entirely honest, I suppose I must confess that I make use of the country. I have never been an ardent gardener, though I love working over my roses because I enjoy the end-product so much. Being large and strong, there are certain aspects of outside work that I find agreeable: sawing logs, pruning trees and shrubs, lighting bonfires, building brick steps and paths. But I take no part in what people think of as the country life.

Sometimes I wonder whether I am not a victim of the English disease. The one (among many) that I refer to is a jealous passion for the landscape, well conserved of course, a passion that is chiefly expressed in looking at it. Your real countryman strides over his acres with gun or rod in his hand and murder in his heart. Richard Jefferies shot everything that moved, including kingfishers. He knew the names of birds and wild flowers and trees, but I am sure he would never have scrupled to cut down a flourishing woodland specimen if he needed logs for his fire or a few pounds in his pocket. His modern counterpart is far more ignorant, greedy and destructive. He rips up hedges, ploughs out footpaths and farms his land as a business with little regard for its future well-being or indeed for any consideration but immediate profit. He is often a town-bred manager who wouldn't know a sparrow from a woodpecker. Like T.F. Powys' disagreeable farmer, Mr Bugby, in *Innocent Birds*, he may well refer to birds in general as 'they flying things' and shoot them as pests, being careful to except the partridge and pheasant which he hand-rears for other rich farmers and businessmen to shoot at, for fat fees.

Very well, then. I love the countryside with an urban heart. A true countryman does not hanker after the town. A sentimental townee usually has rural longings. Perhaps we English have inherited these fantasies from the Romans, who built their villas all over our countryside but made sure that they were miniature towns, with hot baths, sewage systems, and hosts of servants, as well as the rural delights of fresh fruit and vegetables. Their modern counterparts descend upon the villages to buy up the 'Georgian town houses' provided for them by knowing speculators. They have what they want: *urbs in rure*. Like the Romans but, alas, without classical taste and a sense of proportion.

> The clock on the night storage heating
> Ticks like a taxi waiting

Yes, indeed. I have night storage heaters myself, a telephone, a car, a cleaning lady. Just as much *urbs in rure*, you will say. I provide a saucer of milk for a hedgehog I find on the terrace one evening, hoping that it will love me and stay. I watch it drink the milk with creaturely absorption. Both of us absorbed. Then it departs, never to return. Heartless, witless nature, as Housman rightly observed.

Yet I will not condemn myself as wholly sentimental in my passion for Dorset and the West Country. They have both played an important part in my life and I draw from them a totally different strength from any I gain from my London life. It is a matter of roots that have reached deep down into my consciousness or, more truly, my unconscious. As I travel westwards, it is not only the scenery or the increasing luminosity of the sky and the colours of the hills that move me. It is the sense of returning to a part of England that not only saw my own birth but the births and deaths of so many generations of my family.

My feelings for the country, my deeper feelings that is, are closely bound up with a lifelong love of Wordsworth's poetry. I do not know nature as intimately as he did, nor do I receive from it those visionary gleams that illuminated his life. I read his poetry to convey to my senses the world of nature as I should like to know it. Other writers appeal to me strongly for the same reason: Gilbert White of Selborne, Llewelyn Powys and his elder brother, John Cowper, John Clare, Kilvert. But there is a difference between the value I place upon these writers and that which I place upon Wordsworth and his sister Dorothy, whose journals I have known and loved since I was in my twenties.

Wordsworth is among a small group of writers, pre-eminently Montaigne, Sterne and Rilke, who have provided me with guideposts which I may never have followed successfully for long, none the less they remain the pointers by which I have tried to live my life. 'The words of the wise are as goads, and as nails fastened by the masters of assemblies, which are given from one shepherd.' That quotation makes me add to the list of my inner guides Ecclesiastes. The words come near the end of that Old Testament book of philosophy. The two last chapters (the one before starts with the words: 'Cast thy bread upon the waters', another cardinal guidepost in my life) were read to us in chapel at the end of every term by Chief and, after hearing them for the six years of my boarding-school life, I can still say them almost by heart.

To return to Wordsworth, the most valuable concept he gave me is contained in the words: 'The pleasure that there is in life itself'. How difficult, how arduous, I have found the way to this, yet at last in my seventies the steepness of the ascent has levelled off and I recognise Wordsworth's concept as a more frequent visitor to my inner self.

For Wordsworth, nature was a passion that pervaded far more than his senses. He based his entire philosophy of life upon his intimate relation to the natural world, and this has strongly influenced me, though I have never aspired to more than one or two aspects of his philosophy:

> But 'tis not to enjoy, for this alone
> That we exist; no, something must be done.

Wordsworth's sense of election, his belief that he was not privileged merely to observe and explore the natural world, but that there was laid upon him an imperative to draw from it strength to carry out his work as a philosophic poet – this appealed strongly to my mind, especially to the puritanical side of my personality. It may well have been the seed that eventually grew into my desire to teach, believing that only through education could the world be saved. The nagging words, 'something must be done', help to keep me politically aware and

prevent me from using the country as an escape from a world which I
see in darker and darker colours as I grow older.

Wordsworth's celebration of the simple virtues of leech-gatherers
no longer moves me to condone human behaviour in the village or
anywhere else. My love of Wordsworth is on a more personal level.
When I read his poetry, especially 'The Prelude', I find lines and
phrases which illuminate some aspect of myself, often one I did not
realise. I came across a passage not long ago which surprised me into
recognition of something essential in my own life, hitherto only hazily
acknowledged:

> There are in our existence spots of time
> Which with distinct pre-eminence retain
> A fructifying virtue whence, depressed
> By trivial occupations and the world
> Of ordinary intercourse, our minds –
> Especially the imaginary power –
> Are nourished and invisibly repaired.

I have *consciously* felt this on rare occasions, and most notably in
retrospect. When I came to write *The Chinese Garden* and evoked
my feelings for the derelict park and pleasure grounds, and for the
secret places that I made my own, I wrote with what I now see was a
truly erotic passion but more significantly, with Wordsworthian
perception:

> It was my fourth winter at Bampfield and I had seen the cold park
> dawn-flushed many times before . . . here was a scene of extra-
> ordinary beauty and a mood of heightened awareness to record it. I
> could only have felt as I did on my birthday. I had reached the stage
> of my lover-like relations with Bampfield of regarding the park and
> grounds as my personal demesne, and looked upn the sunrise as a
> personal greeting.

> O my America my new-found land!

> I might have quoted Donne if I had read him then, and without any
> sense of ineptitude at the substitution of a place for a person, for
> my attitude to Bampfield was very much that of a lover. I felt pos-
> sessive and was possessed.

Perhaps some of my readers will have experienced for themselves these
'spots of time': 'moments of vision' in Hardy's phrase; 'moments

of being' in Virginia Woolf's. As well as I can put it myself, they are moments when the world of observation and of thought, of emotion and memory, of joy and unhappiness, falls away into silence, to release what lies deeper than language, the poetic image for which words may later be found. As a writer I know this to be true. I have tried in this book to put a few of these 'spots of time' before the reader.

In this chapter I have led you along the banks of a stream, almost all the way sparkling and sunlit. Now I am prepared to pause, to persuade you to look into a deeper, stiller stretch of water. And I will abandon metaphor to do this.

These pleasures of friendship, of books and music and the countryside, how deep do they lie? How powerful is their influence when it comes to ousting 'the chatter of the mind', the bitter and dangerous thoughts that corrode my life? Music is often the most cogent. To listen to great music with the absorption it deserves brings me into that communion where the hearer is the heard and thoughts are banished, a state which, alas, is rarely sustainable, especially when the applause begins. Yet of course I applaud, too, and release my critical faculty in so doing. Thoughts rush in where they did not dare to tread while the music and I were one sound.

If this condition is rare when listening to music, so it is with walking in the country, with reading, and conversations with friends. I think the country takes precedence as offering the best way of stilling the mind's endless prattle, though the deepest happiness will always come to me from the love and communion with my close friends. Not only in the country, of course, but in a city I can practise the pleasure that comes from absorbed observation of a pavement, tree, a rain-washed road, a ring of sunlight on a dark roof. I am as yet a poor practitioner in this art of observing without identification (i.e. approval), without criticism. Still more difficult is it to observe my own thoughts. Not to analyse them or direct them, or weigh up their merits and demerits: simply to contemplate, to experience the disturbance they cause, or occasionally, of course, the pleasure, perhaps the joy of discovery or a reward bestowed by that Janus, memory. It is the search to be aware of what *is* that drives me on, when I am willing to give myself to it, and I am learning to include in 'what *is*' my own turbulent and obsessive mind.

I have not often admitted you to the pessimism that underlies my life, the profound sense of the futility of it all, the bleakness summed up in that unforgettable image of Bede: the sparrow flying through the lighted hall from darkness to darkness. I have deliberately sought, as I usually do in conversation, to drown an inner voice that echoes in my skull from centuries ago, a voice that spoke readily enough of the laughter and good company that I so love myself, yet sounded a knell that persistently rings in my inner ear:

> What is this world? What asketh men to have?
> Now with his love, now in his colde grave
> Alone, withouten any compaignye.

These words of Chaucer would have brought forth an echo in the heart of my dear friend, Alyse Gregory, whose words about friendship I quoted earlier in this chapter. Despite her enthusiastic response to life, there was in her nature a melancholy amounting at times to profound pessimism. It was a strong bond between us, yet we rarely spoke of it. I only came to recognise it fully when I read her diaries after her death, nearly twenty years ago. More and more I have come to admire and value her uncompromising despair, her rejection of easy consolations, and the wisdom she gained from her many ruses to trick melancholy and win the freedom to enjoy so much in life. The words that I now quote come from her diaries, those secret pages where the pessimist as well as the life-lover records a grief or a joy that would seem excessive, expressed publicly in conversation. They are a bridge from this chapter to the next:

Yesterday I stood in the cup of the valley and looked up into the sky far, far above me and saw some gulls, there must have been about a dozen, flying rapidly and silently across the heavens, sometimes in zigzag formation – and it gave me the same kind of incommunicable rapture that I have received from listening to certain music – as if it spoke direct to some secret knowledge of the spirit – it was both in the beauty and the rhythm of this silent flight of white birds across a firmament without limit or solution. It is by such memories that I live. Our strength lies within ourselves and in our power of poetic vision so that we are ever receptive to the sights and sounds of nature, our hearts more open to others.

19
A Rare Occasion

'Each friend,' wrote Alyse Gregory in her book of essays, *Wheels on Gravel*, 'has the key to one side of us,' and a little later she wrote of those 'rare occasions when friendship, like love, springs to life at a glance . . . when whole years of intimacy might have been shared to reach such a happy culmination.'

This chapter commemorates a relationship which sustained and enriched me during a crucial ten years of my life, the years of my affair with Elizabeth and its breakdown, my suicide attempt and its aftermath. My friendship with Alyse Gregory is a celebration of friendship itself and of those women and men who have given me their love. I cannot describe them and I am sure that they will recognise this. Alyse must stand for all my close and valued friends.

I first met her – and this must come first before I explain who she was – when she was living quite alone in a remote farmhouse called Chideok on the Dorset cliffs near Lulworth, with the village of East Chaldon about a mile or a little more inland from the house which had once been a pair of farm labourers' cottages. I had sent her a copy of my first Mary Voyle novel, *Remaining a Stranger*. The setting is a Dorset village near the coast, very much the country of East Chaldon which I had known well. She wrote back to me at once. The letter was dated 22 March 1956.

Dear Miss Voyle,
   When your book with the letter came yesterday afternoon I thought I should have to put off reading it until I had finished reading a borrowed book, a library book. But glancing at the first page all was forgotten and I was drawn in irresistibly, without choice or conscience, recognising a mind so *simpatica* – a wit so lively and original, indeed, an exciting discovery. My brother-in-law (T.F.

Powys) once said to me that wit was defence against fear. If that were the case I think it would not be so rare. I have not quite finished your book – I read it in bed last night until my eyes gave out.

What writer would not be lifted into the seventh heaven by such praise for her first novel? The letter ended with an invitation to come and see her, and I set out from Weymouth by car along the coast to East Chaldon, a visit that was at the outset dramatic, indeed alarming.

I left the small village and drove to the top of the downs, up a rough chalk track. Suddenly it began to descend precipitously on the far side of a deep valley, thick with fog drifting in from the sea. More by guess than anything else, I made my way through folds in the downs that filled me with fears that I should lose myself. The track was only a grassy ribbon along the floor of the valley. There were, of course, no sign-posts. From time to time the shoulder of a hill loomed up and then disappeared again. Suddenly the ground began to rise a little and out of the mist, to my enormous relief, materialised the grey walls and steep roofs and chimneys of Chideok.

Alyse Gregory was the widow of Llewelyn Powys, the writer, almost the youngest of that extraordinary and gifted family headed by the novelist, John Cowper Powys. She was an American and a New Englander and, as a young woman during and after the Great War, had worked in New York and become part of its radical and literary life. In the early twenties she was appointed the Managing Editor of *The Dial*, a distinguished literary review, in which were published writers like Thomas Mann, Virginia Woolf, D.H. Lawrence and T.S. Eliot, whose *Waste Land* first saw the light in its pages. She met John Cowper Powys, at that time lecturing all over America, and later, about 1921, his brother Llewelyn, who was having some success with articles for American periodicals. John moved into the top of Alyse's small house, Number 4 Patchin Place in Greenwich Village, and Llewelyn, enchanted with Alyse's beauty and with what he called her 'grave, delicately ironic' presence, moved into the ground floor, as her lover. In 1924, somewhat against her will, for her passion for freedom extended to sexual love, Alyse married Llewelyn, left the brilliant world of *The Dial*, and came to England. They settled on the Dorset coast, first in some coastguard cottages, and then at Chideok. In nearby East Chaldon lived T.F. Powys, author of *Mr Weston's Good Wine* and many other novels, soon to become a close friend of Alyse.

Llewelyn had suffered from tuberculosis from his youth, and when the disease reappeared in the thirties he and Alyse went out to Switzerland. He died there in December 1939, and Alyse returned to Chideok to live in the double cottage, one half of which had for years been occupied by two of Llewelyn's sisters, Gertrude, a painter, and Katie, novelist and poet. Alyse was herself a writer and, in addition to her essays, *Wheels on Gravel*, had published four novels, and was in 1948 to publish in America a somewhat evasive and tantalising autobiography, *The Day is Gone*, describing her life from childhood up to her marriage. This book, however, is in no sense a search for the self, or even informed by her reflections upon the human predicament like her essays of ten years earlier. Both of these books she gave me early on in our friendship, inscribing *Wheels on Gravel* with a quotation from George Santayana: 'To understand oneself is the classic form of consolation, to elude onself is the romantic.' I had only known her for two or three months, I see from the date of the inscription, but I was clearly subject to her searching glances and what John Cowper Powys described as her 'quicksilver intelligence'.

I can still remember this first meeting vividly, although, curiously enough, I mentioned it only briefly in my diary. She met me at her doorway with a nervous, quick welcome, scanning me keenly with her bright blue eyes, a half-smile fluttering over her mouth. She was tiny, clothed in a long grey woollen skirt and a high-necked blouse with an old silver brooch at her throat. Her hair was silvery, neatly done up in a little bun at the nape of her neck. Above all, I remember the texture of her skin on her cheeks and hands, soft and creamy. When I later read Llewelyn's autobiographical book, *The Verdict of Bridlegoose*, it is her skin that he notices almost first of all when he meets her at Patchin Place: 'Her round white arms . . . as delectable as dairy junket,' he writes.

She took me up to her first-floor room where she read and wrote. I recall her darting, bird-like movements as she showed me books she was engrossed in at that moment, pressed me to eat a simple but delicious tea. The teapot, like many of her objects, was Victorian, covered in a pearly grey pattern that reminds me when I use it today of the soft grey skirt she always wore. She picked up my novel and began to tell me what she had most liked about it, and asked me questions as to what I was now engaged upon. I was enchanted by her humour and by her lively, sometimes gently critical interest in the various facets of my indecisive, hesitant self that she drew out of me so tactfully. I had never been treated like this before, with such warmth and appreciation and, I must add, New England courtesy, as if I were a glass of rather rough, immature wine, in which she yet found some individual and distinctive flavour. And I was fascinated by her knowledge not only of books, but of music. As a girl, she had had a beautiful soprano voice, and had lived for some time in Paris, studying singing with a view to making it her career. She was widely read in French literature, with an abiding passion for Proust. She once told me that when Llewelyn died, it was Proust to whom she turned for comfort, for he created a total world in which she could immerse herself and find relief from the pain she was suffering. Later I learned that she never stopped reading Proust. When she reached the end – she read the volumes in a leisurely way, of course – she began the books anew, a permanent background to her other reading.

Always she treated me with warm affection, listened to me patiently, persuaded me to think better of myself, to believe in what gifts I had. When I look back on the person I was then in my late forties and early fifties, I am appalled to remember how hard it must have been for her at times to put up with my unhappiness, my self-laceration, my variable moods, my lack of self-knowledge.

Alyse's rare qualities brought her a wide circle of friends, and a large volume of correspondence, for many people found it difficult to visit her in this remote spot. Often she would initiate a relationship by writing to some author whose work she had admired, or to someone who had written a letter to a newspaper with which she strongly agreed, or perhaps disagreed, for she spoke out when her New England conscience prompted her to. A notable example of her courage is quoted in Gerald Brenan's autobiography, *A Personal Record*. Alyse was a close friend of Gamel Woolsey, Gerald's wife, and went to stay with them in Spain. While there, she found herself attending a large dinner, at which the guests were mostly Spanish. The conversation turned at one point to bullfighting. Alyse stood up at the table, a diminutive figure, and in quiet but emphatic tones denounced the mindless cruelty of this so-called sport.

Alyse and I corresponded regularly throughout our ten-year friendship. I think no letter did more to restore me than the one she wrote to me after I had told her of my attempt to kill myself. I would like to quote some of it:

I have just read your letter and feel shattered, not only because it brings home to me most penetratingly how much your presence in the world means to me but because I suffer *with* you in this abysm that seems to yawn so wide and that must seem so black and inescapable to you. Is death too easy an escape for us poor mortals? Must we be driven back to pick up the load *once more*? I have planned it so often myself, and of course, still do.

I know it is no use my giving you assurances, but I am as certain as I can be of anything in this life that if you can hold on, *see it through*, just *keep alive*.– somehow, *anyhow*, yield all to fate, make your mind a blank, the will to live will gradually return. Many have had the best years of their lives after failing as you have failed – Mary Wollstonecraft for one –

She quoted a long verse of Matthew Arnold, and ended:

Stay alive *for my sake* – you don't know what your friendship has meant to me – and to so many others – and I feel so anxious, so when you can send me another line. In a review in the T L S I read yesterday 'Those inner tensions, erosive doubts, torturing lucidity, the self-denial of intelligence, the death wish of the thinker are infinitely more anguishing experiences than open war with society' – How true that is. I send you a heart full of anxious love and sympathy.

Alyse.

I wish I had kept some record of the conversations I had with her, not only then but for the few years that remained afterwards. The best I can do is to fill out her portrait with a few excerpts from her own writing. In addition to the books I have mentioned, she contributed reviews and essays to *The Dial* in the U S A and *The Adelphi*, *The Freethinker* and one or two other periodicals in England. No matter what the subject, there always comes across quite clearly Alyse's characteristic and uncompromising opposition to prejudice, to easy answers, to ignorant assumptions, as well as her passionate concern for the underprivileged and badly treated, whether human beings or animals. Her brother-in-law John Cowper Powys, in his Preface to *Wheels on Gravel*, refers to her 'subversive reflections' and this well expresses her fearless plain-speaking on controversial or unpopular themes, given in a quiet but cogent tone, whether spoken or written. I have told the story of the Spanish dinner. Here is the end of a long review written for *The Dial* magazine in August 1928, a time when public reference to homosexuality without condemnation or disapproval was certainly not usual, the book under review being Proust's *Cities of the Plain*:

> By society at large sexual inversion has been regarded either as a vice so revolting and unnatural that a conspiracy of silence has prevailed, or so dangerous that it must receive immediate public castigation. Since the newer psychology has explained it in terms of a malady, another attitude has among the enlightened come into fashion, but even this attitude, so supercilious in its tolerance or so vulgar in its frivolity, veils a contempt which betrays a sense of superiority and a limited sympathy. No writer before Marcel Proust has dared, or has perhaps been permitted, to touch with so free a pen on so dark a subject. We can imagine no author who could have possibly done it with so relentless yet so tender an understanding, with such consummate art. And be it said, we are not among those who discover a 'defect' in his 'moral sensibility' because of the inclusion of certain much-discussed episodes. Candour absolves everything, and for the artist curiosity, combined with spiritual detachment, is essential. Sensitiveness is the unique virtue.

Although Alyse Gregory might not satisfy the more rigid feminists, there is a strong feminist streak in her writing which is part of her liberal and radical attitude. In *Wheels on Gravel* she writes brilliantly of women and their friendships.

> Friendships between women are often deeper and last over a longer period of time than do those between men, for they are based on the insight of slaves, the perfidy of harlots, the irony of queens, and the recklessness of the dispossessed. Women understand each other as negroes stealing sugar-cane understand each other, as village witches understand each other, as gracious court ladies in a barbarian's country understand each other . . . What is often conveyed in a single conspiring glance between two women would fill many thick volumes and might well startle a man from his too innocent complacencies.

Alyse never lost her keen interest in world affairs even in old age and ill-health. Often, when I entered her room, she would almost run to greet me, waving an opened newspaper or magazine and exclaiming: 'Have you *read* this monstrous article? Have you seen this account of . . . ' perhaps some incident in Vietnam, or the treatment of blacks in some incident in South Africa. I cannot resist one more short quotation from a brief review in *The Dial* of two books by one Gabriel Wells, the first on *Capital and Labour*, the second entitled *The Great English Strike*. This was, of course, the strike of 1926 and her review reads very freshly today, nearly sixty years afterwards. Alyse would have appreciated the irony of this. After condemning the two books for their 'stale generalisations' she ends the notice with these indignant words: 'One needs to recall that when all has been said and done the miners are . . . being forced by starvation to return, one by one, into those dark caverns of travail, where philanthopists of Mr Wells' kidney are content to abandon them to their salvation.'

When I wrote *A Time and a Time* in the mid-sixties, I dedicated it to Alyse Gregory. She read it in manuscript just before she died, by her own hand, in August 1967. I had spent the previous day with her, a Sunday. I left her soon after six to drive back to Dorset from the home she had moved to in north Devon. A blazing sunset flared in the sky behind me and Bach's B-minor Mass was being sung on the radio. Alyse had spoken to me about her resolve to take the sleeping pills she had obtained abroad as soon as she felt that her increasing frailty had reached a state where she might be hospitalised. I did not attempt to dissuade her. It was impossible to imagine that free spirit caged in a hospital ward or, even worse, an old people's home.

As I listened to the Mass, I wondered if she was listening to it as well, if she had decided to spread Llewelyn's old cloak over her bed, as she had once told me, and take the pills that night. I became increasingly convinced that she had made her decision and found myself hoping with a kind of lift of the heart that she was making sure of her final freedom, that the trumpets and drums of the 'Dona Nobis Pacem' were accompanying her on her journey.

When the telephone went early the following day, I knew what I was going to hear. I didn't immediately drive over to Devon. I went for an hour's walk. I crossed the fields opposite my house and climbed the farm track that ran to the top of the downs. The valley head was a triangular wood of beech trees. I went round the edge of the woodland and down into the fields again, along a hedge where two butterflies were mating in the early sunshine. I often walk it still and remember Alyse, who so enriched my life. It is for me one of Wordsworth's 'spots of time'.

Her last journal contains far fewer and briefer entries than the earlier ones. It begins with the words: 'November 10th 1964. This will see me to the end.' She reflects on her life and her enduring love for Llewelyn and on her own growing ill-health:

> Perhaps the discovery of a weakness in oneself hitherto unknown and unforeseen should be treated with a hospitable detachment and curiosity as a fresh source of light on experience. Everything fights now against lucidity and effort, the increasing weakness of the body, the dimness of the senses . . . love alone can still animate us, still give us the courage to hold to the light and the intermittent flashes that resurrect the spirit. The leaves drifting down through the autumn haze. To be strange to others or rather to have others strange to us can be borne, but the alienation from ourselves – to refrain from taking one's life requires courage but to take it requires even greater courage.

A year later, in September 1965, she is writing: 'I can still look out of the window – contemplate – the garden this morning glittering with frost! The autumn!'

An even later fragment, very near the end: 'What have we to show for life but the survival of our curiosity and our tribute to wonder?'

20
Ding Dong Bell

Curiosity and wonder . . . How deeply personal these attributes are, beyond betrayal, beyond loss, beyond pain. How Alyse would have savoured the short episode that follows and how immediately she would have understood without any prompting its importance to me.

I am reaching the end of the corridor and this small mirror is like one of those tiny vignettes so often painted by Victorian and early-twentieth-century artists. I have one in my room now, a warmly coloured glimpse of a quayside in pure art deco style. It is like a Cornish or French harbour and matches well with the sombre but rich colouring of the Penwith moors that are the background in this autumnal mirror.

In the church of Madron, a village north of Penzance, hangs the bell of the Ding Dong mine that still stands on the nearby moors. It was last tolled to bring up the final shift of miners when Ding Dong closed in 1878. Mine buildings punctuate the Penwith landscape. Ding Dong is a tall, grey-brown structure with an even taller chimney at one corner, giving the whole the appearance of a hand with a fore-finger pointing to heaven.

I saw it recently at its most mysterious. It was All Souls' Eve and an autumn drizzle blanketed the moors. I was alone in Cornwall for a few days and I had last seen Ding Dong mine with Jan many years before. In the late morning I drove to a moorland track and set out to walk to it. Behind me, the sun broke through cloud to light up a corner of Mount's Bay, but around me the hills struggled for a moment out of fine rain only to disappear again completely. Suddenly, ahead of me, a mile away, I saw the minatory finger of the mine rising from the shrouded moors. Its threat materialised in my mind. It was a warning to view it exactly as it was: a solitary, disused mine building; to dismiss all association, all memories.

It raised acutely the problem of those shackling past feelings which too often cripple the life of the present. On that October morning I heeded the warning almost with fear and as I walked – the lane was bordered by huge grey stones and russet bracken of piercing beauty in the overall mist – the outlines of the mine became firm, and I felt my thoughts, my memories, disperse and fade into the moors. I knew that their solid presences were still there, as much as the invisible hills with their ruined mines, farms and ancient stone groups – Lanyon Quoit and Men-an-Tol – once familiar to me on our walks over Penwith's moorland.

I strode on doggedly and allowed the powerful shape of Ding Dong to absorb me. No one else was about. The only living things I saw were cows, two of which pressed against a wire fence and gazed at me. I stopped and gazed back. The silence deepened and some creaturely affinity kept us absolutely motionless in a triangle of absorption.

At last I went on to the mine. On one side a brick arch gives entrance to it. On the opposite wall and higher up, a slender 'Norman' arch is cut in the stonework with that innate sense of proportion that inspired the old craftsmen. The solid stone walls, when I pressed them with my hands, were damp and cold yet friendly. All Soul's Eve. Yet if the old miners had materialised and gathered around the ruined mine that had ruined them and sent so many of them into exile overseas, I should not have been afraid. I felt an empathy with them, as I had with the cows which, like miners, were simply objects of use and exploitation to their owners.

When I stood inside the roofless walls of Ding Dong, it was neither sentimental or even reminiscent that I felt. The stone structure braced me and held me firm. No painful memories of sunlit days on the moors with Jan or of dark days when the bell of that relationship had tolled for the last time for me, when Cornwall was shut away by the weight of the past and I thought I should never want to see it again.

For a few moments I stood in a state of blessed suspension without thought. The observed was the observer. Memory . . . how fast old scenes, old thoughts, crowd in upon the brain, and how hard it is to reduce them to order. At a point in one's life when loss has been experienced, the power of memory can invade and dominate the spirit. Here in Cornwall, I was forewarned. I knew that memory would grasp at every association and load it upon my sense of loss. I was prepared for it. The week spent in the Penwith peninsula was a deliberate challenge to memory, that problem child of the psyche whose activities can bestow both delight and misery.

Whether we like it or not, memory will act upon us, often powerfully, and of course I have cultivated it, for I regard it as the store from which I extract much of my writing material, being by nature an autobiographical writer rather than a teller of tales. Even a narrative author must find memory invaluable, although maybe his material comes from a different drawer of the cabinet.

Memory is a major part of being human and one of the attributes that separates us from other living creatures. Is life really life without memory? Imagine your old age, your senility even, if you can, and you will find the answer to that question. To be without one's faculty of memory must be to live in fear and confusion. To lose it little by little, as I find that I am beginning to do, is hateful to me. How near am I to that period of general helplessness and incoherence which will be the prelude, all-too-long prolonged, to blessed finality?

In constructing my own survival kit now, I have to take decisions about the intrusive activities of memory, so eager to rush in where angels fear to tread. What is to be done? That something *must* be done is certain, for I want freedom and order in my mind. I want to rid it of the din of experience. I am finding that the only technique is to look one's thoughts sternly in the eye and ask them where they have come from and why they have chosen to appear at this particular juncture. It is awareness of *what is now* that must make up the web of one's living and give it an alert strength. One cannot afford to have the delicate fabric tattered by the probing fingers of the past.

There is a proper use for memory, however, apart from its everyday reminders of such matters as the time when the train leaves. First, one has to sort out pleasant memories from unpleasant. It is peculiarly difficult to dwell on some memories without a measure of pain, and how this is to be done I cannot suggest except by adopting the same process of challenging one's thoughts. It almost amounts to shouting at the approaching figure in one's mind: 'Who goes there?' Only when it answers 'Friend' dare you let it come nearer.

On the other hand I would not be without those delicious memories which John Cowper Powys, who thought deeply upon this matter, likens to 'penetrating odours rising out of the earth at the touch of rain'. They are always there for our refreshment, once divested of the pain they often hold, and no pundit gives us the technique of dealing with those memories which let in the flood waters of unhappiness.

When I made my way through the mist to Ding Dong, I absorbed myself in the stones, the bracken, the brown eyes of the cattle, the tall grey building blurred with rain. If memories approached the steps of my mind, I endeavoured to observe them coolly, to distance them, to handle them as though they were parcels of old papers, the contents of which no longer had any concern for me. My mind was at peace and well ordered that All Souls' Eve. I was enjoying Powys' 'pure and undiluted awareness'. Except for one moment. Walking back along the rough road, with Ding Dong fading into the cloud behind me, I was suddenly so overwhelmed with the sense of all that I had lost that I was compelled to halt in the track and reach out my hand for support. I stood, my fingers pressed to whiteness against the cool surface of a boulder, an anchor against the storm that was shaking me. Slowly it subsided in the weight of the silence. The memories of past days on Penwith moors faded like Ding Dong into the mist. I realised around me the intensity of the present in which I stood, a vast now which subdued the past and future into utter silence and contained my mind within its ordered pattern.

21
The Fishing Party

I have been over three years writing this book. At the beginning of it, I said that I had changed more in the previous seven or eight years than I had changed in my whole life. And I've altered still more during these three years of work.

The infusion of fresh ideas, especially from feminist sources, and the exploration of myself during the walk down this corridor of mirrors into my past, did not, however, at first bring the benefits of greater insight. This is especially true of the account of my attempted suicide given in Chapters Two and Thirteen, for it is an account I have lived with for over thirty years and such things become dear to one. Like unhappiness. I have always held strong views on the right of every individual to end her or his life when it seemed the necessary thing to do. I still believe that this is valid and hope that when times are more enlightened we shall be helped to end our lives when we become irrevocably damaged or diseased, or when senility and incapacity come upon us. The kind of person I was then – and you must remember the stoic influence upon me since early youth – made me determine that unless I had found the life I longed for by the time I was fifty, that would be the appropriate age to bring things to an end. When Elizabeth left me to get married, I acted as I had always believed to be my inalienable right.

As I have said, I left the account of my suicide attempt and the analysis of my reasons just as they were when I first wrote of them in *A Time and a Time*, twenty years ago. After writing this book, I analyse the matter differently, for I have come to realise that my attempt had far deeper roots than the break-up of my love affair with Elizabeth. Those roots go back to a childhood of competition with my siblings and quasi-siblings, every one of them male, a childhood fuelled with secret aspirations to achieve just what they achieved, especially the eldest, the almost legendary Tom who won the larger share of my mother's love.

Here an odd memory has suddenly floated free, something I have not thought about for years. Reach for your Freud. Tom entered the war as a bluejacket. Invalided out, he was then given a commission in the RNAS. His stiff bluejacket's uniform lay in a drawer, and when I was about eight or nine there was nothing I enjoyed more than dressing up in it, with all its complicated tapes and buttons and knots. Why? Oh, dear me, as Gertrude Stein sometimes says when she wants to avoid further analysis of a disaster or a problem of morals or politics. I feel rather the same about childhood behaviour. Does the dressing-up need further explanation? I have travelled from suicide far back to impersonating my brother Tom, or perhaps it is the other way round. Oh, dear me.

To wish you were other than you are sets in motion a deep discontent which grows with time and can burgeon into self-hatred. In fact I have never wanted to be a man. I like being a woman, though I did learn early on that the race was to the strong, and this usually meant the male and that women were handicapped from the start. I did not pause to analyse why this should be so. I was too preoccupied with my personal problems. Once I had found Elizabeth and, more important, had discovered and begun to exploit my writing talents, it no longer worried me, but I now know that I should not have been so blind to what affected my sisters. Suicide is, I suppose, the ultimate act of solipsism and it cut me off from others and prevented me from moving towards the women's movement, where I should soon have discovered how far-reaching and how devastating were the effects of patriarchy, and how it had affected me all my life.

Must I go back and rewrite those early passages about my suicide attempt? No, that is something I will not do. They will have to stand as a monument to my ignorance. A more pertinent question might be: Why write this book at all? Why indeed? I have often wondered during these three years. However, it is done now. What can I add? First, that I regret that it isn't funnier. When I attempted so inexpertly to hang myself at the age of seventeen, the coat-hook to which I tied the noose proved to be set too low and I landed ignominiously on my toes, after taking what I thought was the fatal leap from the top of two trunks. This startled me out of despair into laughter: not quite that short-lived, extravagant laughter that results from shock, but amusement that has retained its sharp tang for me all my life. That leap dislodged a piece of me which lost its seriousness in the fall and became self-mocking. The inability to take myself quite seriously has remained, though you might hardly think so from reading this book. It disappoints me. It was not always so. When I reread *A Time and a Time* recently, I thought it the funniest book I had ever written.

Irony about life and about oneself are essential, but I have found it difficult to let it play over the surface of this autobiography. Will it seem to the reader unutterably glum? And as I've been recycling the debris of my past, nagging at my mind like a thorn in my thumb has been a further doubt. Why am I not using the material or some of it in a novel? Well, of course, there is some material left over. I have not consumed the whole stock in the cupboard. However, there is little point in speculating about the next book until I have finished this and I am finding it hard enough to capture a clear picture in this last mirror in the corridor, because the moods in which I write are so variable. My life has never proceeded with the even tenor of an equable personality and has been presented here much as I was living it during the three years of writing.

There is no one truth, a problem which has beset me all along the way. As Gertrude Stein said: 'You are of course never yourself.' When I look back, for instance, over my life with Jan, I see it unclouded, but my diary shows that it was often fraught with misunderstandings, discontents and inner loneliness, and so it must have been for her. But how far is the reality of a situation important as distinct from the memory of it that we live with in the present? Looking back, I feel those years with Jan suffused with warmth and I let the diary evidence (only intermittent in any case) of strains and disagreements go. It was the intimate shared life I had always longed for. The experience remains the most rewarding in my life. Anything perfect, apart from being impossible, would prove intolerable, I believe. Ours was a living relationship and what above all keeps it living in memory is that its ending did not leave a sour taste in the mouth.

Reading that last statement again, it seems rather high-minded. It is true in essence, but elevated into a somewhat rarefied atmosphere lying well above the actual situation in which I live, where I still battle with that habit of unhappiness described in Chapter Two. Habits are parts of oneself – usually deplorable and unlikeable – that endear themselves to their owners like nasty, smelly pets. The simile is peculiarly apt, for the owner of a pet usually loves it too dearly to have it put down. So it is with habits. We – I, that is, am reluctant to carry it to the vet. But I am coming round to the idea. 'Poor Fido.

Looking back to 1962, I know that I then felt that I had to rebuild my life after my suicide attempt, but was this the right decision? With hindsight, I do not think so. To rebuild implies an act of reassembling the rubble and putting up a replica of what was there before, a kind of personal Dresden. That was what I did. What I should have done, I can see now, was to create a new life, to build a new self using only the valuable fragments of my shattered personality as material in the new house. I did not even attempt to do this. I allowed my circumstances to remain the same. To pursue the building metaphor, I did not move to a new environment. I rebuilt where I was standing instead of breaking away from teaching, possibly even from London and my friends. In an attempt to escape my inner emptiness on which so mistakenly I placed no value, I entered upon the love affair with Kay which, when she went, left me as much in the wilderness as before.

My suicide should have been symbolic of the death of those masculine values in me which I had adopted from the patterns presented to me when I was a child, and the death too of the waste and aridity of so much of my life: a cutting away, a paring down. Suicide was altogether too wholesale. This leads me to add a footnote to what I have already said about my novel, *Man on a Tower*, written shortly after the attempt. The central character of George represented an aspect of myself, I have admitted, and this is true, but my adoption of a male persona now seems suspect. It wasn't entirely a device for concealment. At the time, it certainly seemed to me the only way I could write about love, and other lesbians, like Adrienne Rich in her early poetry, have done this. But in George I was tacitly subscribing to masculine values as well, especially the idea that it is necessary for an artist to become a devouring egotistical monster in order to write or paint well. I still believe that it's a valid point that an artist in any field must expect to sacrifice personal happiness to a greater or lesser extent, must accept and come to terms with loneliness. None the less, I am sure that it is sometimes possible, particularly between women, to bring creativity and human relationship into a harmonious bond, releasing energy and imagination. Women stand on a basis of equality with each other. Few men will see a woman companion beyond her usefulness, and I suspect that this is particularly true of male artists and writers.

There are loose ends to be tied up, I realise, before I can end this book. My affair with Jan is the most important. How and why did it end, for I know that I have referred to the loss of her with a repetitiveness that might be regarded as tedious? In 1976, after we had been lovers for many years and had shared a home for five, Jan decided to leave me and return to the circumstances in which she had lived before. I cannot say more than this. For her, it was the right decision. Few choices affecting two people, however, are likely to be satisfactory to both of them. Perhaps there is a sliding scale of gains and losses. If Jan gained when she left me, there must also have been loss for her. For me the gain – though I still find it difficult to use this term – came much later, when endurance and my fundamental love of life brought me the rewards of new and old friendships, music and books and painting, and an always deepening love for my Dorset home and its countryside.

At the time of her going, I suffered a loss more serious than any I have ever known. Worse than the loss of Elizabeth, which nearly ended in my death? That can be left out of the reckoning. When Jan left I was older and I saw my affair with her as undoubtedly the last in my life. With her I had experienced the joy of sharing a way of life with a lover for the first time. I had far more to lose. There is nothing more I can add to this statement. I am not in the business of making comparisons between Jan and Elizabeth.

I have described at the outset of this book my immediate reactions to that loss and the deliberate way I went about creating a new life, harvesting every experience that could provide me with consolation and support. None the less, the last ten years look more like a battlefield than anything else, in retrospect.

I am thought by others, I know, to be what they call 'life-enhancing'. I wish I did not find it so hard to enhance my own life. Does not make enough effort, as the school reports used to say. At this point, I put my work aside and, despite the cold, pull on my old trousers and dirty fisherman's smock, to go outside. I have to fetch in logs and peat, chop firewood and get the house ready for Christmas. This physical work I enjoy. It employs my hands and arms and gives me a physical warmth and well-being that goes back to those enchanted hours at Bampfield when I crossed the park with the horse and cart to pick up fallen branches and bring them back to saw into logs. How is it possible not to regret that the side of me that extended my sensual warmth to the woman I love, has now had to be set on one side like a dish on a stove, to grow cold?

> What you have abandoned
> is not behind but far ahead
> where we shall never
> now arrive.

Marge Piercy sums it up. In whatever light it places me, I confess that I still long for the future that once would have contained the shared experiences 'when music and moonlight and feeling were one'; that magical lift of the heart when the phone goes and she is there: she's left the office early, will I meet her? The new directions I have taken, the resources on which I've drawn, the radical alteration of much of my life and many of my ideas, have given me no redress for the fact that Jan no longer returns to me in the evening. I have no philosophy to meet this. Only one surety remains: work. Believe me when I say: in the last resort, work is all there is. If out of pain and solitude you can 'breed one work that wakes' you will be blest beyond belief, but usually it is not creative work but the mere physical labour of cutting down overgrowth or cleaning a room that will restore you. So I repeat: work is all there is.

When I wrote those words a few months ago, I intended to end the book at that point. But it was Monday's truth. Today is Tuesday. It is early June. I have been walking for some three hours over the downs, free of all associations, free of pain, over tracks I knew when I was in my twenties; nót the Dorset hills but the Sussex downland from Harting to Cocking. Not long after I left college, I slept out on these hills, I remember, rolled up in bracken. My friend, Diana, was with me. It was warm weather like today, and it didn't seem worth driving back to London. We stayed out on the downs under the stars and awoke drenched with dew. I knew these Sussex tracks with Edith; I walked them, camped in them, pubbed in them with Elizabeth. Later I experienced their pleasures afresh and put a seal on them with Jan. Today I walked alone – though I was staying with some of my oldest and dearest friends – walked alone above a deep valley that I first saw forty years ago. I gathered up the past in my mind without a single regret and it became a concentrated happiness and a conscious recognition that all this is still mine and contains so much past love and companionship. I sat down for a while and contemplated it all, the green contours of the hills, the deep woods, the winding chalk track. I knew that here in Sussex and not in my native Dorset I had discovered forty years ago a truth that belongs to no single time or experience: that for me 'love is the sum'. It might be said that this must be a chimera since I have been singularly unsuccessful in keeping my lover with me. And there is that undeniable dichotomy between writing and love, between writing and private life, that has bedevilled things so often. And yet . . . in the last analysis, whatever inner satisfaction writing has given me, and despite its importance to me as a lifeline, love is the perfect sum.

Since some of my readers may not know the poem from which I have taken these words and also the words I used as the title of Chapter Sixteen, I will set it out here. Singers will know its many musical settings, none of them more lovely than the original early-seventeenth-century version by Tobias Hume. The words are by an unknown poet.

Fain would I change that note
To which fond love hath charmed me
Long, long to sing by rote,
Fancying that that harmed me:
Yet when this thought doth come,
'Love is the perfect sum
    Of all delight.'
I have no other choice
Either for pen or voice
    To sing or write.

O Love! They wrong thee much
That say thy sweet is bitter,
When thy rich fruit is such
As nothing can be sweeter.
Fair house of joy and bliss,
Where truest pleasure is,
    I do adore thee!
I know thee what thou art,
I serve thee with my heart,
    And fall before thee.

I have pursued love like Ariadne's thread through a maze of illusion, disappointment, humiliation even. Looking back as I have done so often with distaste for the many mistaken choices of my life, I can never regret the experience of love and friendship. I believe that love alone stands between us and the abyss. Worldly success, money, creativity, even those passions that absorb us wholly at times and shield our eyes from the approaching dark, must in the end be discounted. Nothing but love has the power to redeem our days.

I have moved into what is left of my life with rather more hope than I have ever before entertained and with more radical and sustaining ideas in my mind. I have acquired, too, a determination to net and land that carp-like fish, unhappiness, upon the bank of my river. It is not such a difficult operation as I used to think it, for I have reached a better appreciation of who I am. A new-found and unfamiliar liking for myself is fortified by old friendships and by new ones, especially among women. I have moved into a world of warmth and understanding in the commonality of women, a world I have looked for all my life. Perhaps it is only now, late in my life, that I am capable of accepting them, so isolated has been my inner self in the past. As I have moved outwards towards them, as I never did in the bleak years of the sixties when I needed them so badly, women have taught me much about the art of living, and no one more than the new lover who has come into my life to make nonsense of the statements I have written earlier about sexual love having ended for me.

I repeat those words of George Sand: 'Escape oblivion . . . write your own history, all of you who have understood your life and sounded your heart.' I may have understood my own life and heart only imperfectly, but in this book I have attempted to explore myself and my past with honesty and in a reflective manner very different from the urgent impulse to come to terms with loss of love and attempted suicide which drove me to write *A Time and a Time*. In that autobiography I allowed humour to play over the surface, I suppose because I feared to expose the black abyss that lay beneath. This book has been more thoughtful and more searching, and all in all rather serious. There is a frivolous or, better perhaps, a fun-loving side of me that has hardly appeared. Now, faced with this last mirror on the wall, I feel inclined to indulge this aspect of myself. I'll organise a fishing party for my friends. We will gather at the river . . . and then I'll throw into it, like a real litter-lout, my rod and line and that stinking fish of unhappiness.

And what then is reflected in the last mirror of the corridor? Not the solitary figure of myself, but the fishing party, our rugs and picnic baskets on the green bank. In this especial rural scene, my friends and I, in a final gesture, toast our loves and toss our champagne corks into the river at our feet.